Taboo, Personal and Collective Representations

Taboo, Personal and Collective Representations examines the symbolic nature of taboo, asking what is the purpose of a taboo and how does it vary across cultures. The book focuses on the concept of taboo as an in-between, organizing principle that differentiates stages through a ritual process of separating ***order*** as clean/blessed from ***disorder*** as polluted/disassociated.

This book uses an interdisciplinary approach that compares the anthropological, ethnological, sociological, and depth psychological perspectives of renowned scholars in their examination of taboos. Unconscious/conscious taboos influence how we perceive transitional, indeterminate states across margins in the maturation and individuation processes. The book argues that a taboo embodies the perilous, symbolic meaning of such a rite of passage and that its emotional value and intensity in the form of symptomatology varies across cultures.

Taboo, Personal and Collective Representations will be of great interest to researchers, academics, and postgraduate students in the fields of anthropology, ethnology, origins of religion, race, gender, and depth psychology.

Elizabeth Brodersen is an accredited Training Analyst and Supervisor at the CGJI Zürich. Elizabeth received her doctorate in Psychoanalytic Studies from Essex University, UK in 2014, and works as a Jungian Analyst in private practice in Germany and Switzerland.

Taboo, Personal and Collective Representations

Origin and Positioning within Cultural Complexes

Elizabeth Brodersen

Routledge
Taylor & Francis Group
LONDON AND NEW YORK

First published 2019
by Routledge
2 Park Square, Milton Park, Abingdon, Oxon OX14 4RN

and by Routledge
52 Vanderbilt Avenue, New York, NY 10017

First issued in paperback 2020

Routledge is an imprint of the Taylor & Francis Group, an informa business

British Library Cataloguing in Publication Data
A catalogue record for this book is available from the British Library

Library of Congress Cataloging in Publication Data
Names: Brodersen, Elizabeth, author.
Title: Taboo, personal and collective representations : origin and positioning within cultural complexes / Elizabeth Brodersen.
Description: Abingdon, Oxon ; New York, NY : Routledge, 2019. |
Includes index.
Identifiers: LCCN 2018052084 (print) | LCCN 2019001576 (ebook) |
ISBN 9781351039901 (E-book) | ISBN 9781138488595 (hbk) |
ISBN 9781351039901 (ebk)
Subjects: LCSH: Taboo—Cross-cultural studies. | Taboo—Psychological aspects. | Jungian psychology.
Classification: LCC GN471.4 (ebook) | LCC GN471.4 .B76 2019 (print) |
DDC 390—dc23
LC record available at https://lccn.loc.gov/2018052084

ISBN 13: 978-0-367-66049-9 (pbk)
ISBN 13: 978-1-138-48859-5 (hbk)

Typeset in Bembo
by Cenveo® Publisher Services

This book is dedicated to Professor Dr. med. Dr. phil. Rustan R. Brock (1927–2017) in loving memory and deep gratitude.

Contents

Acknowledgements viii

1 Introduction 1

2 The nature of taboo in indigenous practices 18

3 Taboo, order, disorder, abjection, and dirt 41

4 Totem and taboo, animal categories, and kinship structures 58

5 The origin and positioning of incest taboo 79

6 Taboo and emotional ambivalence 97

7 Taboo, rites of passage, and indeterminate states 126

8 Taboo, shamanism, and Jungian psychoanalysis 147

9 Conclusion 165

Index 175

Acknowledgements

I would like to thank my husband, Christian, for his strong support throughout writing this book and to the late Professor Dr. med. Dr. phil. Rustan R. Brock, psychoanalyst, for his invaluable psychoanalytical knowledge, who sadly died before the book was completed. I have dedicated this book to him.

I wish to acknowledge the space that was given to me by the IAJS South Africa Conference co-chairs, Dr. Marybeth Carter and Stephen Farah, to present this topic at the 2017 International Association for Jungian Studies (IAJS) conference in Cape Town. It made me reflect on the space that taboo occupies at the margins of the 'other' within the conference theme of the *Spectre of the 'Other.'* I developed further clinical perspectives from the helpful feedback of the conference participants, as well as from the comments of diploma candidates at the CGJI Zürich, where I held a seminar on this topic during summer semester 2018.

I am indebted to two of my past analysands for giving me insights into their own personal and cultural symptomatology of taboo and how it manifests in liminal states caught between the margins of cultural complex processes connected to the unconscious 'other' as 'dirt.'

I also wish to thank Routledge for their excellent publishing and editorial support.

All references from Jung's *Collected Works* listed in the material are translated by R.F.C. Hull and edited by H. Read, M. Fordham, G. Adler, and W. McGuire, published by in the UK by Routledge and Kegan Paul, London.

Chapter 1

Introduction

The term *taboo* attracts academic interest for two main reasons: first, its ambiguity of meaning leads to the concept being wedged between academic disciplines such as anthropology, myth, religion, sociology, politics, and psychosocial and psychoanalytic studies that include Jungian and post-Jungian studies on the rites of passage, liminality, and indeterminate states. The original definition, as a result, needs more clarification. This new enquiry attempts to create more interdisciplinary space within and between these approaches. Second, the term taboo has taken a negative turn during the nineteenth and twentieth centuries with its focus on inhumane racist and misogynist prohibitions attached to miscegenation taboo. I aim to understand the original subtlety and complexity of the term taboo and release its original indigenous meaning as a creative potential for analysing *danger* and its *contagious* nature imbued in taboo as an individual and collective term. The term taboo, itself, denotes untouchability, which reflects the difficulty of pinning down the term.

Background to the study of taboo

The term taboo has been the subject of intense controversial anthropological scrutiny since the nineteenth and twentieth centuries, which I describe in detail in chapter 2. Taboo has been analysed at some length by idiographic and nomothetic anthropologists including Fraser (1910; 1922) Robertson Smith (1889), Radcliffe-Brown (1952), Eliade, (1958a), Douglas (1966), van Gennep (1960), Levi-Strauss (1963), Steiner (1956), and Turner (1964; 1969). I expand the frame to include psychosocial-psychanalytical perspectives of Freud (1912–13), Kristeva (1982), and Jungian/post-Jungian contributions on associative, archetypal medicine such as Jung (1911–12/1952a), Hillman (1979; 1997), Ziegler (1983), Woodman (1982; 1985), Starr Costello (2006), Harris (2009), Haule, (2011) and Merchant (2012). I show progressive interpretive links between Fraser, Radcliffe-Brown, Steiner, Douglas, van Gennep, Levi-Strauss, Turner, Jung and post-Jungians on taboo in their emphases on rites of passage, associative thinking and symbol formation within taboo.

Ethnological idiographic enquiry from factual, direct observation or contact of people differs from history, as it is not derived substantively from written records. The theoretical or nomothetic study of social institutions that practice taboo is usually referred to as sociology; in 1908, Fraser, in his inaugural lecture as the first professor of social anthropology, defined social anthropology as a branch of sociology that deals with premodern societies (Radcliffe-Brown, 1952, pp. 2–3). Therefore, initially, taboo was studied under social anthropology and later under comparative sociology. Social anthropology as an empirical pursuit was represented as field monographs mainly by students of anthropology whereby field techniques were discussed and debated. Comparative sociology made use of ethnography and field data from various cultures and underwent a double scrutiny, that of the collector and that of the theorist. Steiner (1956, pp. 21–30) explains that comparative sociology has retained its term, but the earlier term of social evolutionary anthropology was reinvented and named analytical and descriptive sociology. Radcliffe-Brown (ibid, p. 3) emphasises that comparative or analytical sociology, of which social anthropology is one branch, now combines theoretical or nomothetic studies to provide structural comparisons of different single types of societies to arrive at an accurate description and meaning of taboo. Structural comparisons of taboo practices that include differences as well as similarities importantly add the psychological, symbolic, *affective* dimension. Such considerations have led to socioanthropological interdisciplinary perspectives that partially or out-rightly disagree on the properties contained within taboo to better clarify its usage.

The definition of taboo, itself, can be explored under various ethnological and social aspects: first, as social mechanisms of obedience that have ritual significance; second, as specific and restrictive behaviours in dangerous situations that could be interpreted as the *sociology of danger* itself; third, as the protection of individuals who are in danger; and fourth, the protection of society from those endangered and therefore dangerous persons. Steiner, (1956, p. 21) suggests that taboo has elements of all the above situations where values are expressed in terms of dangerous behaviour. One salient feature of taboo is its *untouchability*: if a forbidden taboo is touched, be it involving a person or object, both become taboo and untouchable, until the appropriate rite is performed.

Early voyages into taboo

The term *taboo* first came to notice in Europe through Captain James Cook's 1784 description during his exploratory world voyages carried out under British Royal patronage, the Royal Navy, and the Royal Geographical Society to describe the *mysterious significance* of certain practices of South Sea Islanders in the Polynesian archipelago during the last quarter of the eighteenth and the first part of the nineteenth centuries. Cook noted that the people of *Atooi* were particularly concerned about whether a particular item was taboo and applied it to all cases where things were not to be touched. Steiner (1956, p. 23) notes that Cook is the first European to take note of the term: no Dutchman or Spaniard had used the term before, and Cook's log book from his first voyage bears witness that taboo was more often seen than spoken. Cook's successor, James King, in writing Cook's travel logs after his death, observed that taboos created social stratification and social distance. King also noticed that women were particularly tabooed, ate alone, forbidden to feed themselves or others, or eat certain kinds of meat, particularly during menstruation and funeral rites. King observed that the term taboo was multifaceted in its application and used to express social distance as well as anything deemed sacred, eminent, or devoted. For example, the king was *Eree-taboo;* a human victim *tangata taboo,* and the island Tonga, where the king resided was named *Tonga-taboo* (Cook III, pp. 163–164).

Other explorer-ethnologists' expeditions to the South Sea Islands under different royal patronages (Russian; German) added to the knowledge of the practice of taboo, such as von Krusenstern, commander of the *Nadjehad* and *Neva*, accompanied by Captain Lisiansky and naturalist von Langsdorff in 1802. Each produced a separate account of taboo: von Langsdorff (1812), considered a reliable ethnographer, gave a 21-point list of taboo customs showing a mix of social and religious elements; von Krusenstern (1812) stressed its religious implications; while Lisiansky (1914) described taboo as a sacred prohibition. In 1817, von Kotzebue, accompanied by ethnologist de Freycinet, wrote arguably the best account of taboo (1839), describing both civic and religious aspects (von Kotzebue, 1821). A later voyage headed by Wilkes in 1836, under the British flag, produced a largely unread five-volume ethnography of the South Sea Island (Wilkes, 1845).

Etymology of taboo

The etymology of taboo reveals a linguistic problem of meaning. Steiner (1956, pp. 31–40) offers a clear etymology of the word *taboo* based on the work of Shortland (1851) and Lehmann (1930). One possible root is the combination of *ta* (to beat) and *pu* (as conch), linking the word to a chieftain's proclamations of taboo as heralded by conch blowing and drum beating. A popular etymology is that taboo means 'marked off' or 'marked thoroughly' and only came to signify sacred or prohibited in a secondary sense. Steiner suggests that the common form of the word is *tapu,* which in some cases can sound like *tafu;* the Hawaiian form is *kapu;* and the Tongan form is *tabu.* The word is also used outside Polynesia: in Fiji *tabu* means unlawful, sacred, and superlatively good; in Malagassy, *tabaka* means profaned or polluted. Steiner suggests (ibid, p. 33) that the word taboo, derived from two main meanings in Polynesian languages as prohibited and sacred, has been assessed in European terms as prohibition and sacredness, but these concepts cannot be expressed in Polynesian terms.

Steiner argues that taboo is a single term that embraces ritual impurity implying awe, obedience, abstention, or keeping of distance. He suggests that the Polynesian word *noa* is the opposite of taboo in terms of polarity, not prohibition. *Noa* means unspecific, undersigned, free, and common that does not come under the influence of taboo in terms of ritual or civil law. The breath of meaning within taboo is well-illustrated by Lehmann's (1930, pp. 301–312) description of the social and political aspects of mana and taboo. Lehmann categorises taboo under three headings: i) socially conditioned taboos; ii) taboos of individual parts of the body and special bodily functions; iii) religious taboos.

Under the first category, Lehmann lists taboos connected to persons holding high office, separated into the power of high officials to give commands and declare taboos, taboos resulting from the sanctity of chiefs, taboos connected with priesthood, and taboos of rank and status. Further, taboos in this category concern the segregation of women, taboos in economic activity and crafts, in times of war, taboo as a legal symbol of a claim or appropriation, and finally, the custom of *tapa-tabu* already referenced. The second main category includes head and dorsal taboos, taboos of special bodily conditions of temporary impurity connected to menstruation and childbirth, and taboos concerned with illness and death. The third main group concerns taboos connected with priesthood. The power of priesthood to impose taboo keeps political power of the chieftains in check. The Polynesian method of exercising power called *mana* is measured by a person's status on the basis of the kind of taboos s/he could impose (Steiner, ibid, pp. 39–40). The graded power of prohibition is accumulated in the authority of the chieftain who held within this office the social tension of the clan. The chieftain simultaneously personified the awe of power, the taboos expressing it, as well as the ability to use segregation taboos to isolate her/him; for example, walking on the ground would become correspondently taboo for his ordinary subjects, but this would be impractical to implement on a daily basis.

Douglas (1966, p. xiii) introduces the notion that 'taboo is a spontaneous coding practice which sets up a vocabulary of spatial limits and physical and verbal signals to hedge around vulnerable relations.' Cultural theorist, Bauman (1973, p. 123) contends that 'ordering involves transmuting what is fundamentally a continuous shapeless stream of perception into a set of discrete entities' and offers the perspective that 'non-things' do not and cannot constitute the target of taboo. The target of taboo is found not in the areas short of culturally bestowed meaning but in those areas of awe and anxiety inspiring regions overloaded with meaning, particularly contradictory meaning. Bauman sees taboo as an attempt to dispose of confusing meanings rather than account for culturally translucent ones (Bauman, ibid, p. 124). The praxis of order is culturally imposed and it threatens to unleash danger if the code of order is not respected, particularly in terms of *contagion*, which extends the danger of a broken taboo to the whole community.

Douglas stresses that taboos depend on community commitment, credibility, and complicity. The implicit theory is that physical nature, including the human body, water, earth, vegetation, and animal life automatically form an armoury to avenge broken taboos to defend the founding principles of order in any given society. I agree with Douglas, Bauman, and Steiner's (1956, pp. 145–147) varied assessments that all dangerous situations are socially and culturally defined. To face danger is to face another power, suggestive of the older meaning of the English word *danger* as *power, jurisdiction* or *dominion.* Danger becomes narrowed down by taboo from unseen threats into specific danger spots that can be controlled. Through contagion there is *social* participation as well as *individual* fear of danger. As Bauman so adroitly expresses (1974, pp. 124–125), the ambiguity of the attitudinal complex associated with taboo is a match for the equivocality of situations and objects to which the taboo provides the institutionalised or instinctive response. Taboo unites attitudes otherwise incompatible: awe and repulsion, admiration and abhorrence, attachment and hatred, explorative curiosity and escape drive.

Methodology

Referencing and furthering Douglas' innovative work on taboo and that of others, particularly van Gennep and Turner, in their emphasis on taboo as ritual separation between status values, my method of amplification focusses on the concept of taboo from *interdisciplinary perspectives* as an *in-between, organising principle* that separates and differentiates stages through a symbolic ritual process of separation of *order* as clean/blessed and *disorder* as pollution/disassociated. Despite Bauman's slightly different perspective on 'non-things,' I examine how bodily fluids transmitted across bodily margins as *me* but *no longer me* become tabooed and influence how one perceives kinship structures, gender roles, incest, propagation, and animal categories (edible/inedible). Such perceptions have particular relevance to modern clinical practice when addressing obsessive compulsions. I assess *dirt* as a term to describe *disorder* and how this meaning has been used to transfer unconscious, undifferentiated tabooed shadow emotions, including tabooed gender potential, onto an outer object as 'other,' making this person or race be experienced as risky, polluted, dirty, unblessed, unhuman, and disassociated. I question the validity of Freud's premise of incest taboo as an innate, universal, structural phenomenology as he ignores Palaeolithic-Neolithic kin clan evidence to the contrary. Instead, I draw on anthropological studies on totemism of Tylor (1903), Fraser (1910), Morgan (1877), Radcliffe-Brown (1952), Levi-Strauss (1962), and Lewis-Williams and Pearce (2005) to uncover an *associative,* creative logic attached to taboo that points to a wider ontology.

Moving through anthropological perspectives, both comparative and structural, I introduce Jungian psychosocial and *archetypal*[1] depth psychological perspectives to widen the study of taboo, linking and comparing indigenous shamanic practices to working with unconscious processes such as dreams, symbols, and active imaginative in modern clinical practice. Although Jung's work on symbols[2] is not specifically mentioned by comparative, sociostructural anthropologists such as Turner, Levi-Strauss, and Tambiah, his definition of symbol formation is nevertheless both helpful and pertinent in analysing the important function that associative, differentiated thinking plays in taboo ritual and liminal states as I will show in each chapter, particularly chapters 2, 4, 6, 7, and 8.

Unconscious/conscious taboos influence how we perceive transitional, indeterminate states across margins in maturation and individuation processes. Both these processes are experienced as awful and fearful because the initiate, male or female, enters and navigates the border*land:* the old developmental stage and safe status is left behind to enter into a new, as yet, unexplored and risky one. I argue that taboo embodies the perilous, symbolic meaning of these rites of passage and that its emotional value and intensity in the form of symptomatology varies across cultures. Such variation reveal hidden unconscious cultural complexes attached to internal and external lines of separation and their responsiveness and flexibility toward change and loss. I expand upon a taboo as an invisible window into which one can explore, mirror, reflect upon, and incorporate the disallowed differences between 'me' and 'not-me.' An important aspect of archetypal factoring is that taboo emotions, normally invisible, personify into rich complex images that become visible and, as such, can be analysed and re-experienced, allowing for a regenerative teleological awareness of their value so that none of their ambivalent, emotional, experiential symbolic content and meaning is lost.

I examine the colour black and its relative shades of darkness as *archetypal* creative death and rebirth processes whereby one moves from the visibility of *known* consciousness into the invisibility of the *not yet known* unconscious process associated with taboo, peril, and dread. Blackness is connected to night-time, the time for dreams, resting, and reflection. I examine how the colour black has been negatively used to separate, marginalise, and dehumanise people making them tabooed as *other.*

Subjective experience of taboo in twinship

My personal interest in taboo stems from my own experience of being a tabooed anomaly as the second-born, same-sex twin. Twins have been discussed as taboo subjects by social anthropologist Fraser (1922, pp. 79–81) and cultural theorist Girard (1977, pp. 41–70). In some indigenous cultures, one or both twins are killed at birth and sometimes the mother. Twins are regarded as taboo and sacred because their double birth arouses suspicious awe due to their unexpected simultaneous arrival that contradicts the rules of normal propagation (Peek, 2001). Newman (1942, pp. 14–15) links such fear with the belief that the birth of single offspring distinguishes man from 'lower' animals with multiple births. The birth of twins, therefore, signifies a nonhuman anomaly or bestial entity. Some tribes believe that no man can father more than one offspring at a time and that the mother must have had sex with two men to produce twins, injecting the added suspicion of female betrayal and promiscuity that deserves ostracism. In China, one twin is considered evil (Hall, 1928). Girard (ibid, pp. 41–75) points out that the sacrifice of one twin restores vital equilibrium by eliminating that dual *monstrosity* imbued in the baleful doubling of nature. In Dahomey Africa, a special ceremony is performed to prevent twins reverting back into monkeys; in other tribes twins are believed to be transformed salmon and could change back into fish.

As the second-born, unexpected, same-sex twin, personifying the family 'shock' at my anomalous arrival, I occupied that forbidden, enclosed, invisible, tabooed space whereby I was initially not given a name and had difficulty finding a gendered voice to articulate that space 'betwixt and between' my expected first-born twin sister. That restricted space began in the womb. Although I was conceived first, my twin sister was blocking the birth canal so I had to push her out of the womb first to separate and be born second, otherwise I would have remained stuck in that liminal passage of the birth canal. I describe the position of twins as an archetypal phenomenon in a recent interdisciplinary post-Jungian research study whereby one twin, as first-born, symbolically personifies visibility/containment/safety/blessing and the other, as second-born, personifies invisibility/separation/risk/damnation on a microlevel irrespective of their actual attributes, which is simultaneously reflected in macrosocietal structures (Brodersen, 2016, pp. 93–105). However, the second-born twin as the taboo 'shadow' of the first-born also personifies a creative widening and acceptance of hitherto individual/collective forbidden traits at the margins of twin interaction, which is based upon a bilateral rather than a closed hierarchical one.

This enquiry into taboo follows on from my twin research to examine more closely these forbidden, in-between, invisible, tabooed spaces in indigenous premodern and modern Western cultures within cultural complexes that manifest during times of transition at the margins. I explore how taboo creatively stretches the borders between the known and unknown and allow *differences* to emerge despite collective pressures for *sameness*. I present empirical clinical material from two client cases to show how taboo operates within collective symptom formations (obsessive compulsions and anorexia) whereby a person is lodged within an individual and cultural complex (betwixt and between) as a forbidden, liminal, transitional space, in-between life and death, until understanding and meaning deepens the archetypal experience of taboo with all the attendant invisibility and anxiety that moving from one status to the next generates, and becomes *visible*.

Any in-between state that breaks down the original structure by introducing ambiguities and anomalies that stretch and change borders in unexpected ways is fearful and risky. I define taboo as the *unexpected*, the *shock* of change that hides within and between borders between the ego (consciousness) and the other (unconscious components of the *shadow* and the *contra-sexual other*). Fraser (1922) and Radcliffe-Brown (1952) note that taboo is not limited to indigenous belief in magic but extends worldwide to include modern Western civilisations in that certain phenomena are guarded and protected by the taboos they generate. This progressive interdisciplinary approach introduces separate chapters that discuss anthropological, socio-political, and in-depth psychological perspectives of a particular aspect of taboo still open to academic debate. My aim is to widen and deepen the understanding of taboo and show how the concept is ever present and provocative in the twenty-first century with its negative application of the miscegenation taboo, the marginalisation and dehumanisation of individuals and races considered dirty, unblessed, and thus unfit for progeny. Researching into the original meaning of taboo and touching that sacred, ritualised, transitional in-between space could ameliorate its present negative use as forbidden and untouchable.

Outline of chapters

Each chapter describes an aspect of taboo that I open to further debate. Chapter 2 analyses Fraser's (1922) mainly descriptive analysis of the origin and practice of taboo firstly, as sympathetic or imitative *magic* and, secondly, as contagious *magic*. I expand upon these definitions. I discuss the relationship between taboo and loss of soul through separation or death, and how these losses are held and structured within sacred rituals. I explore examples of both types of *magical*, analogical thinking and the role taboo plays in relationship to ritual, the origin of religion, and scientific thinking. I place the concept of taboo within Jung's two kinds of thinking (Jung, 1911–12/1952b), archetypal theory (Jung, 1932, 1947; Hillman, 1983), and synchronicity (Jung, 1952, and von Franz, 1994). I include a broad spectrum of anthropological research such as Tylor (1873), Malinowski (1931), Evans-Pritchard (1937), Homans (1941), Radcliffe-Brown (1952), Webster, (1942), Eliade (1958a,b), Tambiah (1973), Finnegan and Horton (1973 eds.), and Greenwood and Goodwyn (2016) who differ in degree from Fraser's interpretation of taboo as an erroneous application of the notion of causality. They support the use of indirect *associative* thinking in taboo prohibition as akin to scientific logic. Finally, I discuss the value of taboo rituals within modern clinical practice.

In chapter 3, I discuss the work of structural anthropologist Douglas (1966; 1968) and cultural theorist and psychoanalyst Kristeva (1982) in relation to taboo. Both academics, using different approaches and source material, widen the parameters of discussion about the origins and positioning of taboo. I present material from anthropologist Leach (1964) and Radcliffe-Brown (1952) amongst others. The chapter argues that language gives names to distinguish and separate things; taboo inhibits the recognition of those parts of the continuum that separates things. Under taboo, they become non-things, 'not-me' as anomalies that fall out of classification and fill the interstices as dirt or waste products. Taking her research from Leviticus in the Biblical *Old Testament,* Douglas states that ritual blessing is the source of all good and the withdrawal of blessing as the source of all dangers. Holiness is defined by strict categories of classification, cleanliness, and order. Diet is classified into clean and unclean foods and animals are separated into edible/clean and inedible/ unclean. However, dirt is necessary because purity is the enemy of change and deadens creativity. Douglas' ideas on purity and danger are evaluated in relation to Julia Kristeva's work on *abjection*. Kristeva maintains that contrary to whatever enters the mouth as forms of nourishment, whatever is expelled from the body, out of its pores and orifices, gives rise to abjection. Kristeva suggests that how faeces and sexuality is ritualised allows the 'two universes of filth and prohibition to brush lightly against each-other without necessarily being identified as *object* and *law*.' On account of this flexibility, Kristeva argues that the rites of defilement as the anomalous 'speaking being' stand at both edges of the unnameable as the non-object *and* the off-limits. Both descriptive analyses deepen the ongoing enquiry between taboo and filth in connection with cultural complexes.

Chapter 4 analyses the connection of *totem* with taboo, the origins of religion, and kinship structures. Totemism dominates two worlds: the symbolic and the material. I include Freud's perspective of totem and taboo and expand on the work of Levi-Strauss' (1962) concept of totemism as containing an internal, logical thinking component that challenges the view that the totemic relationship is primarily a sensory phenomenon. I examine the relationship between *taboo, human propagation, and animal categories*. Leach (1964, pp. 23–63) extends Douglas' (1966) categories of creatures (edible/inedible) to incest taboo and propagation categories. Taboo serves to separate the Self from the world: the world is divided into zones or margins of relative social distance corresponding to 1) very close (taboo); 2) close but further afield (partially permissible); 3) afield (permissible) and 4) too remote (taboo). A fifth category contains animals and persons classified as tabooed filth.

This fifth category has important ramifications for the development of dehumanisation through taboo. I explore the *miscegenation taboo between races*. What characteristics are shared with a sex, clan, or group that makes one part of that group and gives one a feeling of belonging, containment, and structure? Colour of skin and hair is a visible manifestation of demarcation between groups whereby people of black or darker skin colour have been labelled as inferior and less racially pure. Such a taboo may apply to people of different world cultures, races, and skin colour where the *mixing of blood* between races is prohibited and ethnic cleansing practiced to rid cultures of *impurities*. Dark colours emanating from the margin (skin) that cannot be purified through ritual washing is particularly tabooed and dangerous, linked to fear of unknown 'shadow' animalistic, nonhuman aspects crossing over the margin between the known and unknown. I examine racial and gender differences (supposedly smaller brains, less intelligence, etc.) used to marginalise and dehumanise races and women through the works of Gellately and Stoltzfus eds. (2001), Naimark (2001), Picot (2001), Brickman (2003), Bergner (2005), Bain, Vaes, and Leyens eds. (2014), and others. The denigration of animals is in marked contrast to their ancestral position under totemism.

Of all the taboos, incest taboo creates the most debate and ongoing fascination. The origin and positioning of this taboo has generated much controversy within anthropology, cultural theory, and psychoanalytical theory. In chapter 5, I attempt to unravel the complex issues surrounding and underpinning this taboo by examining the origin of incest taboo versus the origins of sex avoidance, analysing when incest prohibition manifested itself as a taboo and the psychosocial conditions behind it (Westermarck, 1891; Fox, 1994; Turner and Maryanski, 2005). I question Freud's (1938) premise that incest taboo is a universal, innate phenomena because no one knew who the biological father was during Palaeolithic-Neolithic eras, and, therefore, could not be castrated by him. Inheritance passed through the female gens not through the father (Morgan, 1877; Coontz and Henderson, 1986). Patrilineal inheritance developed with the onset of civilisation c. 3000 BCE with the introduction of primogeniture as the exclusive right of the first-born son to inherit property, and rationalised by the Genesis myth that subordinated women as creators (Brodersen, 2016). I examine and unbind psychoanalytical and psychosocial interpretations of the Oedipus complex (Girard, 2004), one of the main cornerstones of psychoanalytical incest taboo theory, and point out its shortcomings, particularly in relation to the development of totemism and exogamy that arguably developed from food taboos rather than an incest taboo (Reed, 1975). Some anthropologists suggest that the most widespread sex taboos had nothing to do with genital functioning but served as a prohibition against eating together. Others suggest that food segregation was part of a wider segregation between male hunters and mothers and children based on the *taboo of spilt blood*. Finally, I explore the development of the need for incest taboo, with offspring leaving home past puberty, and the symptomatology arising from its violation (Anderson and Shafer, 1979; Green, 1984).

Chapter 6 examines the correlation between taboo, the development of conscience and emotional ambivalence. Freud (1912–13) suggests a link between emotional ambivalence and a taboo incest wish (Oedipus complex). This chapter ties together the emotional components of taboo, how they develop into symptomatology, and questions Freud's overemphasis on incest wish as the basis for symptomatology, such as obsessive compulsions. I stress that the aetiology of such symptoms develop from the need to cross over margins into the freedom of the 'other,' a movement that is prohibited in totalitarian, monistic, hierarchal cultures that interpret the 'other' as risky and sinful. I reference Reddish's (2014) new theory of conscience to further question Freud's positioning of a *patrilineal* totem in relation to taboo. I examine authoritarian dynamics through the research of Stenner (2005), Stein (2017), and psychoanalyst Luci (2017) for in-depth psychosocial perspectives on the relationship between terror, love, and brainwashing, as shown in authoritarian-totalist disorganised attachment mindsets. Noting clinical vignettes on compulsive behaviour (Bisagni, 2017), I compare Freudian developmental perspectives with the Jungian/post-Jungian *archetypal* positioning of taboo as *disallowed space* for independent thinking using the work of Hillman (1979), Woodman (1982, 1985), Ziegler (1983), and von Franz (2000) on the *puer* and *puella* phenomenology. I describe the painful conflict between safety/obedience/blessed and freedom/disobedience/sinful that are played out at the orifices/margins of the body as *illegitimate tabooed subjectivity* by illustrating two clinical case studies from German clients (both sexes) from Catholic ethnic-German post-war immigrant backgrounds suffering from obsessive compulsions such as excessive washing on contact with bodily discharges of others, and eating disorders such as anorexia nervosa related to taboo on food as their invisible markers.

In chapter 7, I examine the importance of rites of passage as periods of margin or liminality as an interstructural phenomenon subject to taboo referencing mainly the work of van Gennep (1960), Eliade (1958a), Turner (1964, 1969) and Goodwyn (2016). Rites create meaning in that space at the margin of Turner's 1964 definition of 'betwixt and between.' Meade (1995) and Bell (1992) suggest that the radical dismantling of institutions, boundaries, and belief systems in the twentieth and twenty-first centuries, through two world wars and interregional migratory upheavals, leave cultures bereft of the capacity to handle death and embrace life fully. Without some spiritual vision and ritual structure, helplessness in face of war, forced migration and separation is covered up by displays of force and greed. If there is no conscious ritual of loss and renewal this means that individuals lose their capacity to experience the sorrow and joy essential to feel fully human. When original meaning has been lost, without a meaningful container and structure to aid such difficult passages, life flattens out into a death of meaning and there is an increase of compulsive meaningless repetitions to find it.

This chapter critically examines the rites of passage of indigenous people and modern Europeans as they navigate painful separations that occur at birth, puberty, and, particularly, death through the works of Turner (1964, 1969), Boyer (2001), Taylor (2002), McCauley and Lawson (2002), Hernlund and Shell-Duncan (2007), Lifton and Olson (2009), and others. In such initiation rites, persons as neophytes are structurally defined as *transitional beings*. They have a physical, but no social reality, hence they are invisible, tabooed, and hidden with no status, kinship rank, or personal clothing to demarcate them structurally. As they are no longer classifiable, the symbols that represent them are drawn from the biology of death, phases of the moon at nighttime (Baring and Cashford, 1991; Cashford, 2003), decomposition, and other physical bodily taboos denoting important changes in status value. Such rites accompanied through painful taboo rituals at birth, puberty, and death, give meaning and courage to endure separation and change that simultaneously facilitate rebirth.

Chapter 8 discusses rites of passage—leading to a new development status—that take place away from daylight in secluded darkness, similar to working with unconscious processes at night-time through dream work. Within this dark and invisible frame, we enter the liminal night-time, taboo journey of transformation, analogous to the sun as it sets in the west and disappears into the darkness of the unseen 'other' side (Tylor 1902, Jung 1911–12/1952a, Brodersen 2012). This chapter explores the colour black as a night-time colour of invisibility—which is not considered negative, but as a potential to be explored in the unconscious—not yet realised in consciousness. Blackness, itself, has many shades: black that recedes and absorbs; black that dampens and softens; black that sharpens and etches; and black that shines with effervescence (Hillman 1997). From this analysis of black, I examine the role of shamans who undertake the difficult, symbolic journey into the unconscious where ancestors are thought to reside in order to give advice and restore lost tabooed soul aspects of the self. I use the work of Rasmussen (1929), Levi-Strauss (1963), Eliade (1964), Needham (1967), Sonne (1997), Haule (2011), Merchant (2012), and others on shamanism. I give two examples of shamanic practice and compare their journey into the symbolic *land of the dead* to the work of psychoanalysis, Jungian analysis in particular. I conclude that taboo is best addressed through working creatively with unconscious processes whereby tabooed, untouchable, dissociated emotions *personify* and *gain visibility* as *archetypal images*, such as Sedna, the dirt ridden, abandoned, vengeful, underworld sea goddess; Hades, the Greek underworld god, the invisible, tabooed hidden hider; and Penthos, the tattered, angry and forlorn, dark-skinned, transsexual god of loss, grief, and mourning, who all give diverse form to the intense, passionate, contagious, dangerous emotions.

I conclude with a summary of my findings in chapter 9 and suggest opening up the subject for fresh research. I stress that the original indigenous emphasis on the *sacred* within the term of totem and taboo in kinship structures has been lost and needs to be recovered and reinstated. Taboo prohibitions rely on imaginative associative thinking to focus on and contain vital energy that is in danger of being lost, or has been lost, and provides a spotlight and insight into such leakage in order to repair it.

Notes

1. I define the term *archetypal* and *archetypal image* more fully in chapter 2. Briefly, Jung (1954, paras. 1–4) describes archetypes as stemming from the realm of the collective unconscious or the objective psyche that does not depend on a personal acquisition but are, as yet, unborn. The content of personal and cultural unconscious can be made known through feeling toned complexes that constitute the personal and collective psychic life. The archetypes, however, can only be discerned through

their images or motifs that appear in myths, dreams, and fairy tales where specific archaic or universal primordial types emerge and influence psychic life through their energetic charge.
2. The symbol as defined by Jung, (1921, paras. 823–828) is a product of a complex nature that is neither rational nor irrational. The collaboration necessary to form a symbol entails a genuine conflict where thesis and antithesis negate each-other and a new position is forced to acknowledge its absolute participation in both. A new content emerges as a *living* symbol that stands in a compensatory relation to both, forming a mediatory product whereby the conflict is resolved and energy flows into a common channel, which Jung defines as the *transcendent function*.

References

Anderson, L.M. and Shafer, G. (1979). The Character Disordered Family: A Community Treatment Model for Family Sexual Abuse. *American Journal of Orthopsychiatry* 49, 436–445.

Bain, P.B., Vaes, J., and Leyens, J-P. (2014). Advances in Understanding Humanness and Dehumanization. In Bain, P.G., Vaes, J., and Leyens, J-P. (eds.) *Humanness and Dehumanisation*. New York and London: Routledge, pp. 1–9.

Baring, A. and Cashford, J. (1991). *The Myth of the Goddess, Evolution of an Image*. London and New York: Penguin Books.

Bauman, Z. (1973). *Culture as Praxis*. London and Boston: Routledge and Kegan Paul.

Bell, C. (1992). *Ritual Theory, Ritual Practice*. Oxford: Oxford University Press.

Bergner, G. (2005). *Taboo Subjects: Race, Sex and Psychoanalysis*. Minneapolis and London: University of Minnesota Press.

Bible (1989 edn.) *The Revised English Bible*. Oxford and Cambridge: Oxford University Press.

Bisagni, F. (2017). *Obsessions; The Twisted Cruelty*. London: Karnac Books.

Boyer, P. (2001). *Religion Explained: The Evolutionary Origins of Religious Thought*. New York: Basic Books.

Brickman, C. (2003). *Aboriginal Populations in the Mind; race and primitivity in psychoanalysis*. New York: Columbia University Press.

Briffault, R. (1931). *The Mothers, The Matriarchal Theory of Social Origins*. New York: Macmillan.

Brodersen, E. (2012). 'In the Nature of Twins: a Study of the Archetypal Realm of Universal Duality, Opposition and Imitation Between the "First" and "Other" in Creation Myths.' *International Journal of Jungian Studies* 4(2), 133–149.

Brodersen, E. (2016). *The Laws of Inheritance. A post-Jungian study of twins and the relationship been the first and the other(s)*. London and New York: Routledge.

Cashford, J. (2003). *The Moon, Myth and Image*. London: Cassell Illustrated.

Cook, Captain James and King, Captain James (1803). *A Voyage to the Pacific Ocean from 1776–1780*, Vol. III. London: Champante and Whitrow.

Coontz, S. and Henderson, P. (1986). Property Forms, Political Power and Female Labour in the Origins of Class and State Societies. In Coontz, S. and Henderson, P. (eds.) *Women's Work, Men's Property, The Origins of Gender and Class*. London: Verso, pp. 108–155.

Coontz, S. and Henderson, P. (eds.) (1986). *Women's Work, Men's Property, The Origins of Gender and Class*. London: Verso.

Costello, M.S. (2006). *Imagination, Illness and Injury: Jungian Psychology and the Somatic Dimensions of Perception*. London and New York: Routledge.

Douglas, M. (1966). *Purity and Danger*, (new preface, 2002). Abingdon, Oxon, and New York: Routledge.
Douglas, M. (1968). Pollution. In *Implicit Meanings; Selected Essays in Anthropology*, 2nd edn. London and New York: Routledge, pp. 106–115.
Eliade, M. (1958a). *Rites and Symbols of Initiation. The Mysteries of Birth and Rebirth.* Woodstock, CT: Spring Publications, 1995.
Eliade, M. (1958b). *Patterns in Comparative Religion*. Lincoln and London: University of Nebraska Press, 1996.
Eliade, M. (1964). *Shamanism, Archaic Technique of Ecstasy*. Princeton: Princeton University Press.
Evans-Pritchard, E.E., (1937). Witchcraft Explains Unfortunate Events. In (1979) Lessa, W.A., and Vogt, E.Z. (eds.) *Reader in Comparative Religion. An Anthropological Approach*, 4th edn. New York: Harper Collins, pp. 362–366.
Finnegan, R. and Horton, R. (eds.) (1973). *Modes of Thought. Essays on Thinking in Western and Non-Western Societies*. Eugene, Oregon: Wipf & Stock.
Fox, R. (1994). *The Challenge of Anthropology. Old Encounters and New Excursions*. New Brunswick, NJ and London: Transaction Publisher, 1995.
Fraser, J.G. (1910). *Totemism and Exogamy, a Treatise on Certain Forms of Superstition and Society*. London: Macmillan.
Fraser, J.G. (1922). *The Golden Bough, a Study in Magic and Religion*, abridged edn. London and New York: Penguin Books.
Freud, S. (1912–13). Totem and Taboo. In *The Origins of Religion, Collected Works*, Vol. 13. London: Penguin Books, 1990.
Freud, S. (1938). Application. In Moses and Monotheism (III). In *Collected Works*, Vol. 13. *The Origins of Religion*. London and New York: Penguin, 1985.
de Freycinet, L. (1839). *Voyage autour du Monde, enterpris par ordre du roi* 1817–1820. Paris: Smithsonian Library.
Gellately, R. and Stoltzfus, N. (2001). Social Outsiders and the Construction of the Community of the People. In Gellately, R. and Stoltzfus, N. (eds.) *Social Outsiders in Nazi Germany*. Princeton and Oxford: Princeton University Press, pp. 3–19.
Gellately, R., and Stoltzfus, N. (2001). *Social Outsiders in Nazi Germany*. Princeton and Oxford: Princeton University Press.
Girard, R. (1977). *Violence and the Sacred*. London and New York: Continuum, 2005.
Girard, R. (2004). *Oedipus Unbound*. Stanford, California: Stanford University Press.
Goodwyn, E. (2016). *Healing Symbols in Psychotherapy: A Ritual Approach*. London and New York: Routledge.
Green, A.H. (1984). Child Abuse by Siblings. *Child Abuse and Neglect*, 8(3), 311–317.
Greenwood, S. and Goodwyn, E.D. (2016). *Magical Consciousness. An Anthropological and Neurobiological Approach*. New York and London: Routledge.
Hall, H.U. (1928). Twins in Upper Guinea. *Museum Journal of the University of Pennsylvania*. Philadelphia: University of Pennsylvania.
Harris, J.R. (2009). The Imaginal Realm of Dissociation. The Archetypal Nature of Trauma in light of Quantum Physics. In Aizenstat, S. and Bosnak, R., (eds.) *Imagination and Medicine, The Future of Healing in the Age of Neuroscience*. New Orleans, Louisiana: Spring Journal Books, pp. 61–75.
Haule, J.R. (2011). *Jung in the 21st Century, Vol. 1: Evolution and Archetype*. London and New York: Routledge.

Hertz, R. (2009). A Contribution to the Study of the Collective Representation of Death. In Robbins, A.C. G.M. (ed.) *Death Mourning and Burial: A Cross-Cultural Reader.* Malden, MA: Blackwell, pp. 197–212.
Hillman, J. (1979). *The Dream and the Underworld.* Toronto: Harper Collins.
Hillman, J. (1983). *Archetypal Psychology: A Brief Account.* Dallas, Texas: Spring Pubs, 1993.
Hillman, J. (1997). The Seduction of Black. In Hillman, Hogarth, et al (eds.) *Haiti or the Psychology of Black.* Woodstock, Conn: Spring Publication.
Homans, G.C. (1941). Anxiety and Ritual: The Theories of Malinowski and Radcliffe-Brown. In (1979) Lessa, W.A., and Vogt, E.Z. (eds.) *Reader in Comparative Religion. An Anthropological Approach*, 4th edn. New York: Harper Collins, pp. 57–62.
Jung, C.G. (1911–12/1952a). Symbols of the Mother and Rebirth. In *Collected Works,* Vol. 5. *Symbols of Transformation*, 2nd edn. London: Routledge and Kegan Paul, 1995.
Jung, C.G. (1911–12/1952b). Two Kinds of Thinking. In *Collected Works,* Vol. 5. *Symbols of Transformation*, 2nd edn. London: Routledge and Kegan Paul, 1995.
Jung, C.G. (1921). Definitions. In *Collected Works*, Vol. 6. *Psychological Types*, 2nd edn. London: Routledge and Kegan Paul, 1989.
Jung, C.G. (1932). The Structure of the Psyche. In *Collected Works,* Vol. 8. *The Structure and Dynamics of the Psyche*, 2nd edn. London: Routledge and Kegan Paul, 1991.
Jung, C.G. (1933). King and Queen. In *Collected Works*, Vol. 16. *The Practice of Psychotherapy*, 2nd edn. London: Routledge and Kegan Paul, 1993.
Jung, C.G. (1947). On The Nature of the Psyche. In *Collected Works,* Vol. 8. *The Structure, and Dynamics of the Psyche*, 2nd edn. London: Routledge and Kegan Paul, 1991.
Jung, C.G. (1952). Synchronicity: An Acausal Connecting Principle. In *Collected Works,* Vol. 8, *The Structure and Dynamics of the Psyche*, 2nd edn. London: Routledge and Kegan Paul, 1991.
Jung, C.G. (1954). Archetypes of the Collective Unconscious. In *Collected Works,* Vol. 9i. *The Archetypes of the Collective Unconscious*, 2nd edn. London: Routledge and Kegan Paul, 1990.
Kristeva, J. (1982). *Powers of Horror: An Essay in Abjection.* Trans. Rondiez, L.S. New York: Columbia University Press.
Leach, E.R. (1964). Anthropological Aspects of Language: Animal Categories and Verbal Abuse. In (1979) Lessa, W.A. and Vogt E.Z. (eds.) *Reader in Comparative Religion. An Anthropological Approach*, 4th edn. New York: Harper Collins, pp. 153–166.
Lehmann, Fr. R. (1930). *Die Polynesischen Tabusitten.* Leipzig: Voigtländer Verlag.
Lessa, W.A. and Vogt, E.Z. (eds.) (1979). *Reader in Comparative Religion. An Anthropological Approach*, 4th edn. New York: Harper Collins.
Levi-Strauss, C. (1949). *The Elementary Structures of Kinship.* (revised edn.) Boston: Beacon Press, 1969.
Levi-Strauss, C. (1962). *Totemism.* London: Merlin Press.
Levi-Strauss, C. (1963). *Structural Anthropology.* Trans. Jocobson C. and Schoepf, B.G. New York: Basic Books.
Lewis-Williams, D. and Pearce, D. (2005). *Inside the Neolithic Mind.* London: Thames and Hudson.
Lisiansky, U. (1814). *A Voyage around the World in the Years, 1803, 1804, 1805 and 1806.* London: Booth and Longman.
Luci, M. (2017). *Torture, Psychanalysis & Human Rights.* London and New York: Routledge.
Malinowski, B. (1931). The Role of Magic and Religion. In (1979) Lessa, W.A. and Vogt, E.Z. (eds.) *Reader in Comparative Religion. An Anthropological Approach*, 4th edn. New York: Harper Collins, pp. 37–46.

Meade, M. (1995). Introduction to Eliade, M. (1958). *Rites and Symbols of Initiation. The Mysteries of Birth and Rebirth.* Woodstock, CT: Spring Publications, 1995.
Merchant, J. (2012). *Shamans and Analysts: New Insights on the Wounded Healer.* Hove and New York: Routledge.
Morgan, L.H. (1877). *Ancient Society.* New Brunswick, N.J: Transaction Publisher, 2000.
Naimark, N.M. (2001). *Fires of Hatred, Ethnic Cleansing in Twentieth-Century Europe.* Cambridge, Mass. and London: Harvard University Press.
Needham, R. (1967). Percussion and Transition. *Journal of the Royal Anthropological Institute* (Man) 2(4), 606–614.
Newman, H.H. (1942). *Twins and Super Twins: A Popular and Scientific Account of the Causes, Frequency, Heredity, Intelligence, Psychology and Affinity of Twins, Triplets, Quadruplets and Quintuplets.* London and New York: Hutchison's Scientific and Technical Publications.
Peek, P.M. (ed.). (2001). *Twins in Africa and Diaspora Cultures.* Bloomington: Indiana University Press.
Pichot, A. (2001). *The Pure Society from Darwin to Hitler.* London and New York: Verso, 2009.
Radcliffe-Brown, A.R. (1952). Taboo. In *Structure and Function in Primitive Society. Essays and Addresses.* Glencoe, Ill: The Free Press, pp. 133–152.
Rasmussen, K. (1929). A Shaman's Journey to the Sea Spirit. In *Report of the Fifth Thule Expedition 1921–1924, Vol. VII, No.1 Intellectual Culture of the Iglulik Eskimos.* Copenhagen: Gyldendalake Boghandel, Nordisk Forlag, pp. 123–129.
Reddish, E. (2014). *The Petrified Ego. A New Theory of Conscience.* London: Karnac.
Reed, E. (1975). *Women's Evolution. From Matriarchal Clan to Patriarchal Family.* New York and London: Pathfinder Press.
Robertson Smith, W. (1889). *The Religion of the Semites.* Edinburgh: A & C Black.
Shortland, E. (1851). *The Southern Districts of New Zealand.* London: Longman Brown, Green and Longmans.
Sonne, B. (1997). Mythology of the Eskimos. In (1997) Larrington, C. (ed.) *The Woman's Companion to Mythology.* London: Harper Collins, pp. 162–185.
Stenner, K. (2005). *The Authoritarian Dynamic. Cambridge Studies in Public Opinion and Political Psychology.* Cambridge and New York: Cambridge University Press.
Stein, A. (2017). *Terror, Love & Brainwashing. Attachment in Cults and Totalitarian Systems.* London and New York: Routledge.
Steiner, F. (1956). *Taboo.* London and New York: Routledge.
Tambiah, S.J. (1973). The Form and Meaning of Magical Acts. In Horton, R. and Flannigan, R. (eds.) *Modes of Thought.* London: Faber and Faber.
Taylor, T. (2002). *The Buried Soul: How Humans Invented Death.* Boston: Beacon.
Turner, V.W. (1964). Betwixt and Between: The Liminal Period in Rites De Passage. In (1979) Lessa, W.A. and Vogt, E.Z. (eds.) *Reader in Comparative Religion, An Anthropological Approach*, 4th edn. New York: Harper Collins, pp. 234–243.
Turner, V.W. (1969). *The Ritual Process, Structure and Anti-Structure.* New Brunswick US and London: Aldine Transaction, 2008.
Tylor, E.B. (1873). Animism. In (1979) Lessa, W.A. and Vogt, E.Z. (eds.) *Reader in Comparative Religion. An Anthropological Approach*, 4th edn. New York: Harper Collins, pp. 9–19.
Van Gennep, A. (1960). *The Rites of Passage.* Chicago: The University of Chicago Press.
Von Franz, M-L. (1994). *Archetypal Dimensions of the Psyche.* Boston and London: Shambhala, 1997.

Von Franz, M-L. (2000). *The Problem of the Puer Aeternus.* Toronto: Inner City Books.
Von Langsdorff, G.H. (1812). *Bemerkeungen und der Reise um die Welt in den Jahren 1803 bis 1807.* Frankfurt: Verlag Friedrich Wilmark.
Von Krustenstern, A.J. (1812). *Reise um die Welt in den Jahren 1803 bis 1806.* Berlin: Haude und Spener.
Webster, H. (1942). *Taboo: A Sociological Study.* New York: Octagon Books, 1973.
Westermarck, E. (1891). *The History of Human Marriage.* London: Macmillan.
Wilkes, C. (1845). *Narrative of the Unites States, Exploring Expedition, During the Years 1838 to 1842*, 5 vols. Philadelphia: Lea and Blanchard.
Woodman, M. (1982). *Addiction to Perfection, the Still Unravished Bride.* Toronto: Inner City Books.
Woodman, M. (1985). *The Pregnant Virgin. A Process of Psychological Transformation.* Toronto, Canada: Inner City Books.
Ziegler, A.J. (1983). *Archetypal Medicine.* Woodstock, Connecticut: Spring Publications.

Chapter 2

The nature of taboo in indigenous practices

Introduction

This chapter describes in some detail the taboos that pervade indigenous thinking in the form of taboo rituals and taboo personages. This material will be further analysed and differentiated in the subsequent chapters of this book under distinct headings, but in this chapter, I want to first explore the nature of taboo and why and when it occurs. This chapter is, therefore, separated into five main aspects. Aspects one and two analyse Fraser's (1922) mainly descriptive analysis of the origin and practice of taboo, firstly, as sympathetic or imitative magic and, secondly, as contagious magic. The third aspect discusses the relationship between taboo and loss of soul through separation or death, and how these losses are held, structured, and realized within sacred rituals. In aspect four, I explore examples of both types of *magical,* analogical thinking and the role taboo plays in relationship to ritual, the origin of religion, and scientific thought. I place the concept of taboo within Jung's two kinds of thinking (Jung, 1911–12/1952), archetypal theory (Jung, 1932, 1947; Hillman, 1983) and synchronicity (Jung, 1952, and von Franz, 1994).

I include a broad spectrum of research on taboo, such as Tylor (1903), Malinowski (1931), Evans-Pritchard (1937), Homans (1941), Radcliffe-Brown (1952), Webster (1942), Eliade (1958), Tambiah (1973), Finnegan and Horton (1973 eds.), and Greenwood and Goodwyn (2016), who all differ by degree from Fraser's interpretation of taboo (sympathetic or homeopathic magic) as an erroneous application of the notion of causality. In all cases, associative thinking described by Jung as *indirect* needs to be revalued as a *directed* thought structure used for problem solving. Finally, I discuss the value of analysing taboo rituals in connection to their relevance in healing psychosomatic illnesses in modern clinical practice.

The nature of taboo: some definitions

The nature of taboo and its function has been variously delineated through describing premodern indigenous practices. In indigenous societies, the rules of ceremonial purity observed by divine kings, chiefs, and priests are the same rules that apply to homicides, mourners, women giving birth, girls at puberty, hunters, and fisherman. As I describe in the introduction of chapter 1, Steiner's (1956, p. 32) analysis of the etymology of the Polynesian word *tabu* reveals that *ta* means 'to mark' and *pu* as an adverb of intensity means that *tabu* could be translated as 'marked thoroughly.' Steiner suggests that the logical opposite of *tabu* is neither *sacred* nor *defiled*, both of which are encompassed in the word, but *profane* in the sense of being common as non-things. Fraser contends (1922, p. 269) that the premodern mind does not differentiate between the concept of holiness and pollution. Their common feature is more important: they are dangerous and in danger—the danger in which they stand and to which they can expose others is what we could describe as spiritual and imaginary.

Radcliffe-Brown (1952, pp. 133–152) asserts that the early Polynesians use the term taboo to refer to prohibitions of a special kind, such as to avoid touching a newly born infant, a corpse, or a person of the chief. A person who touches these *tabu* objects becomes *tabu,* which means two things: firstly, s/he must observe a number of special restrictions on his/his behaviour, for example, s/he may not use her/his hands or feed her/himself. The *tabu* person is in a state of danger and if s/he fails to observe the restrictions of taboo, s/he will become ill or even die. Secondly, s/he is dangerous and highly contagious in the same sense as the thing s/he has touched. For example, if s/he comes into contact with utensils or the fire in which food is cooked, the dangerous influence would spread further and injure anyone who partakes of it. A person who is *tabu* can be restored to normality (*noo*) through rites of purification.

Mana

A *tabu* person has contracted a powerful, *living* force that must be regulated and neutralised at all cost. Jung (1928, paras. 116–138) stresses that the word *wakonda* used by the Dakota Native Americans and *manitu* by the Algonquins is similar to the Melanesian concept of *mana* as the all-pervasive, universal, invisible, transferable life energy. *Mana* as energy is powerful, effective, productive, awesome, and terrible—a psychic phenomenon perceived as inseparable from the object. On contact with such power, taboos are necessary as a regulatory structure. Taboos not only embody the prohibitive energy, they contain and structure it at its margins so that it does not escape without proper observation and control. The power to restrict or veto behaviour in the form of a taboo is the measure of a person's political authority (Steiner, 1956, pp. 38–40). Thus, the greatness of a chief's personal mana, his fertility in begetting mana, and the self-imposed restriction of his sacerdotal function are diverse aspects of the same phenomenology. The exercise of taboo provides a means of allocating a person his/her social position hierarchically between the chief and his subjects and also horizontally between sections of society and the sexes. Energy as mana is particularly dangerous in times of transition that need specific rites to move energy across margins into new terrain. I discuss this aspect of taboo specifically in the next chapter, chapter 3, with Douglas' contribution (1966) and again in rites of passage in chapter 7. As I show under the section of menstruating women and warriors of this chapter, the veneration and fear of losing mana in spilt blood as a vital life fluid undergoes the strictest taboos in order to contain its properties.

Taboo as imitative and contagious magic

Fraser (1922, p. 13) suggests that holiness, and the pollution of it, is based on two principles: sympathetic or imitative magic and contagious magic. The first is based on the idea *'that like produces like, or that an effect resembles its cause,'* and, the second, *'that things which have once been in contact with each-other continue to act on each other at a distance after the physical contact has been severed.'* The former principle may be called the law of similarity, and the second, the law of contact or contagion. Both principles assume that entities act on each other at a distance through a secret sympathy, the energetic mana contagion being transmitted from one to the other as a kind of invisible synchronicity or telepathy. Taboos fall under the category of sympathetic magic and are meant to protect its members and keep them safe. The sympathetic tie between peoples at a distance underlines the concern and affection of wanting to help and accompany each other through ordeals that have no certain outcome. Taboo rituals give both structure and security to uncertain, risky situations. Fraser's definition of taboo as sympathetic and contagious magic has come under criticism that I shall detail, but, first, I want to describe the manifestation of taboos put forward by Fraser. He (1922, pp. 316–318) acknowledges the debt modernity owes indigenous people and that the shared similarities outweigh some of the differences in approaches to safety and problem solving.

Imitative (sympathetic) magic

Fraser postulates (1922, pp. 13–45) that magic comprises a large number of negative precepts, that is, prohibitions. The positive precepts are charms; the negative precepts are taboos. If the consequence of an act could prove dangerous or undesirous to the community, one must be careful to avoid acting that way. The consequence could prove fatal. Among the Inuit of Baffin Land in Canada, for example, boys are forbidden to play cat's cradle because if they did their fingers might become entangled in later life in the harpoon lines. Among the *Huzuls* of the Carpathian Mountains, the wife of a hunter may not spin fibre while her husband is eating, for fear hunted game will turn and wind like the spindle, evading the hunter's aim. Among other tribes, a pregnant woman may not spin or twist ropes for two months before her delivery so that her child's guts will not become entangled like the thread. In some regions, no one may stand or loiter on the ladder of a house where there is a pregnant woman, for such delays may retard the birth of the child. In various parts of Sumatra, a pregnant woman is forbidden to stand at the door or on the top rung of a house-ladder under pain of suffering a hard labour for her neglect in ignoring such precautions. In many cultures, pregnancy is a tabooed state full of peril and danger.

Fraser (ibid, p. 26) maintains that food taboos are based on homeopathy. For example, in Madagascar, soldiers are forbidden to eat a number of foods on the principle of sympathetic magic—that they would be tainted with the same dangerous properties: they cannot not eat hedgehogs as they may ingest the same 'shrinking into a ball' disposition; a soldier should eat a knee of an ox in case he becomes weak in the knee and unable to march. They must not eat kidneys because it means the same word as 'shot,' which he would be if he ate one.

Other aspects of taboo concern the emotional, sympathetic, and synchronistic connection between peoples at a distance. For example, many of the indigenous tribes of Sarawak believe that if their wives commit adultery while the husbands searched for camphor, the camphor obtained by the men would evaporate; in the Key Islands, to the South west of New Guinea, as soon as a vessel sets sail for a distant port, the part of the beach where it was launched is covered with palm branches and becomes sacred. No one is allowed to cross that spot until the vessel returns home. To cross over would cause the vessel to perish. Moreover, three or four girls are chosen to remain in sympathetic connection with the vessel. They must remain in a room assigned to them and sit motionless, as their movements would cause the vessel to pitch and toss. They may not eat sticky foods, such as rice boiled in coconut milk, for the stickiness would clog the passage of the vessel through the water (Fraser, 1922, p. 29).

As other examples of imitative magic, when men are away fighting, their wives imitate their warlike gestures in dances performed at regular intervals. The female dancers flourish their knives and spears in a symbolic act to draw danger away from their male partners (ibid, pp. 32–33). In Laos, when an elephant hunter is starting for the chase, he warns his wife not to cut her hair or oil her body in his absence as both actions would have negative effects. When a *Dyak* village has turned out to hunt wild pigs in the jungle, the people who stay at home may not touch oil or water with their hands, for if they did, the hunters would lose grip on their weapons or game.

Mutual homeopathic connection also exists between humans, animals, and vegetation. If a woman were to eat bananas growing from a single head or a double grain of millet, she would give birth to twins. The Sundanese believe that if a house is built of the wood of thorny trees, the lives of the inhabitants would be equally thorny and troubled. Homeopathic connections to animals give the same value as lucky charms: some *Bechuanas* wear a ferret for a charm because ferrets impart a tenacity of life that makes them difficult to kill. Others wear the hair of a hornless ox and the skin of a frog on their mantel because a frog is slippery and the ox, having no horns, is difficult to catch; rat hair connotes nimbleness; ashes of roasted spider legs, when sprinkled, promote litheness and nimbleness when playing the one-stringed lute (Fraser, 1922, pp. 37–38). A similar connection applies between a wounded man and the agent that inflicted the wound; whatever is done to the agent also affects the wounded (ibid, p. 49).

Contagious magic

Indigenous peoples believe that a contagious connection between themselves and every part of their body continues after the physical coaction has been broken (Fraser, 1922, pp. 45–47). As illustrated above, reciprocity exists between the wounded, the wound, and the agent of the wound that affects the condition of the wound itself. They believe they will suffer from the same harm that might befall any severed parts of their body, such as hair, naval cord, teeth, and nail clippings, which still contain living aspects of their soul when severed. Care is thus taken that these severed, marginalised portions of themselves are left in safe places, as to avoid exposure to accidental injury or sorcerers who might use them to their detriment or death. The belief is that the sorcerer can take hair, spittle, blood, nail clippings, teeth, and other bodily refuse and wrap them up in a leaf, knot it in a certain way, and bury them with specific rites that will cause the victim to waste away and die if not retrieved.

Often shorn hair and nail clippings are stored in a safe place also for resurrection purposes. For example, in Turkey and in Ireland, not only nail clippings and hair but a person's real name should be kept secret/taboo in case it is stolen. In ancient Egypt, a person received two names; the great and the little name. The great name is carefully concealed. Indian tribes of British Columbia have a taboo on telling their names or the names of their relatives or diseased persons, as names represent identity that can be stolen or misused.

Taboos are enacted on eating and drinking because, at these times, the soul might escape from the mouth with the common belief that the indwelling spirit leaves the body and returns to the mouth, however, equally, a homeless spirit could take advantage and enter the body. The *Zafimanelo* in Madagascar lock the doors when they eat; hardly anyone sees them eat—they take a cloth to their faces to hide the act. The penalty is death if the witness observes the king eating. The remnants of the king's food are buried so they do not fall into the hands of sorcerers who might use the wasted food to cast a fatal spell over the king. This taboo is not only beneficial for sanitary reasons but helped the custom slowly develop into the acceptance of eating food together in social groups. By participating in the same food, men are physically united through the same food in their stomachs.

There are also taboos at showing the orifices of one's face. The Sultan of Darfur wraps up his face in a piece of white muslin so that no evil spirits can enter through his nose and mouth. Muslim women today hide their faces behind veils. Many cultures regard the head as particularly scared. The Siamese think that a spirit called *khuan* dwells in the head and must be protected at all times. The Cambodians think that it a great offence to touch another person's head and will not enter a place that could be above someone's height. Hence, houses are built on one story only so they do not have to walk over someone's head. In Tahiti, anyone who stood over the king or queen or passes his/her hand over their heads might be put to death. A Tahitian infant's head was particularly taboo. If a branch or tree touched the child's head the tree was cut down as unclean and unfit for use.

As the head is considered so sacred, cutting hair is a delicate operation. Among the Maoris, spells are uttered at hair cutting ceremonies. One spell is spoken to consecrate the obsidian knife with which the hair is cut and the other is announced to avert thunder and lightning, which hair cutting is believed to cause (Fraser, ibid, p. 285).

Tabooed personages

Kingship

Kings come under special taboos because of their perceived power, *mana*, and elevated status, which must be contained and controlled at all times. Taboos on kings leaving the house means they must never go beyond their precinct. The kings of Ethiopia were worshipped as gods but kept shut up in their palaces. Earlier, the Kings of Sheba were mobbed or stoned if they left their palaces: sacredness must be contained, otherwise violence can ensue. *Sacredness* also involves containing all unacceptable emotions such as anger, jealousy, envy, feelings of intense injustice, and revenge. Such feelings are transferred onto one person as King who is elevated in value but also kept under close surveillance and strict taboo rules of both food and movement in case these difficult emotions suddenly erupt. For example in Mexico, the emperor Montezuma never set foot on the ground; he was always carried by nobleman. The Japanese Mikado never touched the ground with his feet. For kings of Egypt, although worshipped as gods, every waking hour was governed by prescribed rules that limit freedom.

Apparently, each kingly, holy or tabooed person is charged with a physical substance or fluid called *mana,* discussed earlier, which can be discharged or drained away with contact with the earth. S/he must be insulated and isolated if not to be emptied of that precious vitality, not just for her/his sake but for others. This powerful explosive substance might be detonated with the smallest touch. Thus, the sun may not shine on a holy person because the sun is not worthy to shine upon him/her but, equally, because the sun's rays might ignite even more power in an already overheated and potentially dangerous personage (Fraser, 1922, pp. 204–209).

Menstruating women

The two taboo prohibitions on touching and being placed in the sun, also apply to girls in some indigenous cultures at the onset of menstruation. For example, in New Iceland, girls are confined for four to five days in cages being kept in the dark or secluded in a hut (Fraser, ibid, p. 251). Sometimes girls of seven or eight are kept for several years in secluded huts until they are of marriageable age. They emerge pale, pure and thin, like newborns ready to take on their new role. The seclusion of girls when they reach puberty is caused by the intense fear that menstruation blood evokes. Menstruation blood is thought to contain such vital, dangerous mana that it could cause all sorts of disasters should it come into contact with crops, cattle, or food. Lebanese peasants think that the shadow of a menstruating woman causes flowers to wither and trees to perish. If she mounts a horse, the horse might die, or she boards a boat, a thunderstorm would ensue. In European countries, menstruation is often called a curse (Delaney, Lupton and Toth, 1976). The odour of menstrual blood can turn beer sour, cause bread to fall, a theory backed by the discovery of menotoxins, an alleged bacterial toxicity found in menstrual blood (cf. Montagu, 1957; Ford, 1945). However, as Buckley and Gottlieb (1988, pp. 19–23) attest, menstrual blood despite its odour, was used extensively to encourage the growth of wheat, and in the medical treatment of gout, goiter, inflammations, puerperal fever, worms, and headaches. Menstrual blood is still used in fertility rites, love potions and to ensure fidelity. The general rule of keeping menstruating women suspended between heaven and earth means that their dangerous energy remains neutralised. When enveloped in a hammock and slung up to the roof as in South America or raised above the ground in a dark and narrow cage as in New Ireland, they are both protected from themselves and others. These taboos for kingly personages and for menstruating women are intended to preserve life by keeping the mana within these states contained and insulated.

The connection between kingship and menstruating women, both occupying liminal spaces that signifies the presence of an anomaly gives credence to the idea of menstrual discharge as *out of place,* breaching the natural bounds of the body. Douglas (1966) defines pollutants, coded *dirt,* as caught between the margins of *me* and *not me,* as I expand in chapter 3. As Buckley and Gottlieb (1988, p. 26) argue, menstrual blood does not flow randomly or accidently, but purposely from a single source as the only act that women perform to let blood flow. The monopoly of bloodletting is generally in male hands of hunting, butchering, warfare, and rituals involving sacrifice. In this context, menstrual blood would be seen as an anomaly.

Among primitive taboos, menstruation blood contains the strongest taboo because it is so powerful in the generation of human life. Menstruating women are segregated from the community, forbidden to touch or use any objects of communal usage—sometimes even their own food—for risk of contamination (Peters, 1921, p. 59; Girard, 1977, pp. 36–38). Menstruation blood needs to be seen within the general category of bloodletting. Fraser (1922, p. 277) contends that the reluctance to shed blood on the ground is in the belief that the soul exists in blood and that any ground upon which it falls must necessarily become taboo or sacred. Most indigenous peoples take utmost care to avoid contact with spilt blood unless it is associated with sacrifice, which purifies it. When people enjoy peace and security, blood is a rare sight. When anger is unleased through acts of violence, blood appears everywhere, forming great pools. Its very fluidity gives form to the contagious nature of violence. Blood stains by its very presence and proclaims violence, wounds, death, and vengeance.

Girard (1977, pp. 34–37) suggests that menstrual blood is singled out for impurity and taboo because of its association with sexuality and the strong emotions it arouses. Intimate sexual contact through contagion is the origin of various illnesses, real or imaginary: it culminates in the bloody, painful labours of childbirth, which may entail the death of the mother, the child, or both. Sexual activity leads to quarrels, jealous rages, competition, and mortal combats. By means of a taboo on menstrual blood, a transfer of violence has been affected and monopoly established that controls that source. Girard attributes the term 'violence' to the eruption of such emotions, but I classify them as 'dangerous' and contagious to stress the wide range of ambivalent emotions present in taboo such as fear of loss, anger, competition, and jealousy.

Only blood itself can cleanse the impurity and danger attached to blood and loss of soul. The blood of sacrificial victims achieves that aim. Blood that dries on a victim soon loses its viscous quality and first becomes a dark sore, then a roughened scab. But it is still an impure product of violence, illness, or death as opposed to the free-flowing, crimson blood of newly slaughtered victims. This blood is never allowed to dry or congeal but is removed without a trace after the sacrifice. Menstrual blood, on the contrary, flows in a variety of colours and textures. In the Swazi culture, menstrual blood is considered part of the foetus in utero and its discharge is analogous to a miscarriage and death. In other situations, menstrual blood cleanses a woman after childbirth (Kuper, 1947, p. 107) but, through haemorrhaging, can kill.

There is considerable evidence to suggest that menstruating women far from being devalued by their community are, in fact, elevated through their taboo status. Buckley and Gottlieb (1988, pp. 7–15) show that close cross cultural studies reveal a wide range of distinct rules with quite different, even opposite purposes and meanings, making menstrual taboos ambiguous and multivalent. Their purpose may be to explicitly protect women by means of ensuring their own autonomy rather than protecting society from a universal feminine evil. Buckley and Gottlieb ask whether menstrual seclusion in separate huts may have arisen from women's own voluntarism rather than from masculine coercion. Seclusion is not always onerous bringing with it the possibility of privacy and sexual autonomy (Kahn, 1931, p. 130).

Pubescent boys

Such taboos include the rites of separation of *pubescent boys* 10 to 12 years of age from their mothers. Gillison (2002, pp. 112–114) describes the initiation rites of these boys from Papua New Guinea which take between three to four days, where the boys will undergo sleep deprivation and a type of brainwashing in order to drive the mothers out of their lives in the process of making them men. When the boys emerge from the *hausman,* they will never live with their mothers again. Once the boys live in the *hausman* for the initiation procedures, the only people allowed to approach them are their maternal uncles and paternal clan elders. The *Herowana* boys are allowed little or no sleep; when they need to go to the toilet, they are carried on the backs of their mentors and held over the toilet pit so that their feet do not touch the ground. The carrying and much of the procedures in the initiation ceremony is said to mirror their first birth from their mothers. Like a baby in the womb during the period of rebirth, they must not be contaminated by forces outside the womb of the *hausman.* The relationship between rebirth and the male initiation process is further emphasised as they prepare to leave the compound: their faces are covered with red oil, then red orchids and red plumes from the Raggiana bird of paradise representing the blood of parturition; the behaviour of the Papuan hornbill is imitated where the father *horses* the fledging on its back flying just beneath the fledging so that it does not fall down.

The clan collects brightly coloured leaves to decorate the pathway as the boys' uncles place the initiates on their shoulders as the women sing of the beauty of their born-again birds. There are further initiation rites to be endured after the ceremony when the boys are forced to swallow long strands of flexible cane which cause them to vomit up the last traces of mother's milk still residing in their intestines after the initiation ceremony. A second level initiation rite for young fathers is to remind them to strictly adhere to traditional food taboos. They must not eat female 'things,' that is, food that comes from animals that live in caves or holes in the ground, as that may weaken their resolve and independence as warriors. I describe these taboos in puberty rites of passage for both sexes more fully in chapter 7.

Warriors

Because of indigenous taboos on spilt blood, *warriors,* just as menstruating women or women in childbirth, are in spiritual danger and strict taboo rituals must be observed. For example, Maoris and Australian aborigines on the warpath are sacred and taboo to the highest degree. The vessels they used are sacred; they have to practice continence and personal hygiene as their bodily waste could be used by the enemy. Also in some indigenous American tribes, similar to girls when they first menstruate, the vessels from which the warriors eat and drink must not be touched by another person. The warrior is forbidden to scratch his head because his hands are also taboo; he has to use a stick. Men on the warpath always sleep at night with their heads turned to their home country. They may not sit upon bare ground, nor wet their feet, nor step over the legs, hands, or body of another member who was sitting or lying on the ground. Warriors abstain from sexual intercourse and expect the same continence from the villagers in a mutual sympathetic connection. Fraser (1922, p. 255) conjectures that warriors abstain from sexual intercourse lest close contact with women would infect them with feminine weakness and cowardice and enfeeble their weapons, although this argument has been overturned. Warriors fear contaminating women with the blood of killed animals. The taboo is to protect menstrual blood from mixing and thus being contaminated with deceased animal blood.

Among the hill tribe of Assam, when under the taboo of war, warriors are not permitted to address their wives or eat food cooked by them before they leave. When successful warriors who have shed the blood of enemies return with the heads of their vanquished victims, special ceremonies are performed to appease the anger of the deceased. A special hut is prepared for the warrior where he resides for two months undergoing bodily and spiritual purification before he can resume physical contact with others. One purification ceremony consists of a dance accompanied by a song where the death is lamented and his forgiveness entreated so that the soul of the victim does not harm the warrior or his clan.

Taboo and loss of soul

An important aspect of indigenous beliefs is the taboo involved with soul elements of the self that are thought to be migratory and, thus, open to loss or theft. Such taboos tie into indigenous beliefs that the soul of a person takes the form of an inner animal, a manikin, a shadow, or a reflection that has a life of its own (Fraser, 1922, p. 215). This inner force or *mana* embodies life energy. When a person is inactive, as in sleep, the soul as her/his double leaves the body and can be stolen or expropriated by others, leading to sickness or death. To safeguard his/her soul, a person might put it in a safe, hidden, tabooed place far away so that it comes to no harm. It is a common rule not to rudely awaken a sleeper because his/her soul is away and may not find the way back. Still more dangerous is to move or alter the appearance of the sleeper as the soul may not be able to find or recognise its body and return to it.

The *Karens* of Burma (ibid, p. 221) believe that the soul may leave the body and not return. In the Congo, some tribes believe that when a person is ill, his soul has left his body and a sorcerer is called in to capture the vagrant spirit and restore it. Pining, sickness, great fright, and death are ascribed by the *Bataks* of Sumatra to the absence of the soul from the body. The departure of the soul may not be voluntary, but extracted from the body against its will by much-feared envious and vengeful ghosts, demons, or sorcerers. The soul of the sleeper is able to wander, visit places, and perform the acts s/he dreams about. The absence of the soul during sleep has other dangers, as it might be permanently detained, meet another soul in a battle, or the soul of the deceased may steal it. The shadow or reflection of a person is considered as the soul and if injured or walked over, the action will resonate with its owner.

An important aspect of taboo is the rule of containment that it gives to the soul and loss of soul through separation. Animism expounded by Tylor (1903, pp. 6–9) is similarly concerned with the difference between a living person and a dead one and the causes of waking, dreams, trances, disease, and death. As I mention earlier, many indigenous people think that each person has two components belonging to him/her: a life and a phantom or soul. These two have close connections with the other, but in animist belief, the phantom is able to exist after death in the form of a shadow or ghost-soul. Indigenous people make no distinction between animals and humans, a point which I elaborate on in chapter 4. Animals are considered to have souls and can share a human one. Transmigration recognises the idea of animals, trees, and plants being animated by the human souls of the dead. The soul is supposed to escape by the natural orifices of the body, especially the mouth and nostrils, and sometimes is conceived as a bird ready to take flight as an intermediary state between heaven and earth (Tylor, ibid, pp. 7–17).

Tylor importantly sees a continuum between early indigenous animistic beliefs about the existence of spiritual beings after death and later monotheisms such as Buddhism and Christianity (Jong, 2017, pp. 47–61). The idea of bodily resurrection in Heaven or Hades is technically an indigenous transmigration of the soul: both exist on a detailed cognitive level.

Soul making

When both modern and premodern people leave their native home, their souls might feel isolated among different customs and ancestral spirits, so they need to find a safe place to put their soul for safekeeping. Sometimes animal, plants, people, or inanimate objects are used. As mentioned before, birds are often images of the soul of a person in flight. In the Gimi tribe of Papua New Guinea, when girls leave their homes to start a new married life as 'marrying in' wives elsewhere, their souls become homesick and return in the form of birds to check on their families during their absence. Gillison (2002, p. 99), who experienced the Gimi initiation ceremonies first-hand in 1970s, states that the Gimi believe that when people die, their spirits travel to the land of the dead, but along the way they may tarry with their soulmates, the birds of paradise. Spirits of the dead or clan members who have left the village, lonely for their own kind, sometimes return and live with a group of birds of paradise to watch over their kinfolk. The soul's hiding place itself becomes taboo and sacred. The knowledge of the soul's secret whereabouts must be protected out of the fear that if the safe place is destroyed, the soul itself could meet the same fate. Similarly, the modern psychoanalytical container can offer a safe haven for reconnecting with lost soul aspects when people have moved away from their roots and become disorientated, which I will discuss fully in chapter 8. The lost soul aspects are transferred unconsciously onto the analyst who contains and absorbs such tabooed losses while working simultaneously with the unconscious parental and cultural complexes. Once soul aspects are restored, the withdrawal of the projection from the analyst can begin.

Funerary taboos

Taboos concerning death contain and structure the difficult emotions signifying an eternal loss and separation. The names of the dead are tabooed (Fraser, 1922, p. 303), possibly as a deterrent and a precaution so that their souls are not encouraged to linger in their old identity. At a funeral in China, the mourners will step back from the coffin, in case their shadows fall into the coffin and their health is endangered. There is also the widespread custom of covering up mirrors or turning them to the wall after a death has taken place in the house (Fraser, ibid, p. 232). It is feared that the soul projected out of the person into the mirror reflection may be carried off by the ghost of the departed commonly supposed to linger in the house until the burial. That is the reason why sick people should not see themselves in the mirror and the mirror in the sickroom is therefore covered. The same fear also applies to portraits. A portrait contains the soul or a vital part of it, so whoever possesses it can exercise a fatal influence over the original. In various parts of Europe, for example in West Scotland, there is the belief that illness, even death, would ensue if people had their portraits painted or photographed.

The taboo on touching corpses and how mourners are treated seems to be universal in Polynesia. In Samoa, those who attend the deceased are careful not to handle food and are fed by others as if they are helpless infants. Baldness and loss of teeth are the punishments inflicted if they violate the taboo. Among the *Shuwap* of British Columbia, widows and widowers in mourning are secluded and forbidden to touch their own heads or bodies. They must build a sweat house beside a creek, sweat there all night and rub their bodies with branches of spruce (Fraser, ibid, pp. 248–250). No hunter must come near the mourners for their presence is unlucky. Behind these rituals is fear of a malignant ghost who may be hovering near them. In the *Mekeo* district of New Guinea, a widower loses all his civil rights and becomes a social outcast.

I suggest that the mourning process itself is emotionally and physically draining. The overwhelming emotions attached to death as the final departure of a loved one into unknown territory can be dangerous, even contagious, hence the pollution rituals involved toward handling the process of dying and of dead bodies. The fear that a ghost takes over the soul of the living can be interpreted as one's own longing to be reunited in death with the deceased; this must be contained in order to go on living (see chapter 7 for more detail).

Interpretative paradigms: analogical or symbolic thinking versus scientific thinking

Although Fraser appreciates the efficacy of associative thinking found in taboo prohibitions, he thinks it is erroneously applied to magical thinking (1922, p. 59), which he describes as the 'bastard sister of science.' Taboo practice is haunted by the emotional obsession of situations out of human control. The existence of personal attachment and the fact that change, particularly death, is the most upsetting and disorganising of human calculation lends itself to the affirmation that death is not real, that man has an immortal soul. Whether the solutions are found in the associative thinking of taboo practices or in science, these sentiments arise out of the deep psychological need to deny personal destruction as well as an equally determined cultural need for co-operation, empathy, and problem solving.

Taboo, Jung's two types of thinking, archetype, synchronicity

Jung's analytical framework has much to offer the study of taboo. His inclusion of *indirect associative thinking* (Jung, 1911–12/1952, paras. 21–46) gives a legitimate frame when dealing with the mythological, associative thinking found in taboo practices. Jung describes directed thinking as thinking in words and a product of the objective social sphere (ibid, para. 17), which Freud characterises as progressive thinking. Jung defines mythological, associative, *indirect* thinking in dreams and active imagination as fantasy thinking based on subjectivity and instinct; it is not readily accessible and belongs as much to the unconscious as to the conscious realm. The definition of two types of thinking is not new. James (1890, pp. 44–75) distinguishes between two types of thinking that informed Jung's definition: first, sharp bright *images* in colour and form as imaginative, subjective, associative thinking and second, objective, abstract thinking that loses its intensity when transferred to generality. James (ibid, p. 53) suggests that imaginative pictorial perception is contrary to the requirements of generalised abstract thinking (logos), pinpointing an apparent incompatibility between subjectivity and objectivity. Jung and Jungian analysts, such as Adams (2001, p. 121, 2004, pp. 2–19), however, use associative, imaginative thinking through amplification as a *directed* analytical tool to sharpen fantasy and dream *images* in order to transform subjective, disassociated taboo emotions into legitimate ego and cultural/collective analytical discourse. Through contact with indigenous, primordial, shamanic practices described fully in chapter 8, a reconnection with nature, prehistory, and ancestral memories revitalises a dried-out directed, hierarchical thinking into an emotional immediacy and intensity for life (Jung, 1961, p. 270).

Jung's theory of *archetypes* is applicable to the nature of taboo as taboos deal with the universal fabric of human emotions and found not only in indigenous cultures but worldwide. Taboos give form, pattern, and containment to intense personal and collective anxiety attached to the unexpected and developmental changes in status through *rites of passage* within the clan system. Jung (1937, para. 136) defines archetypes as inherited possibilities, discernible in images and motifs that describe their primordial (*Arche*) structural elements and their energetic charge. Jung (1947, para. 411) depicts the feeling-value of the archetype: 'As a numinous factor, the archetype determines the nature of the configuration process and the course it will follow as though it were already in possession of the goal to be circumscribed by the centring process.' He describes the archetypal function of an indigenous East African rite to welcome the sun each morning and at the first phase of the new moon. They step out of their huts hold their hands before their mouths and spit or blow into them vigorously offering their soul substance (spit and breath) to welcome the sun god. Knowledge of mythology penetrates and corresponds to the deeper layers of the psyche where emotional connectedness is derived from *images* as recurring motifs of the collective unconscious (Jung, 1951, para. 309; 312). Jung's willingness to personify the archetypes as animate beings with purposeful properties is a controversial aspect of his theory (Walker, 2002, p. 16; chapters 7 and 8).

Jung (1947, paras. 408) suggests that 'psychic processes behave like a scale along which consciousness slides.' At one end, instincts dominate and at the other, the spirit. Taboos move along this spectrum easily by incorporating the physical, affective, as well as the spiritual dimension, particularly attached to rites of passage. The harsh emotional physicality of taboo rituals are met with their spiritual significance without which prohibitions would have little meaning or efficacy. As Goodwyn (2016, p. 14) correctly surmises: 'Human nature is seen as a capacity that includes and operates from *within*, *through* and *from* culture that is not separate from biology and psychology but tightly interwoven within it.... The interaction of both leads to self-organising universals with the psyche.' Hillman (1983, p. 1) equally suggests that archetypes personify not just the human psyche but simultaneously in physical, sociocultural, linguistic, aesthetic, affective, and spiritual form (cf. Brodersen, 2016, pp. 3–5).

Jung's concept of *synchronicity* (Jung, 1952, paras. 818–871) can be applied to Fraser's concept of imitative and contagious magic. Through the *affective* strength found in both types of consciousness, a bridge is formed between psyche and matter: a synchronistic, interactive field is constellated, which breaks through the barriers of space and time, between the ego and the collective unconscious. Synchronicity seems magical: each person has an electrical and magnetic field, an attractive and/or repellent force, which activates when touching something or someone with a similar affective charge (Jung, ibid. para. 860). Von Franz (1994, p. 386) stresses the importance of Jung's discovery of the synchronicity principle, that is, that 'symbols produced sporadically and spontaneously by the unconscious through the action of the archetypes tend to coincide in a meaningful way with the material occurrences in the external world.' Synchronicity incorporates an objective psyche that organises psyche and matter simultaneously in a form called *magical consciousness* by Greenwood and Goodwyn (2016).

Magic, religion, and science

Fraser accounts for taboo practices amongst indigenous peoples as stemming from an erroneous process of thinking that is accidental rather than purposeful when compared to religious rites that maintain a stable, orderly society. Malinowski (1931, p. 43) offers a more neutral approach than Fraser by asserting that taboos exist whenever humans come to an unbridgeable gap, a hiatus in knowledge, or lack the power of practical control over their environment. Standardised traditional magical fixes, organise and impose on its members a positive solution that arises from human impotence. The raw material for sympathetic magic dwells on the desired end and the best way of achieving it. The fixed time, the determined spot, the preliminary isolating conditions, the taboos to be observed by the performer, as well as the psychological and sociological nature, all place the magical act as an integrative force that organises practical activities to manage existential anxiety. Every human crisis implies a strong emotional upheaval, mental conflict, and possible disintegration. Taboo rituals help to structure and contain these crises. Malinowski proposes that taboos have a definite and practical purpose known to all who practice them and easily elicited through their affective transmission. Indigenous people 'through their taboo practices are capable of exact observation, sound generalizations and logical reasoning' (1931, p. 39).

Radcliffe-Brown (1952, pp. 133–152) notes the cross-cultural nature of taboo. Fraser similarly concludes that the practice is not confined to indigenous people but has a wider meaning that includes European and Westerners as 'forbidden.' Radcliffe-Brown gives the example in Britain of spilling salt and eating meat on Friday or in Lent. It is bad luck to spill salt, but to disobey a religious church rite is guilty of *sinful* wrongdoing. In Fraser's definition, spilling salt is a question of magic, while eating meat on Friday is a question of religion. Similar to Malinowski, Radcliffe-Brown does not make a clear distinction between magic and religion as both give confidence, courage, and a sense of security as well as giving structure and containment to human fears and anxieties (1952, p. 149). Webster (1942, pp. 4–5) equally argues that taboo rituals although employed for civic as well as sacred purposes, were entirely religious ceremonies with an emphasis on the *sacred* and could be imposed only by priests or persons called *kiaimoku* as representatives of civic authorities. Taboos contribute to the build-up of the complex fabric of society that give status *value* that is purposeful, and not accidental.

Douglas (1966, pp. 44–45) goes further in her criticism of Fraser's view of taboo as an aberrant logic. She sees little qualitative difference between indigenous practices of taboo and our own practices of busy scrubbing and cleaning, which, she suggests, also carry symbolic meaning of separation and classification of objects into clean and dirty. She suggests that the modern approach to order/clean/blessed and disorder/dirt/sinful creates many unrelated sub-worlds, whereas as indigenous peoples create one single symbolically consistent universe.

Steiner (1956, pp. 50–51) suggests that defining taboo became historically problematic not only because of the rationalist approach to religion but because British Victorian society itself was one of the most taboo-minded and taboo-ridden societies on record. It was an expanding society in which new groups could rise to comparative wealth but also had to safeguard their newly acquired privileges by increasing awareness of avoidance customs as positive social factors and strictly decompartmentalising vocabulary between magic, religion, and science, which Steiner's maintains influenced both Fraser's and Robertson Smith's theory of taboo.

Expanding on the work of Radcliffe-Brown and Malinowski, Homans (1941, pp. 57–62) notes that for indigenous practices, a taboo contains at least seven *functional* elements to combat anxiety that need consideration: first, *primary anxiety*, whenever a wo/man desires an accomplishment of certain result and does not possess the technique to secure these results, s/he feels a sentiment called anxiety; second, *primary ritual* whereby under these circumstances, the person tends to perform actions that have no practical results but are intended to relieve anxiety. Third, *secondary anxiety* in which rituals have been performed, his/her anxiety remains latent and the rites give confidence. S/he will feel anxiety when these rites are not properly performed. This anxiety becomes generalised toward anyone who has not observed the rites. Fourth, *secondary ritual* is a ritual of purification and expiation that functions to dispel secondary anxiety. Fifth, *rationalisation* is associated with ritual giving a reason for them, for example, when certain magical rites ensure the catching of fish. Sixth, *symbolisation* such as Catholic Mass makes an analogical reference to Christ's sacrifice on Calvary; finally, seventh, its *function* as ritual gives humans confidence, meaning, and a formal collective structure by dispelling their anxieties and disciplining their social organisations.

Through examining the dialectics of *hierophanies* (manifestations of the sacred) and *kratophanies*, (manifestations of power), Eliade (1958, pp. 15–19) further suggests that taboos are *purposely* rather than erroneously directed at any phenomena that are ambivalent, unusual, unique, new, perfect, or monstrous in order to contain them. What are called taboo are entities, things, places, or persons cut off or forbidden because contact with them is dangerous. Generally speaking, any object, action, or person that has—naturally or acquired by some shift of ontological level—an uncertain force of nature, becomes taboo. These forces can be impermanent: as soon as things are known and handled, fitted into a primitive cosmos, they lose all power to upset the order of things. Clearly, birth, death, and sickness are phenomena that come into the category of unusual and frightening. Certain things, people, and places belong to a different cosmic order. Frutiful contact with such ambivalent properties found in *hierophanies and kratophanies* helps secure a person's hope for the future and strengthen her/his reality, although s/he may fear that s/he loses contact with reality if s/he is totally lifted to a plane of higher existence other than the natural profane state.

Eliade argues that the ambivalent attitude between safety and risk that simultaneously attracts and repels is based on the idea that the unknown and the extraordinary indicate the presence of something 'other' than the norm of natural entities. In a similar vein, extreme ugliness or beauty plus physical deformities such as dwarfism mark out and isolate those who possess them as anomalies of nature, but also single them out for elevation as *sacred*.

It can be argued that while magical acts are characterised by analogical thought and action, they can be measured and verified by the same standard as science. Tambiah (1973, pp. 199–229) suggests that magical acts usually compounded of verbal utterance and object manipulation constitute performative acts by which a property is imperatively transferred to a recipient object or person on a synchronistic, analogical basis. In contrast, the exploitation of analogical thought in science serves as a model for the incompletely known in the phenomena to be explained. Analogy depends on the recognition of similarities between instances being compared. Tambiah argues that analogical reasoning in taboo is more complex and reflective than the simplistic 'like attracts like' understanding of Fraser's definition of contagious magic because it brings into concurrent view both similarities and differences between objects.

For example, Tambiah discusses the stems of the creeper *araka*, how they lose their leaves and are replaced by a double row of hands, joined to the stalks, just as the extremities of the hands and feet disappear. This creeper is highly thought of by indigenous people as treatment for leprosy. In the case of the creeper, the falling of its extremities is a phase of its growth cycle, whereas in the case of leprosy sufferers it leads to degeneration and death. Thus, this comparison uses the *araka* creeper in the rite as a vehicle or agent of life, the message being that the leprosy disappears and health appears just as the shedding process in the creeper stimulates growth. The object of the *araka* is manipulated and chosen analogically on the basis of similarity and difference. Two objects are seen as having resemblances and differences and an attempt is made to transfer the desirable quality of one to the other that is in a defective state. It would be inappropriate to subject these rites to verify or test whether they are true or false or whether the act has affected a result in terms of a scientific causation.

The treatment of ringworm in children called *imanduruakondo* (*ima* means sickness and *nduruakonda* means fowl house) is another example where positive and negative analogies work together as a whole. It is called *imanduruakondo* because the scabby patches of the disease resemble fowls' excrement as if the children had eaten food grown in the vicinity of the dung house, hence the homeopathic remedy consists of the excrements dried and reduced to ashes mixed into a paste with a little palm oil and applied to the ring worm. This is another interesting case of symbolic thinking. While the 'like attracts like' argument would say that the fowl's excrement is falsely used to attract the scabs on the skin that it falsely resembles, the analogy is creative: the relation of the fowl to excrement is one of elimination of unwanted waste product while that of scaly skin on children is one of unwanted adherence to body. So the fowl's excrement can convey the desired effect of eliminating the scabs when applied to the body because in one sense it is similar to it, it is also essentially different.

In the same way, the properties of sound can be compared to the properties of light in their similarity of relationship. For example, properties of sound, such as echoes, loudness, and pitch can be compared to properties of light as reflection, brightness and colour respectively.

All the above mentioned academics contest Fraser's view of taboo as an accidental happening. Magic is neither simply a science that has failed as Frazer asserts, nor an incipient rational science; rather magical and scientific thinking should not be applied to each other, nor is one type of thinking superior to the other. Thinking and action are intimately linked and connected not only in ritual but in everyday behaviour as well. Their very utterance is itself an action that effects a change in reality. It is on the criterion of persuasion, transference, and expansion of meaning that magical acts must be evaluated and analysed. Evan-Pritchard (1937, pp. 363–366), for example, using his research of the *Azande* tribe, notes that witchcraft is used to explain unfortunate events. The *Azande* do not explain these events by mystical causation, but by a chain of causation derived from natural consequences and by the elimination of alternative plausible explanations (ibid, p. 365). The fact that the *Azande* do not engage in feuds or raids may indicate the ability of accusations and angers against witches to absorb latent hostilities. Science cannot tell us what happened beyond the laws of probability. In their rationalisation of why an unfortunate event takes place despite the normal procedures being followed, the *Azande* find comfort, the flexibility to adjust to new life conditions, and the opportunity to retaliate all in one explanation.

Greenwood and Goodwyn (2016, pp. 5–6) equally emphasise that magical thinking as magical consciousness cannot be adequately assessed by classifying it according to methodologies assigned to scientific thought. They argue that magic and science have been placed into a false dichotomy, whereby science tends to override the precepts of magical thinking. They suggest that a truly open-ended scientific approach that goes beyond the cultural bias of scientism might arrive at a creative synthesis without one discrediting the role of the other in human thought processes. Magical consciousness tends to work through analogical rather than logical thought patterns, although this premise is being gradually eroded in favour of a combination of the two modes of thought interacting with each other (cf. Finnegan and Horton, 1973). Sorenson (2007) shows that magic is a culturally pervasive integrative mode of thinking that uses metaphor and metonymy to express and create a blended ritual space where elements of sacred and profane worlds mix, particularly in stressful human situations.

Relationship of taboo to modern mental health practices

The phenomenon of psychogenic death caused by a taboo violation is common in aboriginal Australia, Polynesia, South America and Africa (Ellenberger, 1970, pp. 22–25). If a taboo has been violated and the purification rites not performed, an afflicted person could die. In Africa, death can be swift: in Samika, in the French Congo, a young boy ate bananas cooked in a pot that had been used previously for manioc. Manioc is a strictly taboo food and his grandparents warned him that if he ate any of it he would die. In a few days, he died of asphyxia. In Polynesia, death from a taboo violation occurs in a less dramatic way as the patient lies down and refuses to eat. What is important is not so much the violation of a taboo but that the violation has been exposed and made public and the offender been made an object of shame.

Cannon (1942), Lester (1974), and Lex (1974) all collaborate that fear through suggestion and autosuggestion through the body's sympathetic nervous system, similarly afflicts the terminally ill patients, modern hypochondriacs, and ulcer patients in a similar despair found in taboo violation. Cannon (ibid, pp. 169–181) relates the experience of aborigines toward tribal taboo in the Northern Territory of Australia in which taboo becomes an effective means of ridding a victim of a taboo violation. It is accomplished in two stages: firstly, all people who stand in kinship relationship to the victim withdraw their sustaining support and place him/her in a new category. S/he is viewed as one who is more nearly in the realm of the sacred and taboo than in the world of the ordinary community. The organisation of his/her social life has collapsed; s/he is no longer a member of a group and alone and isolated. The only escape is death. During the death illness that ensues, the group acts with countless stimuli to suggest death positively as a collective solution. Voodoo deaths are based on a similar premise that when a victim has a bone pointed at him/her, in other words, skinned and boned alive, without intervention, it inevitably leads to voluntary starvation and death (Cannon, 1942, p. 368).

The victim complies and cooperates with the withdrawal. S/he becomes the attitude of the fellow tribesmen want him/her to be and assists in committing a kind of suicide. Before death takes place, the second movement of the community occurs whereby they return to the victim in order to subject him/her to the fateful process and ritual of mourning. The purpose is to cut the victim off entirely from the ordinary world and place him/her in his proper position in the world of the dead. The effect of the double movement, first away and then to return to the victim with all the compulsive force of the most powerful rituals is obviously drastic. The social environment of premodern peoples is more influential than in modern societies because of their intense fear of isolation and the unknown, although fear of isolation and loneliness through an alleged or real misdeed in modern humans just as easily kills the spirit to live.

Fear is one of the most deeply rooted and dominant of the emotions. Great fear and great rage have similar effects on the body; the instinct to attack if rage is present and the instinct to run away if fear is present. When aroused into action, the sympathetic-adrenal system controls the organs and blood supply, liberating sugar from the liver, accelerating the heart, contracting certain blood vessels, discharging adrenalines, and dilating the bronchioles. All these changes make a person more effective in his/her response, but if these reactions are prolonged without the occurrence of action, they produce a profound emotional strain. Without the intervention of a medicine man or shaman to counteract the taboo, Cannon suggests that death is caused by shocking emotional stress that prohibits the intake of food, water and sleep.

We have seen that taboo and prohibition ritual is closely tied to containing the eruption of dangerous emotions that emanated when a change of status is present, whether during pregnancy, childbirth, onset of menstruation and other puberty rites, illness, or death. Ellenberger (1970, pp. 2–52) points to the connection between indigenous beliefs about taboo as the ancestry to modern medical and therapeutic practices. A breach of taboo can result in psychogenic death if not treated. In some indigenous tribes, the concept of sin as a pathogenic secret is identical with that of a breach of taboo that needs a public confession to cure the illness. Certain moral offences come under taboo violation, notably those of a sexual nature. Among physical ailments that result from moral offenses are painful and protracted childbirth and sterility in women. Confessions of a secret (conscious or unconscious) are public affairs and often supplemented by eliminatory procedures such as washing, vomiting, or bleeding.

Among the South American *Mixtex*, sins of theft and offenses against property are particularly taken into account. Ceremonial healing often re-enact the original trauma within a well-structured group involving the patient's entire tribe under the authority of the medicine man. Among the Navaho, if a member falls in to a state of anxious depression as the result of a bad dream, the illusion of having seen a ghost, or fear of having offended a sacred animal, the patient can die of a slow starvation. In such a case, the timely ceremonial cure performed by the right medicine man or shaman can be surprisingly rapid and effective. Ellenberger (ibid, p. 48) and Levi-Strauss (1963; see chapter 8 on shamanism) stress the remarkable affinities between certain features of modern dynamic therapy and indigenous healing. Dynamic therapies can be interpreted as a regression into the past because the scientific approach has proved often insufficient in penetrating the mystery of psychosomatic illness. In chapter 6, I discuss the psychosomatic distress of patients in modern clinical practice who are caught up in endless purification rituals as punishment for unconscious, undiscovered taboo violations.

Conclusion

In this chapter, I have described in some detail the taboo practices of indigenous peoples drawing on the work of Fraser and his critics. I have shown that indigenous forms of taboo are complex and not an erroneously applied logic that Fraser intimates. Some of these details will be repeated in other chapters in this book where I use them to illustrate different perspectives on taboo in each case. The material on taboo practices presented in this chapter is by no means exhaustive. I have chosen but a few of the main researchers and others will be introduced thematically in the chapters that follow. It strikes me how relevant taboo practices still are in modern day life as if there is an underlying, archetypal dynamic in taboo that needs to be made more visible, particularly in its relationship to later religions practices and beliefs about the transmigration of the soul and its dangers. As I explained in the introduction in chapter 1, taboos appear when change needs to be regulated in order to simultaneously facilitate it. Change itself is difficult to pin down and offer a particular image, as it constantly moves within its liminal status. So far, I have not presented an archetypal image of taboo, but I will do so as the book progresses, when certain images become more visible.

References

Adams, M.V. (2001). *The Mythological Unconscious.* Putnam, Conn: Spring Publications, 2010.

Adams, M.V. (2004). *The Fantasy Principle, Psychoanalysis of the Imagination.* Hove and New York: Brunner-Routledge.

Buckley, T. & Gottlieb, A. (1988). A Critical Appraisal of Theories of Menstrual Symbolism. In Buckley. T., and Gottlieb, A. (eds.) *Blood Magic: The Anthropology of Menstruation.* Berkeley and London: University of California Press, pp. 3–50.

Buckley, T. and Gottlieb, A. (eds.) (1988). *Blood Magic: The Anthropology of Menstruation.* Berkeley and London: University of California Press.

Cannon, W.B. (1942). 'Voodoo' Death. In (1979) Lessa, W.A., and Vogt, E.Z. (eds.) *Reader in Comparative Religion. An Anthropological Approach*, 4th edn. New York: Harper Collins, pp. 367–373.

Delaney, J., Lupton, M.J., and Toth, E. (1976). *The Curse, A Cultural History of Menstruation.* Urbano and Chicago: University of Illinois Press, expanded edn. 1988.

Douglas, M. (1966). *Purity and Danger: an Analysis of Concepts of Pollution and Taboo.* (new preface, 2002) Abingdon, Oxon, and New York: Routledge, 2002.

Eliade, M. (1958). *Patterns in Comparative Religion.* Lincoln and London: University of Nebraska Press, 1996.

Ellenberger, H.F. (1970). *The Discovery of the Unconscious. The History and Evolution of Dynamic Psychiatry.* New York: Basic Books.

Evans-Pritchard, E.E. (1937). Witchcraft Explains Unfortunate Events. In (1979). Lessa, W.A. and Vogt, E.Z. (eds.) *Reader in Comparative Religion. An Anthropological Approach*, 4th edn. New York: Harper Collins, pp. 362–366.

Finnegan, R. and Horton, R. (eds.) (1973). *Modes of Thought. Essays on Thinking in Western and Non-Western Societies.* Eugene, Oregon: Wipf & Stock.

Ford, C. (1945). *A Comparative Study of Human Reproduction.* New Haven: Yale University Press.

Fraser, J.G. (1922). *The Golden Bough, A Study in Magic and Religion*, abridged edn. London and New York: Penguin Books.

Gillison, D. (2002). *New Guinea Ceremonies.* New York: Abrams.

Girard, R. (1977). *Violence and the Sacred.* London and New York: Continuum Books, 2005.

Goodwyn. E.D. (2016). *Healing Symbols in Psychotherapy.* London and New York: Routledge.

Greenwood, S. and Goodwyn, E.D. (2016). *Magical Consciousness. An Anthropological and Neurobiological Approach.* New York and London: Routledge.

Hillman, J. (1983). *Archetypal Psychology: A Brief Account.* Dallas, Texas: Spring Pubs, 1993.

Homans, G.C. (1941). Anxiety and Ritual: The Theories of Malinowski and Radcliffe-Brown. In (1979) Lessa, W.A. and Vogt, E.Z. (eds.) *Reader in Comparative Religion. An Anthropological Approach*, 4th edn. New York: Harper Collins, pp. 57–62.

Horton, R. and Flannigan, R. (eds.) (1973). *Modes of Thought.* London: Faber and Faber.

James, W. (1890). *Principles of Psychology.* Vol. 2. New York: Dover Publications, 1950.

Jong, J. (2017). 'Belief in Spiritual Beings:' E.B. Tylor's (Primitive) Cognition Theory of Religion. In Tremlett, P-F, Sutherland, L.T., and Harvey, G. (eds.) *Edward Burnett Tylor, Religion and Culture.* London and New York: Bloomsbury, pp. 47–61.

Jung, C.G. (1911–12/1952). Two Kinds of Thinking. In *Collected Works*, Vol. 5. *Symbols of Transformation*, 2nd edn. London: Routledge and Kegan Paul, 1995.

Jung, C.G. (1928). On Psychic Energy. In *Collected works*, Vol. 8. *The Structure and Dynamics of the Psyche*, 2nd edn. London: Routledge and Kegan Paul, 1991.

Jung, C.G. (1932). The Structure of the Psyche. In *Collected Works,* Vol. 8. *The Structure and Dynamics of the Psyche*, 2nd edn. London: Routledge and Kegan Paul, 1991.

Jung, C.G. (1937). Concerning the Archetypes and the Anima Concept. In *Collected Works,* Vol. 9i. *The Archetypes and the Collective Unconscious*, 2nd edn. London: Routledge and Kegan Paul, 1991.

Jung, C.G. (1947). On the Nature of the Psyche. In *Collected Works,* Vol. 8. *The Structure and Dynamics of the Psyche*, 2nd edn. London: Routledge and Kegan Paul, 1991.

Jung, C.G. (1951). The Psychological Aspects of the Kore. In *Collected Works,* Vol. 9i. *The Archetypes of the Collective Unconscious*, 2nd edn. London: Routledge and Kegan Paul, 1990.

Jung, C.G. (1952). Synchronicity: An Acausal Connecting Principle. In *Collected Works,* Vol. 8, *The Structure and Dynamics of the Psyche*, 2nd edn. London: Routledge and Kegan Paul, 1991.

Jung, C.G. (1954). Letters on Synchronicity. In *Collected Works*, Vol. 18, *The Symbolic Life*, 2nd edn. London: Routledge and Kegan Paul, 1993.

Jung, C.G. (1961). Compiled and edited by A. Jaffe. *Memories, Dreams and Reflections.* London: Fontana, 1963.

Kahn, M. (1931). *Djuka: Bush Negroes of Dutch Guiana.* New York: Viking Press.

Kuper, H. (1947). *An African Aristocracy: Rank Among the Swazi.* London: Oxford University Press for the International African Institute.

Lessa, W.A. and Vogt, E.Z. (eds.) (1979). *Reader in Comparative Religion. An Anthropological Approach*, 4th edn. New York: HarperCollins.

Lester, D. (1972). Voodoo Death: Some New Thoughts on an Old Phenomenon. In *American Anthropologist* 74, 386–390.

Levi-Strauss, C. (1963). *Structural Anthropology.* Trans. Jocobson, C. & Schoepf, B.G. New York: Basic Books.

Lex, B. (1974). Voodoo Death: New Thoughts on an Old Explanation. In *American Anthropologist* 76, 818–823.

Malinowski, B. (1931). The Role of Magic and Religion. In (1979) Lessa, W.A. and Vogt E.Z. (eds.) *Reader in Comparative Religion. An Anthropological Approach*, 4th edn. New York: Harper Collins, pp. 37–46.

Montagu, M.F. (1957). *Anthropology and Human Nature.* New York: McGraw Hill.

Peters, I.W. (1921). The Institutionalised Sex Taboo. In Blanchard, P.M. (ed.) *Taboo and Genetics-A Study of the Biological, Sociological and Psychological Foundation of the Family.* Wroclaw, Poland: Filiquarian Publishing, pp. 53–68.

Radcliffe-Brown, A.R. (1952). Taboo. In *Structure and Function in Primitive Society. Essays and Addresses.* Glencoe, Ill: The Free Press. pp. 133–152.

Sorenson, J. (2007). *A Cognitive Theory of Magic.* Langham, Maryland: Rowman & Littlefield.

Steiner, F. (1956). *Taboo.* London and New York: Routledge.

Tambiah, S.J. (1973). The Form and Meaning of Magical Acts. In Horton, R. and Flannigan, R. (eds.) *Modes of Thought.* London: Faber and Faber.

Tremlett, P-F., Sutherland, L.T., and Harvey, G. (eds.) (2017). *Edward Burnett Tylor, Religion and Culture.* London and New York: Bloomsbury.

Tylor, E.B. (1903). *Primitive Culture. Researches Into the Development of Mythology, Philosophy, Religion, Language, Art, and Custom.* Vol. 2. London: John Murray.

Von Franz, M-L. (1994). *Archetypal Dimensions of the Psyche.* Boston and London: Shambhala, 1997.

Walker, S.F. (2002). *Jung and Jungians on Myth.* London and New York: Routledge.

Webster, H. (1942). *Taboo: a Sociological Study.* New York: Octagon Books, 1973.

Chapter 3

Taboo, order, disorder, abjection, and dirt

Introduction

This chapter is divided into two main parts to discuss, primarily, the work of structural anthropologist Douglas and, second, cultural theorist and psychoanalyst Kristeva, in relation to taboo. Both academics, using different approaches and source material, widen parameters of discussion about the origins and positioning of taboo. I also present material from anthropologists Leach and Radcliffe-Brown, amongst others. When one examines taboo deeper, Leach (1964) proposes that physical and social environment are perceived first in childhood as a continuum that does not contain separate 'things.' A person is gradually taught to impose a discriminating grid through language acquisition. Language gives names to distinguish and separate things; taboo inhibits the recognition of those parts of the continuum that separates things. Under taboo, they become non-things, as anomalies that fall out of classification and fill the interstices. Girard (1977, p. 59) stresses that the dissolution or disappearance of natural difference can bring about the dissolution of regulations pertaining to the individual's proper place in society. An appearance of nondifference as anomaly is *monstrous* and triggers intense feelings of taboo.

Falling out of classification

Leach (1964, p. 158) suggests that taboo is not only a focus of special interest, but also of intense anxiety: '*Whatever is taboo is sacred, valuable, important, powerful, dangerous, untouchable, filthy, unmentionable.*' In developing a sense of personhood, one important task is to establish boundaries: where is the edge of me? Boundaries establish a sense of a core identity, an ontological security and self-containment. Leach emphasises the importance of clear, unambiguous certainty about the difference between *me* and *it*, between *we* and *they* or *me* and *not me*. Related to boundaries are orifices, which allow substances to pass through the body (*me*) into the outside world (*not me*). He argues that faeces, urine, semen, menstrual blood, hair clippings, nail parings, spittle, ear wax, nose excrement, and breast milk are intensely ambivalent because they are both *me* and *not me* as they pass through the bodily orifices. As they travel across the margins into open spaces, they pose a threat to ego identity, collective containment and unity, and meet intense feelings of taboo attached to risk and change.

Douglas (1966, pp. 48–49) positing a different analysis from Fraser's emphasis on sympathetic and contagious magic as misapplied logic, as I have already mentioned in chapter 2, argues that all cultures logically standardise values for the community and provide basic, ordering categories of classification that deal with anomalies and ambiguity. Douglas maintains that indigenous beliefs and religious practices are similar in the way that they structure their margins between order, disorder, and the anomalies that fall in between the margins. She suggests that there are several ways of dealing with anomalies: negatively, one can ignore them, perceive and condemn their existence, or physically control them; positively, anomalies can be deliberately confronted in order to create new patterns of perception, such as in rites of passage from one status to the next. Ambiguous symbols used in indigenous taboo ritual and in religious practices enrich mythological meaning by stressing other levels of cognition that incorporate order/safety/good and disorder/risk/evil into ever more complex and progressive developmental patterns of comprehension.

Leach (1964, p. 158) similarly argues that cultures, whether through indigenous practices or through religion, impose differentiation to establish order and create unity and safety amongst their members. A hypothetical ambiguous 'other' is created at the margin as taboo that embodies both potential and risk. The gap between two logically distinct categories, this world and the 'other' supernatural world is therefore filled with tabooed ambiguity. The margin between safety and risk and the objects that inhabit these margins as the ambivalent 'other' are regarded with taboo, dread, and suspicion. This margin is bridged by supernatural beings of highly ambiguous, indeterminate natures: incarnate deities, virgin mothers, supernatural monsters as half-person-half-animal hybrids, or angels (humans with wings) who are credited with the ability to mediate between the gods and humans. The Virgin Mary, human mother of god, for example, attracts particularly intense taboo veneration as the pure and untouched prelapsarian virgin anomaly. Mary gave birth without sexual intercourse or having experienced the pain of childbirth. Such an image of the protective Virgin Mary can appear in dreams of women in analysis who want to become pregnant but have been sexually abused in childhood. Their dreams can show a preparedness to work with the emotional ambivalence of purity and danger and move forward into the rites of passage to become mothers themselves.

Pollution rules

Taboos appear as pollution prohibitions when they meet one of the following criteria (Douglas, 1966, p. 165):first, when a situation is morally ill-defined, a pollution belief can provide a rule for determining post hoc whether fraction has taken place or not; second, when moral principles come into conflict, a pollution rule can reduce the confusion by giving a simple focus of concern; third, when an action is deemed morally wrong but does not attract sufficient indignation, a violated pollution rule can aggravate the seriousness and marshal public opinion on the side of the right. Finally, when moral indignation is not reinforced by practical sanctions, pollutions beliefs can provide a deterrent to wrongdoers.

Radcliffe-Brown (1952, pp. 133–152), in his assessment of taboo, differentiates between ritual avoidance and ritual prohibitions. A ritual prohibition as a 'taboo' is a rule of behaviour that is associated with a belief that an infraction will result in an undesirable change in the ritual status of the person who fails to keep to the rule. The Roman Catholic Church, for example, prohibits eating meat on Friday and during Lent. A person who breaks these rules must confess and be absolved. Such rituals, including superstitions, develop out the need to relieve anxiety when faced with developmental changes that push the boundaries of known knowledge into the unknown. Rituals provide a focussing mechanism, a method of mnemonics and a control for experience. A ritual focuses attention by framing; it enlivens the memory and links the present with the relevant past. It also formulates experience and can permit knowledge inside its frame that would otherwise not be known. It does not merely externalise experience bringing it into the light of day, it also modifies the experience by expressing it. There are thoughts that have never been put into words, so the thought is changed and limited by the very words selected. Radcliffe-Brown (ibid, p. 138) stresses that indigenous beliefs, as opposed to certain hierarchical monotheistic beliefs, do not recognise the difference between *holy* and *unclean*. The Polynesians, for example, do not recognise a chief as holy and a corpse as unclean. They are both subject to taboo because they are dangerous and they have ritual value to the clan as a whole. Taboos exist as part of a mechanism by which a clan maintains order, maintains existence, and establishes its fundamental values. The beliefs by which rites are justified and given consistency are the rationalizations of symbolic actions and of the sentiments associated with them to protect each member from unexpected and, therefore, dangerous elements attached to change of status.

Taboo, blessing and defilement

Douglas (1966) argues that any enquiry into 'taboo' should examine the principles of power and danger. She suggests that defilement or pollution occurs as a result of a systematic ordering of thoughts and ideas whose keystone, boundaries, margins, and internal lines are held by rituals of separation (ibid, p. 51). Ritual recognises the potency of disorder. Taking her research from Leviticus in the *OT*, Douglas argues that religious ritual blessing is believed to be the source of all good and the withdrawal of blessing as the source of all danger. The blessing of god makes living possible and is essential to creating order. Fertility of women, livestock, and fields is promised as a result and can be obtained through keeping covenant with god; when blessing is withdrawn, the power of the curse is unleashed resulting in barrenness, pestilence, and confusion. Holiness is thus defined by strict categories of classification and order. The relationship to the physical body also reflects this holy state. Being presented at the Jewish temple requires perfection: the animal's sacrifice must be without blemish, women must be purified after childbirth because all bodily discharge, including menstruation blood or physical blemish is considered defiling. Diet is classified into clean and unclean foods.

OT Leviticus uses the classification in *OT* Genesis for separating animals in edible/clean and inedible/unclean. Edible animals fall into correct categories whereas inedible taboo animals fall outside their classification. Douglas (1966, p. 69) points out that *OT* Genesis classifies threefold: earth, water, and the firmament. Leviticus adopts this scheme: in the firmament, two legged fowls fly with wings; in the water, scaly fish swim with fins; on the earth, four-legged animals hop, jump, or walk. Any class of creature that is not equipped for the right kind of locomotion in its element is deemed contrary to holiness, for example, anything living in the water which does not have fins or scales is unclean. Likewise, four-footed creatures that fly are unclean. Any creature that has two legs and two hands and moves on all fours like a quadruped is unclean such as the weasel, the mouse, crocodile, and various kinds of lizards.

The last kind of unclean animal is that which creeps, crawls, or swarms upon the earth. Swarming applies to those animals that teem in the water and swarm on the ground. Carnivores are inedible because they kill their prey and transgress the Jewish commandment of 'thou shalt not kill.' Before any meat is eaten, therefore, the blood must be properly drained. The distinction between carnivores and herbivores is that herbivores chew the cud, so the difference can be clearly seen. Any animal that parts the hoof, has a hoof cloven into two, and chews the cud, is edible. The swine, even though it parts the hoof, does not chew the cud, so is inedible. The camel, hare, and the rock badger chew the cud but do not part the hoof and are thus inedible. Animals that fall out of their classification are considered as indeterminate, anomalous forms of movement. By rules of avoidance, holiness is given a physical expression and defilement of it is assessed at every encounter.

OT Leviticus classifications may seem arbitrary and irrational (cf. Fraser, 1922, and Robertson Smith, 1889) and yet they still form one basis of modern religious practice. It seems likely, however, that these classifications have more than one underlying motive. There are sound sanitary reasons attached to the avoidance of being contaminated by dirty clothes, and infected skin secretions, unwashed foods or unhealthy, obese eating habits as well as their moral connotations. Stein (1957) emphasises the moral symbolic component behind Jewish taboos, suggesting that each law about forbidden foods has its deeper meaning: mice and weasels are inedible, mice because of their destructiveness and weasels as a symbol of malicious gossip. According to

Moses, they must be excluded to encourage devout thoughts and to form character. Edible birds are all tame and clean as they live only from corn. Wild, carnivorous birds that kill lambs, goats, and even humans, are unclean because one should not do violence to the weak. Cloven hoofed animals with parted hoofs symbolise that all actions must portray proper ethical distinction. Chewing the cud, on the other hand, stands for memory. The dividing of the hoof and chewing of cud signify discretion between good and evil. Fish without fins or scales do not rise themselves up by prayer and cover themselves with scales of virtue. Pigs are unclean although they have cloven hoofs because they do not ruminate. As pigs do not give milk, hide, or wool, they are only kept for their flesh, which is seen as a sign of excess and gluttony. Using Plato's use of allegory, Stein further explains that fish with fins and scales symbolise endurance and self-control, while the forbidden ones are swept away by the current unable to resist the force of the stream. Reptiles wriggling upon their bellies are inedible because they signify those devoted to ever-greedy desires and passions. Creeping animals that have legs above their feet so they can leap are edible because they symbolise moral effort.

Douglas also differentiates anomalous categories that fall outside the concept of holiness and involve killing what is deemed dangerous in indigenous practices. For instance, in 'monstrous' births where the line between human and animals is crossed or defiled, a birth may be labelled as a particular kind of event in order to restore the original category or boundary. For example, the *Nuer* treat 'monstrous' malformed births as baby hippopotamus accidentally born to humans. The answer is to place them gently in the river where they belong. In some West African tribes, as I have already mentioned in the introduction chapter 1, twins are killed at birth as anomalies of nature and sometimes the mother, because they believe that multiple offspring belong to lower, four-legged animals.

Potency of disorder and dirt

Special powers, however, can be obtained through relinquishing order. Although disorder spoils patterns, it also provides the material for new patterns. Ritual, both in indigenous and modern religious practices, recognises the potency of disorder and liminality and expects to find power in instances where truth is reached only through abandoning rational control for a time. In chapter 7, I expand on liminality as transformative in rites of passage. Formlessness is also powerful and dangerous, as are people in marginal states. People left out of the normal pattern of knowledge are considered taboo and dangerous, for example, an unborn baby whose sex is unknown cannot approach a sick person in case its proximity through the pregnant mother causes coughing or fever to increase. The unborn baby's voracity can also affect the harvest. All margins are considered dangerous; if they are pulled in a different way, the fundamental experience is changed (Douglas, 1966, p. 150).

Douglas importantly advocates that the structure of ideas is vulnerable at the margins. She sees it as a mistake to treat bodily margins in isolation from sociocultural margins. This explains the unevenness with which different aspects of the body are treated in different world cultures. Each culture has its own risks and problems; which particular bodily margin is attributed to its beliefs about danger and pollution depends on which situation the body is mirroring. In some cultures, menstrual blood is feared; in others excreta is dangerous; in India cooked food and saliva are pollution prone. As Douglas (1966, p. 152) amplifies, four kinds of social pollution can be qualified: first, danger from outside as seen as pressing on external boundaries; second, danger from within, transgressing the internal lines of a system; third, danger within the margins of the lines; and, fourth, danger from internal contradictions so that at certain points, the system seems to be at war with itself.

Orifices of the body are especially vulnerable points. Matter issuing from them is particularly dangerous as it has traversed the body as *me* but *no longer me*. Nail clippings, semen, menstrual blood, tears, sweat, boils and rashes, are symbolic of societal structures and their acceptance as filth/dirt depends on the societal structure and framing of the margins as flexible or difficult to traverse. Douglas (ibid, p. 47) points to the particular quality of stickiness or viscosity using Sartre's (1943) work. Viscosity lies as a halfway state between solid and liquid; it is unstable but does not flow. Stickiness clings as a cross-section, like a trap on the margin between static and change. In this context, ear wax, nasal excrement, faeces, pus, and blood clots all belong to this sticky, anomalous, marginal realm. Stickiness is contagious in its ability to cling. Bauman (1973, pp. 137–138) offers the term *slime* as equivalent to stickiness. He suggests that the 'snare of slime lies in its fluidity.' It seems like a liquid, but to touch it would risk being dissolved in sliminess and being incorporated into an amorphous, jellylike, oozy substance associated with the nature of slippery, poisonous snakes. Snakes are also associated with boundary issues, faeces, the shedding of skin and the overstepping of borders. Menstrual blood is particularly tabooed as I discuss in chapter 2. Girard (1977, p. 35) sees menstruation releasing contagious, strong, conflictual emotions attached to sexuality, which can erupt into violence and hence best avoided. Sexuality leads to quarrels, jealous rages, and mortal combat. Even within the framework of marriage, there is no guarantee of order. I discuss in depth the strong taboos attached to menstrual blood and mothers and their offspring during childbirth as a transitional state as one interpretation in chapter 7.

In India, saliva, nasal, and genital excrements are more pollution worthy than tears. Tears do not defile as they are moving water: they purify, cleanse, and bathe the eye and are unrelated to bodily digestion or procreation. Pollution beliefs provide a kind of impersonal punishment for wrongdoing by supporting the accepted system of morality. In India, human excrements are not forbidden on the streets because they have a special externalised 'defiled' caste of 'untouchable' people who exist to touch that taboo material for the collective. Gidla (2018) reports on the origins of the 'untouchables' in India, called Daliks, who comprise one sixth of India's population. The Daliks are originally nomadic, tribal people who have been denied land and human rights under the Hindu caste system that seized their property. Forced to live beyond the margins of Indian life, they collect human faeces and handle dead animals. One could argue that because status value has been denied them in the form of land and rights, Daliks are positioned in a forever nomadic, liminal, tabooed in-between state of untouchability. Their handling of putrid waste products that cannot be touched for fear of contagion reflects their own impure psychosocial position in the caste system.

Douglas suggests that anxiety about bodily margins expresses danger to group survival. Dirt is created by the differentiating activity of the mind. It is a by-product of the creation of order and its role is to threaten those distinctions. Cleansing rituals work upon the body politic through the symbolic medium of the physical body. In the course of any imposing of order, whether internal or external, the attitude to rejected bits and pieces goes through two stages: they are recognisably out of place, a threat to good order, and brushed away (Douglas, 1966, ibid. p. 197). They still, however, have an identity: hair, nail clippings, food remains and wrappings are the most dangerous as their half identity still clings to them and order is impaired by their presence. Eventually, they lose their identity and become pulverised or dissolved into a mass of common rubbish. As long as identity is absent, rubbish is not dangerous as it provokes no unpleasant memory. Where there is no differentiation there is no defilement. Finally, rubbish returns to its original state of its true indiscrimination and creative formlessness. However, dirt can be examined in its position of power at the margins as boundary transgressions and seen as an attacking force on good order. Eliade (1958, p. 194) refers to the transforming power of water to dissolve dirt, which is why water, washing, and baptism are used in taboo rituals and play an integral role in obsession repetition compulsions. This aspect of taboo is particularly important in clinical work in finding the source behind obsessive compulsive states such as washing compulsions, which I expand upon in chapter 6.

Cultural complexes: internal and external margins

Douglas (1966, pp. 140–159) thus characterises the idea of society as having external boundaries like the human body. It has external boundaries, margins, and an internal structure. Its outlines contain power to reward conformity and reject difference. The structure of living organisms is well able to reflect complex social forms, particularly in the ritual of sacrifice. For example; if an animal is cut longitudinally through its sexual organs, the sacrifice is tended to undo incest taboo violation. Douglas (ibid, pp. 141–159) argues that one cannot interpret ritual unless one is prepared to see the body as a symbol of society and as the powers and the dangers enacted out on the body by society.[1] For example, although not mentioned by Douglas in her research, the British through their access to open shorelines, ports, and sea passages, became adept during the eighteenth century, and earlier, at disposing their human surplus 'waste' across their borders by shipping convicts off to colonies. Deportation and gang pressing became a social experiment to see whether, under different social circumstances, polluted 'waste' could be recycled and transformed into economic value (cf. Hughes, 1986).

How the body and its margins are reflected upon varies between cultures depending on where their internal lines or borders are situated. In some cultures, menstrual pollution is considered a lethal danger, in others not at all. In some cultures, excreta are dangerous, in others not. In India, cooked food and saliva are pollution prone, but Bushman collect melon seeds from their mouths for later roasting and eating. For example, for the Coorgs of India, danger exists from impurities entering their system. Anything coming from the body is never to be readmitted. The most dangerous pollution is for anything that has once emerged gaining re-entry. Once a piece of food has been chewed, one cannot take it out and then put it back in. The Coorgs share with other Indian castes a concept of what is outside and below. For them, the model of exits and entries of the human body is the symbolic focus of their fears for their minority standing. When rituals express anxiety about the body orifices, the sociological counterpart of this anxiety is to care and protect what comes in and out. The threatened boundaries of their people would be mirrored in the care for the integrity, unity, and purity of the physical body. I discuss this point in detail using two case studies in chapter 6.

As we have already discussed, in the Hindu caste system, the lowest cast of untouchables handle the corpses and the excreta faeces in the street. One can argue that the caste system orders social hierarchy. The lowest castes are the most impure and their humble services allow the higher castes to be free of bodily impurities. It represents a division of labour: the stable head does the thinking and praying and the lowest, most nomadic, despised parts carry away waste matter from where it is eliminated. How waste is handled and by whom reflects the social structure and its inflexibility about transforming waste into an aspect of value.

Entry into the Indian caste system is determined through the mother. For this reason, in the higher castes, boundary pollution focusses on sexuality. Female purity is carefully guarded as her vagina is the entry into procreation and lineage. Male promiscuousness is a lighter matter. Through the adultery of a wife, impure outsider blood can introduced and spoil the lineage.

The necessity of dirt

However, as Douglas (1966, p. 200) rightly maintains, dirt is necessary because purity is the enemy of change. Purity classifies into noncontradictions that deaden creativity. Whenever a strict pattern of purity is imposed, its highly uncomfortable tension leads to contradiction and, if not observed, hypocrisy. Life that does not fit into tidy categories still exists and demands attention. It must find a way of affirming what has been rejected. For example, anomalies can be put together into one animal and considered holy in order to maintain creativity. In the *Lele* culture of the Kasai in southwestern Congo, the pangolin cult achieves uniting the anomalies in a creative sense, which allows disorder a proper place. Their cult seems to suggest a meditation on the inadequacy of the categories of human thought. Initiates approach, hold, kill, and eat the animal whose own existence combines all the elements the *Lele* keep apart. The pangolin is scaly like a fish, but climbs trees, lays eggs like a lizard but suckles its young, and unlike other small animals, its young are born singly. Like human twin parents, the forest pangolins are symbols of an unusual, anomalous fertility and are thus able to bring disparate parts of creativity together by overstepping the margins. When humans produce twins, they have transcended the normal human limitations and entered the fecund animal world. Twins are anomalous in an auspicious way. Twins and their parents can be either killed or given special status, depending on whether the culture is dirt affirming or dirt negating (cf. Brodersen, 2016, pp. 93–132).

The creative relationship between death, madness and dirt is well illustrated by the African *Nyakyusa* tribe living north of Lake Nyasa (cf. Wilson, 1957, pp. 78–81). The pollution of death can be treated positively and creatively. The *Nyakyusa* tribe explicitly associate dirt with madness: those who eat dirt, that is, their own faeces, are mad. They believe that madness comes from two sources: from god and the neglect of ritual. Ritual separates life from death as it conserves sanity and life; madness brings filth and a kind of death. In the ritual of mourning, however, filth is actively welcomed. In the face of death, the *Nyakyusa* have given up everything, even claim to have eaten filth as madmen do, in order to keep their reason.

Madness is feared if the *Nyakyusa* tribe neglects the ritual of freely accepting the corruption of the body; sanity is assured if they perform that ritual. Douglas (1966, p. 219) gives the example of the Dinka's use of ritual murder when their aged spear-masters are allowed to choose the time of their death. Rituals, punishment, moral pressures, and rules can only do so much to bring people in harmony with their nature. There must be a free consent and choice to free them from the chains of necessity actualised by death. When someone freely embraces the symbol of death and decay by, for example, eating his/her own faeces, a great release of power for the good can be expected. In painting such dark themes of death and loss, pollution symbols are necessary as is the use of the colour black to imbue darkness, night-time, and faeces. Death is the ultimate leap into the unknown where normal rules of pollution to keep safety and cohesion within the margins do not apply. Pollution is allowed to legitimately cross over into chaos to meet death voluntarily. I expand upon the creative importance of the colour black as faeces during liminal border*land* states in much more detail in chapters 7 and 8.

New perspectives on Douglas' work

Douglas (1966/2002, p. xv) has since amended some of her original arguments due to scholarly criticisms of her work, particularly her analysis of *OT* Leviticus' classification of animals. She concedes that the prohibition on 'unclean' animals was not based on abhorrence or abomination but as part of an elaborate intellectual structure of rules that mirrors god's caring and just covenant with his people. She had misinterpreted the term to *abominate*.

Interesting new international perspectives have developed from Douglas' work on purity, dirt, and rubbish. For example, Dürr and Winder (2016, pp. 52–68) have taken the ambiguities of cleanness and dirt in relation to urban pollution to highlight social hierarchies, power, shifting values, and social meaning as objects that are discarded, rediscovered, and transferred. Dürr and Winder take *Tepito*, a rundown neighbourhood in Mexico, to analyse the contrasting notions of ethics and behaviour toward garbage. They provide an overview of how pollution is framed and develop a conceptual framework by reflecting on urban pollution and purifying practices as they relate to ethical images of good urban behaviour. They suggest that dirt and rubbish are not passive materials *out of place,* but serve as an *active* redistributive urban resource. They see garbage as slippery because it passes between social orders as well as between order and disorder. One *Tepito* activist considers garbage as a valuable recycling material, such as glass and cardboard packaging that can be sold, renaming informal garbage collectors as the real ecologists because they take care of street refuse and transform it into value. The perception of garbage has changed from something stigmatised and useless into something valuable through its recycling.

Another perspective stresses littering as a form of challenging social norms (ibid, pp. 61–63). Nonconformist residents view littering as an act of resistance to the pressures to become *good* citizens in a social environment where poor residents are neglected like rubbish and excluded. Some *Tepito* residents blame foreign traders who sell their merchandise but leave their rubbish as the 'dirty other.' The 'dirty other' is a dominate trope that draws ambiguous boundaries between outsider and insider, self and other. In this vein, rubbish is interpreted as key to shaping sociospatial relations and emphasises the *active* vitality of rubbish and dirt in its own right. In this way, capitalism depends on its own decay, which is ontologically reconstructed within revitalised rubbish for its renewal and agency (Williams, 2016, p. 81).

Kristeva and abjection

Kristeva (1982), developing ideas from Douglas' work on purity and danger, interprets filth at the margins or between the margins, as ***abjection*** and sees it as a major contributor to depressive states. Contrary to what enters the mouth as forms of nourishment, what goes out of the body, out of its pores and openings, points to an infinitude of the body proper and gives rise to abjection. Faeces signify what has never ceased to separate from the body in a state of permanent loss in order to become autonomous. Kristeva (1982, p. 74) suggests that how faeces and sexuality are ritualised allows the 'two universes of filth and prohibition to brush lightly against each-other without necessarily being identified as *object* and *law.*' On account of this flexibility, Kristeva argues that the rites of defilement as the anomalous 'speaking being,' stands at both edges of the unnameable as the non-object *and* the off-limits.

Psychoanalysis interprets anal rejection as the first material separation that is controllable in a human being. Within abjection looms one of those violent, dark revolts of being directed against a threat that has been ejected beyond the scope of the possible, the tolerable, and thinkable. It lies there, but cannot be assimilated. It beseeches, worries, and fascinates desire but does not let itself be seduced. Kristeva argues that *abjection* does not have a definable *object* that can be imagined or named. It only has one quality of the object, that of being opposed to I. What is *abject* as the jettisoned, radically excluded other object draws one toward a place where meaning collapses. Yet from this place, the *abject* continues to challenge its master. On the edge of nonexistence, *abject* and *abjection* are safeguards as belonging to the 'other.' Thus, it is not lack of cleanliness or health that causes *abjection* but that which disturbs identity, system, and order at the margins and seemingly does not respect borders, positions, and rules (cf. client case 1, chapter 6, on the mastery of anal ejection).

The *abject* represents the hidden, tabooed, unacknowledged, and feared parts of identity, the other against which normalcy is defined. Bodily fluids and emissions from the pores and orifices such as pus, sweat, milk, semen, and blood stand as signifiers of the abject of the body without boundaries that threaten the illusion of the contained, rational subject and, as such, stability and social unity. In a similar vein, Gross (1990, pp. 80–103) argues that the female form with it creases and curves, seepages and secretions, as well as its changing boundaries during pregnancy and menopause, signifies association with the animal world where human mortality and fragility are in contrast with the clean, contained, proper body, unspoiled by fecundity. It is no wonder women subject themselves to strict diets to control all signs of fleshy excess. Of course, the female body is not intrinsically abject or polluted, but it has been positioned as such by monism with the inherent connotation of deviance and danger.

Gross (ibid. p. 81) further explains that for psychoanalytical European writers, such a Lyotard, Deleuze, and Derrida, the body is conceived as a fundamentally historical and political object. It is the central object over and through which relations of power and resistance are played out. She suggests that the interlocking of bodies and signifying patterns is the precondition of an ordered and stable identity for the subject and a smooth regulated production of discourses and stable meanings. Any culture is a series of related structures that comprise social forms, values, and cosmology, the whole of knowledge through which all experience is mediated. Certain cultural themes are expressed by rites of bodily manipulation, injection, and expulsion.

The mirror stage

Lacan's (1977, pp. 1–8) understanding of the mirror stage underlines the fantasy of a cohesive, stable identity facilitated by an identification with its own image that can position itself as a subject within and outside the space of its own body through the mirror image. Lacan stresses that the subject's acquisition of the self, of a continuous identity, is the result of the child's ability to locate him/herself within a body of space and to have a spatial comportment as a threshold (mirror) of the visible world. This necessary embodiment of subjectivity must be psychically signified in order for the subject to gain a stable, sexually coded speaking position. Kristeva (1982), however, is more interested in how sociality and subjectivity are based on the expulsion or exclusion of the improper, unclean, and disorderly elements of a corporal existence that must be separated from its clean and proper self. The subject must disavow part of itself in order to gain a stable self; a refusal to do so marks whatever identity it acquires as provisional and open to breakdown and instability. Kristeva's view differs from Freud in that the improper and unclean is never expelled but hovers at the border of the subject's identity. The abject is part of the subject that it attempts to expel. It is a symptom of the object's failure to fill the subject or to define or anchor the subject.

Objects generating abjection

The objects generating abjection—food, faeces, urine, vomit—inscribe the body within those surfaces, hollows, and crevices that become erotogenic zones: mouth, eyes, anus, ears, and genitals. All sexual organs and erotogenic zones, according to Lacan, are structured in the form of a rim between the inside and outside of the body. The rim in a particular bodily zone is a hole or a gap seeking an object to satisfy it. Abjection results when the object does not adequately fill the rim. A gap re-emerges as a hole that imperils the subject's identity, for it threatens to draw the subject, rather than the object, to it. Even at times of its strongest cohesion, the abyss beckons and haunts it. It entices and attracts because it insists on the subject's necessary relationship to death, to the refusal of its corporeality.

Abjection is above all ambiguity (Kristeva, 1982, pp. 9–10). Kristeva distinguishes between three broad categories of abjection: food, waste, and sexual difference (roughly, oral, anal, and genital). Abjection is the by-product of the social and psychical investment in and privileging of certain bodily zones at the expense of others. The abject is undecided whether it is in or out.

It disturbs identity, system, and order demanded by the symbolic laws of the father. It testifies to the precarious grasp of the subject of his/her own identity, an assertion that the subject may slide back into impure chaos. Oral disgust is the most archaic form of abjection.

Kristeva uses the example of the skin of milk. It can make the subject retch and choke because it represents the subject's own skin and he/she chokes on his own corporeal limits. However, the expulsion of food and the refusal to accept it can be interpreted as the refusal of mother's love that is bound up with the need for more oral independence and a refusal to accept parental authoritarian demands. Kristeva does not address this aspect, which I think plays an important role in the aetiology of eating disorders for both sexes (cf. client case 2, chapter 6).

Kristeva's second category of *abjection* is corporeal waste. She interprets it slightly differently from Douglas. All bodily fluids, waste products, and refuse, draw the distinction between inside and outside. Inside the body is the body's ability to regenerate itself; outside it is unclean and filthy. But the subject is implicated in its waste; it cannot be completely expelled. For Kristeva, the corpse is the most horrifying example of waste. It is always surrounded by taboos and rituals to prevent contamination. It exists at the very borders of life. It is no longer I who expels, but I who am expelled. The border becomes its *abject*. It is something rejected from which one does not part and from which one cannot protect oneself. It poses a danger to the ego as it questions its stability and control over itself.

Kristeva's third category is the revulsion of sexual difference, represented in the cultural forms of incest taboo and the horror of menstrual blood. She differentiates excrement and its equivalence that represents the danger to identity that comes from without; menstrual blood stands for the danger issuing from within identity and does not simply differentiate men and women, but men and mothers. Horror of menstrual blood is a refusal to acknowledge the subject's corporeal link to the mother. According to Kristeva, it derives from the pre-Oedipal stage preceding binary opposition and distinct categories. The *abject* is placed on the side of the feminine and it is opposed to the paternal, rule-governed symbolic order of the father. Naming *abject* establishes a distance or space that may keep the dangers of chaos at bay.

The *abject* defines the pre-Oedipal space and self-conception. Like *abjection,* pregnancy is a borderline phenomenon, blurring yet producing one identity and another. Like the *abject*, maternity is the splitting, fusing, and merging of a series of bodily processes beyond the will or control of the subject. In pregnancy, a woman is positioned as space, receptacle, and matter; in lactation and nurturing functions, she takes on the position of part object, a complimentary screen onto which the child's demands are projected and from which images are introjected. 'She' does not exist as such. Kristeva's resistance to the idea of an identity for women is politically problematic as she argues that women have no special link to the maternal body, a view which many feminists, as mothers, would dispute. She insists that only certain men who are prepared to risk summoning up the archaic traces of their repressed semiotic and maternal prehistory are able to evoke, to name, or reinscribe this maternal space-time through religious or poetic discourse where the symbolic is able to tolerate the expression of normally unspoken pre-Oedipal pleasures. Kristeva accepts the validity of the Oedipus complex. She is unhappy with it, but still accepts its patrilineal authority, which I question in chapters 5 and 6.

Kristeva (1982, pp. 113–132) interestingly argues that Christianity developed a new concept on inside-outside distinct from Judaism. Through the abolishment of dietary rules, partaking of food with pagans, and contact with lepers, prostitutes, and mothers, a new arrangement with differences was set up. *Abjection* is no longer exterior. The threat from pollution comes from within (Matthew, *NT* 23. 26.). There is nothing from outside that upon entering the body can defile, but whatever comes out of the body, these are the items that defile him/her. Kristeva points out that the nutritive opening up to the gratifying relationship to the mother, pagan and archaic (matrilineal) re-establishes the oral relationship to the mother as introject. Through the process of interiority, defilement blends with guilt and a new category is re-established, that of *sin*. Christianity is a blend of paganism and monotheism but biblical logic remains intact. Despite all the initial nourishing references, it only keeps the idea of a sinning flesh.

Kristeva cites text after text in the *NT* in which Christian doctrine states that nothing that enters into a man defiles him only that which comes out; tears and sperm are exceptions of the bodily exudates that are not subject to defilement. Sin like excrement is within the body as a permanent condition. The power of horror lies not having let it enter one's body because one is born with it, but in letting it show. To symbolically eat and drink Christ's flesh and blood at mass transgresses the Levitical prohibitions but simultaneously restores innocence through the action. Kristeva points out that the 'brimming flesh of sin' belongs to both sexes but its roots are buried in feminine temptation. Kristeva, however, overemphasises sin as overindulgence of the body flesh (sex, food) and bypasses the importance of hubris, disobedience, and dissent.

Kristeva criticises Douglas for stopping literally at the frontier of the body (MacCannell, 2003, pp. 84–85) as the base for allegorical interpretation of social institutions. She insists that beyond the body are the psychic drives that must be recognised for a complete description of the self-society relationship. Kristeva goes beyond the body into the forces that made it important. She sees the set of drives as universal and not subject to cultural modification. This option frees her from sociology, but limits her explorations into taboo via cultural complexes. She also accepts the pre-Oedipal and Oedipal developmental processes as innate, creationist, monotheistic structures without reimagining the maternal during earlier matrilineal Neolithic times. I discuss the validity of the creationist Freudian concept of incest taboo in chapter 5.

Brickman (2003, pp. 116–117) points out that Kristeva identifies the *abject* ascribed to women culturally through their association with maternity. The biological separation of the child from the mother is the template for the constitution of the subject out of the undifferentiated abject. Freudian theory stresses that subjectivity evolves through separation, differentiation, repudiation, and repression of the maternal surround which, as Brickman reminds us, becomes identified with actual gendered and raced others. Development is conceived in terms of separation with mother/nature/primitivity through the mediation of father/civilising/law.

Stern's empirical studies (1984, pp. 5–12), however, show that infants are never in a state of actual undifferentiated symbiosis with the mother, but from birth onward show an interactive interest in externality. A sense of an emergent self develops as early as two months; from two to six months, a sense of a core self develops; from seven to fifteen months, a sense of intersubjective self is activated; and between eighteen and thirty months, the verbal sense of self takes place (ibid, p. 273). Subjectivity can no longer be configured exclusively as a progressive separation, but more within the context of connecting with and recognising significant others. Winnicott (1971) suggests that it is within the context of maternal dependence, in that mirror stage of intense loving engagement as a *transitional space,* in that joyful *gleam* of the parent's eye that reflects back to the child, rather than in Lacan's image of a self-unity in a double-glass mirror imagery, that holds the capacity for representation, independent subjectivity, and *mutual recognition* to develop. Failure of mutual recognition in an interactive, in-between space turns the parent/child dyad into one of domination and submission, replicated culturally in a totalist mindset that disallows a cooperative transitional space where subjectivity and free will can develop, which I discuss in chapter 6.

Conclusion

I have expressed the broad outlines of the work of Douglas (1966; 1968) and Kristeva (1982) on the subject of taboo. Douglas' work stresses experiential explorations into external and internal lines pointing to developing deeper hypotheses about cultural complexes. Kristeva, on the other hand, places emphasise on the subjectivity of taboo for women's bodies. Their different approaches may well reflect their differing intellectual and cultural aetiologies: Douglas as a British academic with democratic, historically nontotalitarian, maritime roots has a more open, experiential approach to taboo and borders as transitional spaces; Kristeva, born in Bulgaria in 1941, lived through the horrors of World War II and under totalist (see Stein, 2017 on totalist thinking, chapter 6) alternating fascist-communist regimes as a child. In 1966, Kristeva crossed her cultural borders into France and endured the loss of her homeland. The loss of cultural roots and the mother (as home) as well as her adherence to the closed Freudian patrilineal creationism of the

Oedipus complex both deeply elaborates on the status of women in transit but, also, to my mind, restricts her thinking about taboo and borders and how *abject* waste could be recycled into value across borders.

I speculate that the totalist thinking that necessarily dominates Kristeva's mindset in her formative years precludes her imagining the mother's body from a different perspective as an active, positive, independent, and encouraging agent in the liminal process between developmental stages of separation, liminality, and maturation. For Kristeva, women's bodies seem forever *abject* stuck between borders, which has influenced her positioning of the maternal as both promising *and* threatening in a *closed,* abject, liminal cocoon of dread.

Note

1. I discuss this aspect more fully in the next chapter, chapter 4, concerning Nazi Germany's miscegenation taboo.

References

Bauman, Z. (1973). *Culture as Praxis.* London and New York: Routledge and Kegan Paul.

Bible (1989 edn.) *The Revised English Bible.* Oxford and Cambridge: Oxford University Press.

Brodersen, E. (2016). *Laws of Inheritance. A Post-Jungian Study of Twins and Relationship Between the First and Other(s).* London and New York: Routledge.

Brickman, C. (2003). *Aboriginal Populations in the Mind; Race and Primitivity in Psychoanalysis.* New York: Columbia University Press.

Douglas, M. (1966). *Purity and Danger,* (new preface, 2002) Abingduon, Oxon, and New York: Routledge, 2002.

Douglas, M. (1968). Pollution. In *Implicit Meanings; Selected Essays in Anthropology,* 2nd edn. London and New York: Routledge, pp. 106–115.

Dürr, E. and Winder, G.M. (2016). Garbage at Work: Ethics, Subjectivation and Resistance in Mexico. In (2016) Duschinsky, R., Schnall, S., and Weiss, D.H. (eds.) *Purity and Danger Now. New Perspectives.* London and New York: Routledge, pp. 52–68.

Duschinsky, R., Schnall, S., and Weiss, D.H. (eds.) (2016). *Purity and Danger Now. New Perspectives.* London and New York: Routledge.

Eliade, M. (1958). *Rites and Symbols of Initiation. The Mysteries of Birth and Rebirth.* Woodstock, CT: Spring Publications.

Fletcher, J. and Benjamin, A. (eds.) (2012). *Abjection, Melancholia and Love. The Work of Julia Kristeva.* Abington and New York: Routledge.

Gidla, S. (2017). *Ants Among Elephants: An Untouchable Family and the Making of Modern India.* New York: Farrar, Straus and Giroux.

Girard, R. (1977). *Violence and the Sacred.* London and New York: Continuum Press.

Gross, E. (1990). The Body of Signification. In (2012) Fletcher, J. and Benjamin, A. (eds.) *Abjection, Melancholia and Love. The Work of Julia Kristeva.* Abington and New York: Routledge, pp. 80–103.

Hughes, R. (1986). *The Fatal Shore: The Epic of Australia's Founding.* New York: Alfred A. Knopf.

Kristeva, J. (1982). *Powers of Horror: An Essay in Abjection*. Trans. Rondiez, L.S. New York: Columbia University Press.

Lacan, J. (1977). *Ecrits: A Selection*. London and New York: Routledge.

Leach, E.R. (1964). Anthropological Aspects of Language: Animal Categories and Verbal Abuse. In (1979) Lessa, W.A. and Vogt, E.Z. (eds.) *Reader in Comparative Religion. An Anthropological Approach*, 4th edn. New York: Harper Collins, pp. 153–166.

Lechte, J. and Zournazi, M. (eds.) (2003). *The Kristeva Critical Reader*, Edinburgh: Edinburgh University Press.

MacCannell, J.F. (2003). Kristeva's Horror. In (2003) Lechte, J. and Zournazi, M. (eds.) *The Kristeva Critical Reader*. Edinburgh: Edinburgh University Press, pp. 69–97.

Radcliffe-Brown, A.R. (1952). Taboo. In *Structure and Function in Primitive Society. Essays and Addresses*. Glencoe, Ill: The Free Press. pp. 133–152.

Robertson Smith, W. (1889). *The Religion of the Semites*. Edinburgh: A & C Black.

Sartre, J.P. (1943). *L'Etre et le Neant*, 3rd edn. Paris: Gallimard.

Smith, A-M. (1998). *Julia Kristeva, Speaking the Unspeakable*. London: Pluto Press.

Stein, A. (2017). *Terror, Love & Brainwashing. Attachment in Cults and Totalitarian Systems*. London and New York: Routledge.

Stein, S. (1956). The Dietary Laws in Rabbinic and Patristic Literature. *Studia Patristica* 64, 141 ff.

Stern, D.N. (1984). *The Interpersonal World of the Infant; A view from Psychoanalysis and Developmental Psychology*. London: Karnac Books, 1998.

Thompson, M. (1979). *Rubbish Theory: The Creation and Destruction of Value*. Oxford: Oxford University Press.

Williams, R. There's Power in the Dirt. Impurity, Utopianism and Radical Politics. In (2016) Duschinsky, R., Schnall, S., and Weiss, D.H. (eds.) *Purity and Danger Now. New Perspectives*. London and New York: Routledge, pp. 69–83.

Wilson, M. (1957). *Rituals and Kinship Among the Nyakyusa*. Oxford: Oxford University Press.

Winnicott, D. W. (1971). *Playing and Reality*. London: Routledge, 1989.

Chapter 4

Totem and taboo, animal categories, and kinship structures

Introduction

This chapter on the study and origin of taboo is comprised of three aspects: *First,* I examine the connection of *totem* to taboo and to the origins of religion using the works of Tylor (1873) on animism; Morgan (1877), Fraser (1910), Freud (1912–13), Durkheim (1915), Radcliffe-Brown (1952), Lewis-Williams (2002; 2005), and Clottes (2009), amongst others. Animals such as bears, lions, snakes, and beavers, have such strong natural strength that they serve as clan totems. It is forbidden, or taboo, to kill or eat a totemic animal except during special sacrificial rites where the totem is indigested by the clan to enhance their potency. It is also taboo to marry or kill a person from the same totem clan, so exogamy arguably developed from totemism. Totemism dominates two worlds: the symbolic and the material. Durkheim (1915) suggests that the *totem is an elementary religion* and was the first form of demarking and separating people within kin clans. I include Freud's limited and closed perspective of totem and taboo and expand on the work of Levi-Strauss' concept of totemism (1962) as containing an internal, logical, intellectual component that challenges Radcliffe-Brown's (1952) view that the totemic relationship is essentially a sensory phenomenon.

Second, I examine the relationship between *taboo, human propagation,* and *animal categories.* Leach (1964, pp. 23–63) extends Douglas' (1966) categories of creatures (edible/inedible) from chapter 3 to incest taboo and propagation categories. He sees the same set of equivalence in the relationship between edible/nonedible animals and permissible/nonpermissible sexual partners. Taboo serves to separate the self from the world: the world is divided into zones or margins of relative social distance corresponding to 1) very close (taboo); 2) close but further afield (partially permissible); 3) afield (permissible); and 4) too remote (taboo). A fifth category contains animals and persons classified as tabooed filth. This category has important ramifications for the development of dehumanisation through taboo.

Third, I explore the *miscegenation taboo between races.* What characteristics do I share with a sex, clan, or group that make me part of that group and give a feeling of belonging, containment, and structure? Colour of skin and hair is a visible manifestation of demarcation between groups whereby people of black or darker shade of skin colour have been labelled as inferior and less racially pure. In both cases, Leach's fourth category falls under taboo. Such a taboo may apply to people of different world cultures, races, and different skin colour. Dark colours emanating from the margin (skin) that cannot be purified through ritual washing is particularly tabooed and dangerous, linked to fear of unknown 'shadow' aspects crossing over the margin between the known and unknown. I examine racial and gender differences (supposedly smaller brains, less intelligence etc.) used to marginalise races and women considered 'inferior.' Contrary to animals being valued as *sacred* ancestors in indigenous cultures, they are grossly devalued during recent history to protect the supposed purity of any given race or white, male supremacy (Pichot, 2001; Brickman, 2003; Bergner, 2005).

Totem and Taboo

The development of totemism can be interpreted as the first expression of demarcation between peoples as a way of differentiating between 'us' and 'them,' and takes a fundamental form that predates animism and naturalism in its sacred character. Taking examples from the Australian aborigines, Durkheim (1915, pp. 27–33) argues that totemism is an elementary religion and forms the basis of the clan system. Each clan has its exclusive totem. In a large variety of cases, totems belong to the animal or vegetable kingdom, particularly the former. The totem is not just an animal or vegetable; it is also an emblem, a symbol, crest, or sign and serves as part of their religious liturgy. Durkheim suggests that totem clans are not founded on the basis of blood ties, but see themselves as forming a symbolic family based on their shared totem. Out of the 500 totemic names collected among the tribes of southeastern Australia, most are names of plants and animals. While the totem is a collective emblem it also has a sacred character. The tribes of Central Australia make constant use of certain sacred instruments in their rites called *churinga,* which are pieces of polished stones engraved with a design representing the totem of the group. The stones are sometimes attached to a thread made from human or opossum hair and whirled about quickly as bullroarers to produce a humming sound that would accompany any ritual of importance. It is the totemic mark that gives the *churinga* their sacred character.

The aborigine believes that s/he, while a person in the real world, is also an animal or plant of the totemic species. In fact, s/he bears its name, which is a mark of his/her identity with nature. A member of the kangaroo clan calls him/herself a kangaroo; s/he is, therefore, in one sense an animal of this species. The animal represents an impersonal force that no one possesses entirely; it is completely independent of the particular subject in whom it incarnates itself. The animal precedes the individual, is superior in power, and survives him/her. Individuals die, generations pass, but this force remains active, living, animated, and constant. It can be compared to aspects of Jung's theory of archetypes, which I define in Introduction, chapter 1.[1]

Hedman (2018, pp. 16–33) argues that the *Haida* totems or their cedar poles display human form devoid of sexual characteristics as an archetypal image of the primordial person as androgynous or hermaphrodite. *Haida,* the first Peoples of British Columbia, developed an art form over 3,000 years ago, which Hedman argues are rich in archetypal images. Hedman wishes to avoid any reductionism of *Haida* art as warned by Deloria (et al 2009) and Bernstein (2008, viii–xvii), namely, that Native American art is not an extension of Western imagination, but exists within its own cultural sphere. Hedman extends his argument to show that two totem moieties, the eagle and the raven of the *Haida* clans, reflect the celestial and chthonic realms of the collective unconscious. As interstitial people, the *Haida* knew they lived in the border*land* between two cosmic zones, the celestial/sky forest and the chthonic/underground sea. The person of the raven clan is not necessarily more emotional or instinctual, and the eagle clan is not necessarily more intellectual, but together, they symbolise a mediatory balance between two poles: the heavenly *above* and the underworld *below* (cf. von Franz, 2000, p. 145). *Haida* folktales and totem images emphasise the close creative bond between people and animals in that taboo, liminal, intermediary, border*land* realm where they are interchangeable as ancestors, a point I emphasise throughout this chapter.

The animal mythic ancestor

As Tylor argues (1903, p. 16), the doctrine of metempsychosis not only considers that animals have souls, but that these souls transmigrate and inhabit human beings and that the creatures may be, in fact, their own ancestors. Indigenous people believe that they contain within them a principle comparative to the one residing in the totem as present and active within them that transports them into the world of sacred things. It is, therefore, forbidden or tabooed to kill or eat a totemic animal because the totem is placed on a higher rank than a person. Between the person and the totemic animal exists a close relationship, but the animal is considered superior and treated as an elder brother. Even if the totemic principle has a preferred seat within a determined species or animal, it cannot remain localised as its sacred character is highly contagious; little by little, subtotems are attached to form a cosmological system in the collective consciousness, which is given moral value. Therefore totems dominate two worlds: they reside in men but are simultaneously the vital principle of all entities. They animate and discipline the mind, but at the same time, make plants grow and reproduce. This double nature has enabled the sacred to be seen as the womb from which germinate all the seeds of civilisation. One can compare the cosmology of totems to astrology and its symbols, particularly the Chinese animal symbols in their horoscopes. Animals such as bears, lions, snakes, and beavers, have such strong natural strength that they serve as clan totems. Within the totem, clan members experience heightened life-affirming values in keeping with the totemic *natural* characteristics, such as bears or trees, as their mythic ancestors (Lacourt, 2010, 2016).

It is significant that hunter-gatherer *Homo sapiens* c. 40,000 years ago painted animal forms on subterranean cave walls, which, according to Mithen (1999, pp. 159–162; 2009), derives from the development of *cognitive fluidity*, that is, the ability to recombine knowledge through 'mapping across cognitive domains,' which include social, technical, and natural history. Cognitive fluidity expresses itself as the 'emergence of representational re-description' to solve complex, life-threatening problems in uncertain environments and find new creative solutions. Hunter-gatherers put bones in drawing of animals on cave walls as if to contact the animal (*spirit world*) behind the wall that acted as a porous membrane to the other side (Lewis-Williams 2002; Clottes, 2009). According to Eliade (1958, p. 92) 'bone symbolises the final root of animal life, the mould from which the flesh continually arises. It is from the bone that men and animals are reborn.' It seems that premodern peoples have no problem regarding animals as their evolutionary ancestors. Similarly, Levy-Bruhl (1935, p. 24) movingly describes a number of rock paintings in Northwest Australia made by native Australians. They are figures with faces but no mouths and are carefully retouched on the rock wall called *Wondjina* to recreate the power of rain. The *Wondjina's* head in such paintings is retouched or occasionally painted anew to ensure regeneration and renewal through *Wondjina's* connection to *Ungud*, the ancient, mythic, creative time. Experiential continuity with mythic ontology is essential for ensuring present prosperity.

Totemic clan structure

Fraser (1910) elucidates the totemic clan structures from Native America using a wide variety of data drawn mainly from Morgan's (1877) ground-breaking exploratory work on totems and exogamy. However, unlike Freud (1912-3, pp. 53–70) who over-stresses the horror of incest in the formation of totems that facilitate exogamy by separating family members, neither Morgan nor Fraser attribute incest taboo as a main factor within the organisation of totems.

As Kroeber (1920, pp. 20–24) attests, its organisation is much more complex and multifaceted than that, as I will discuss in this chapter and in chapter 5 on the Oedipus complex.

Fraser (1910, pp. 2–3) remarks that totemism tends to flourish among clans such as the Pueblo and the Iroquois and marks a degree of social and intellectual progress. The large communal houses of the Iroquois are constructed of bark boards fastened on a framework of wooden boards. A single house is generally from 50 to 130 feet long and about 16 feet wide. It would contain 10 fires and 20 families. Over one of the two doors positioned at either end is carved the totemic device or crest of the head of the family. Only members of the same totem live together in a communal house. Each of the six tribes that compose the Iroquois confederacy is subdivided into a number of totemic and exogamous clans. Every tribe has the three clans of the Wolf, the Turtle (Tortoise) and the Bear, but whereas the *Mohawks* and the *Oneidas* have only these three, other Iroquois tribes add other totems such as the Beaver, the Eel, and Snipe. The *Tuscaroras,* for example, subdivide the Wolf and the Turtle under Gray Wolf, Yellow Wolf, Great Turtle, Little Turtle, etc. Iroquois clans are exogamous: members must marry into a clan different from their own, but they may marry a woman of any clan in the other group. Through this custom, the purity of the blood through the totem is preserved, while the tie of relationship between the clan members is strengthened or enlarged. Morgan (1877, pp. 38–41) states that there are eight clans arranged into two divisions and named as follows: first are Wolf, Bear, Beaver, and Turtle; and second are Deer, Snipe, Heron, Hawk.

Originally, the four clans of the first division being brothers are not allowed to marry amongst themselves but are free to marry with any of the second four being that of cousins. Whoever violates these laws of marriage incurs the deepest taboo disgrace. The children always belong to the clan of their mother. These laws are now more relaxed as they may marry into any totem clan but their own. It is unclear whether descent always runs through the female line as some clans are divided equally among patrilineal and matrilineal gens.

In South America, long houses called *malocas* replicate the cosmos (Lewis-Williams and Pearce, 2005, pp. 88–93). In the beginning, there was only one universe, which was a house occupied by the *Yeba,* the original ancestor of the *Barasana* who was himself a jaguar. His sons were the ancestral anacondas, and in due course, each of the sons became a father in his own house. These were the *He* people. In present day kinship groups, each *maloca* reproduces the mythic structure. History and myth are telescoped and thus indistinguishable. As the *Yeba* myth suggests, jaguars are avatars and conceived as mediators between the three cosmic divisions of the world, between life and death, between the human world and spirit world of the ancestors, and between nature and culture. The walls of the *malocas* often have three dimensional mural images, which have been re-plastered many times. Renewal of images itself is a meaningful act, not just an aesthetic refurbishing. The act of making and remaking is as important as the finished image (ibid, p. 111). They parallel the same intention as the Upper Palaeolithic practice I discussed previously of placing bones and small objects in the walls of the caves. Walls were not just as spaces, but states of being, as the permeable interfaces between people in the building and the active, energetic spirit world that lay behind the walls. The walls act as membranes between normal, temporal clan existence and the infinite cosmos where spirits and spirit animals can emerge in all their energy when needed.

Totem guardian spirits

The clan totems are, to a certain extent, considered as guardian spirits of the clans and their ancestors. Each clan has a legend to explain the origin of their crests. It is said (Fraser, 1910, pp. 324–326) that the ancestor of the clan came down from heaven as a bird or the sun, or came up from the underworld or out of the sea, wearing the dress, skin, or mask of an animal or supernatural being that s/he later removed to become the human progenitor of the clan, henceforth adopting the animal or object as their crest. For example, the *Neentsa* clan relate how two eagles and their eaglet descended from heaven at Cape Scott where they took off their eagle skins and became humans. Similarly, the *Gigilqam* clan has the tradition where they descended from a mythical thunder bird, and the beak of the bird is carved and fastened as a crest to the front of their house. The descent of the clan from its crest animal resembles the descent of the clan from its totem animal. The *Sisintle* clan have the crest of the sun and explain how the sun in the form of a bird took the likeness of a wo/man. The *Gexsem* clan relate how they inherited their totem, which represents the Spirit of the Sea (ibid, pp. 325–6). These clans use masks to represent and replicate their totem ancestors who give them ancestral roots and a vital connectedness.

For example, the Wolf clan of the *Lillooet* wear masks made like the head and face of a wolf and their dancers are clad in wolf skins. The Owl clan wear a mask representing that bird and use owl feathers attached to their clothes and headdresses. The Bear clan of the *Hailolaux* use a mask that resembles the grizzly bear and wear bear skins—grizzly, brown, and cinnamon—at ceremonial dances. The *Osages* of the *Dacotan* tribes (Fraser, 1910, p. 129) believe that they are descended from the snail and the beaver. Killing the beaver for its skin would be tantamount to killing the brother of the *Osage* and destroying their shared, kinship vitality.

Multifaceted functions of totemism

The origin and function of totemism and exogamy seem to emphasise that it fostered social cooperation within clans and helped develop interconnectedness between clans that embody the same totem. Fraser (1910) suggests that totemism does much to develop cordial cooperation based on mutual trust and good will and on their readiness to subordinate their personal interests to that of the community. The tendency of totemism to knit humans together from different clans in social groups is evidenced by the fact that two people of the same totem in two different clans are closer than two brothers or sisters who have different totems. The enigmatic character of the totem is lodged in the fact that it appears to be an incongruous assortment of unrelated and conflicting phenomena: first, the totem is usually described as a species of animal, less often as a plant, sometimes as a natural object such as a stone; second, the totem is defined as the joint ancestor of humans and animals; and third, the totem is always taboo. Not only is everything connected with the totem taboo, the term totem, itself, means taboo (Reed, 1975, p. 58.) The essence of the totemic taboo is that it eradicates the possibility that a kinsman would hunt, kill, or eat another kinsmen or kin animal. The lives of kin are taboo and sacred because they stem from the same ancestral, mythic creative source as the totem.

Totem taboos also encourage abstinence and discipline that allow species, animals, and humans to be protected, preserved, and to mature in order to multiply their resources. Webster (1942, pp. 322–324) underlines the economic aspects of taboo by stressing that their practical effect is to preserve the supply of a particular kind of food by diminishing the number of clansmen in search of it. If one assumes that each hunter has a different totem, then each man will allow a certain object to go free. Webster argues that food is the first form of property, so the first human laws impose food restrictions through taboo and are maintained by tribal authority. Food taboos secure an abundant supply of food for the elders when young people are inculcated through their rites of passage to ensure strict obedience and an implicit belief in the terrible consequences of any infraction of elder regulations. Reed (1975, pp. 21–42) likewise suggests that taboos began with the necessity to create cooperative social organisations that required a suppression of sexual competition and violence in the sex hunt and in the hunt for food. Reed argues that exogamy ensured enough food for clan members through periods of lean resources without the need to resort to cannibalism.

Twentieth century structural anthropologist, Levi-Strauss (1962), however, analyses totemism from a different perspective. He discerns a tripartite division among totems of the *Ojibwa* (ibid, p. 22): *water* (water spirit, cat-fish, pike etc., which would include all the fish clans); *air* (eagle, sparrow-hawk, goose, and all bird clans); *earth* (consisting of caribou, moose, beaver, racoon, including carnivores, herbivores, and omnivores). Referencing and critically reassessing the work of Radcliffe-Brown (1952), Levi-Strauss (ibid, p. 85) asks why a bear, wolf, and lynx as specific animals as totem are selected rather than another? Plants are not of such interest because of their immobility and thus lack of a perceived vitality. Levi-Strauss suggests that an animal, such as the python, is more than just a simple object of taboo; it is because the ancestors, their human descendants, and the resident animals are all united by a *territorial* link. For example, the African indigenous *Tallensi* society can be compared to a fabric that corresponds to localities and to lineages. As a member of a large clan, a person is related to common and distant ancestors symbolised by sacred animals, as a member of a lineage to closer ancestors symbolised by totems, and lastly, as an individual s/he is connected with particular ancestors who reveal his/her personal fate and may appear as an intermediary, such as a domestic animal or wild game (Fortes, 1945, pp. 141–142). The predominant place assigned to carnivorous animals called 'teeth bearers,' which exist to protect them by attacking other animals or even people, symbolise the vitality and the attacking warrior force of the *Tallensi* clan itself. Such a question brings about a *reintegration of content within form*.

Firth (1930–31) in his study of Polynesian totemism stresses that the totem animal, on land or at sea, is often endowed with striking characteristics in terms of locomotion, versatility of movement, colour, shape and ferocity, or peculiar cries that represent supernatural strength and vitality of the ancestor spirit. Levi-Strauss, however, stresses that such interpretations are incomplete because it is *'not resemblances but the differences, which resembles each other'* (1962, p. 77). The resemblances and difference between the animal species, for example, the kangaroo and the wombat, are translated through myth into terms of friendship and conflict, solidarity, and opposition. The animal world is represented in terms of social relations similar to our own. To accomplish this, the natural species are classed as *pairs of opposites* that have at least one characteristic that permits them to be compared. This structural principle consists of the union of the opposites. Levi-Strauss uses the example of differences and similarities between kangaroos and wombats, both marsupial but of differing size (ibid, p. 89). Birds as totems are adopted because they give a wide of spectrum of behaviour similar to that of humans. When one compares the night owl and the nightjar, both eat meat and live in trees, but there is an opposition within the pair underlying the similarity: while both birds are carnivorous, one is a hunter, the other is a thief. Birds are chosen because they form an *intellectual vehicle* that advances both thought and meaning (ibid, p. 104).[2]

Building on the work of Radcliffe-Brown, Levi-Strauss argues that *associationism*[3] has the merit of sketching the contour of elementary logic as a direct expression of the symbolic structure of the human mind and not an inert product of the environment on an amorphous consciousness. Totemism has served scholars who try to separate indigenous cultures from modern ones and place totemism within sacred beliefs rather than within the social sciences. This placement has over emphasised indigenous mental attitudes as incompatible with the exigency of a discontinuity between man and nature, which monotheisms hold to be essential. It purports a second nature of primitive thinking as an archaic stage of human development.

Totemism can thus be considered as *formulating* a specific problem: how to make opposition instead of an obstacle to integration, serve to produce it.

Within such a perspective, animals in totemism cease to be creatures that are feared, admired, or envied because their perceivable reality permits the embodiment of ideas and relations conceived by *speculative thought* on the basis of empirical observations. Natural species are not chosen because they are 'good to eat,' but because they are 'good to think.' Levi-Strauss suggests that totemism is not a sacred but a social structural expression that responds to *problem solving* in an intellectual way. There is nothing archaic, remote, or mystical about the process. Through all these differing interpretations of totemism, one appreciates the complex thinking it has generated in anthropology of all tropes since Morgan's ground-breaking work in 1877. What is central to totemism is the close positive kin relationship between humans and animals. Animals also contribute a wider range of vital emotional elements into cognition than human form alone. Lewis-Williams, and Pearce (2005, p. 152) point out that a too-hard line adoption of structuralism can present too rigid a framework for oppositional thinking. This type of logical exposition can reduce the role that *emotions* play as creative generators of thought.

Taboo, totem, human propagation, and animal categories

As I mention in chapter 3, Leach (1964) postulates the physical environment of a young child is perceived as a continuum. The child is taught to impose upon the environment a discriminating grid to distinguish between *me* and *it, us* and *them*. We are only able to separate things by suppressing our recognition of non-things that fill the interstices, then, what is repressed becomes especially interesting but also anxiety making. Whatever is taboo is simultaneously sacred, valuable, powerful, dangerous, untouchable, filthy, and unspeakable.

Leach (1964, pp. 153–166) extends Douglas' categories of creatures (edible/inedible) in chapter 3 to taboo and propagation categories to stress again the close connection and overlap between animals and humans as we see in totemism. He sees the same set of taboo equivalence in the relationship between edible/non-edible animals and permissible/nonpermissible sexual partners. Leach suggests that taboo serves to separate the self from the world, and then the world is categorised into zones or margins of relative social distance corresponding to 1) very close (taboo); 2) close but further afield (partially permissible); 3) afield (permissible); and 4) too remote (taboo). Leach (1964, p. 160) extends categories of creatures (edible/inedible) to human sex taboo and propagation categories. He observes the same set of equivalence in the relationship between ambiguity and taboo. For example, sexual intercourse with family members living close together in the same home is under taboo as is eating pets, such as dogs and cats that live in the home. Sex with near relations, such as first cousins, is partially permissible as is eating farm animals that are castrated or not yet reached puberty. Fully permissible sexual intercourse is allowed between peoples in the village and in the same country, who are not related, just as mature untamed field animals and wild game are fully edible. Some animals may only be hunted or shot during certain times of the year. Taboo reappears between peoples who live too far apart and are too foreign in terms of geography, perhaps different races and cultures. Remote wild animals are correspondingly in this fourth category as inedible, such as tiger and elephant meat for Europeans.

Correspondence between sexual accessibility and categories of edibility is more than accidental as shown by linguistic coincidences (Leach, 1964, pp. 161–163). The archaic expression for game was beasts of venery; the term venery itself has various meanings from hunting to venereal disease. The close linguistic link between domestic animals and human sexual bodily parts is noted, for example, cock for penis, pussy for female pubic hair, ass for arse. Leach importantly offers a pertinent fifth category of animal taboo, that of vermin, particularly vulnerable to pollution, which links into Douglas' classification of animals in chapter 3 according to their classification of order/disorder. Leach includes in this category mammals and birds injurious to game and crops such as foxes, weasels, rats, mice, owls, fleas, bugs, lice, parasitic worms, or 'undesirable' persons described as pests that cause the plague. For example, the Jews in the Third Reich racist propaganda were linked to images of rats that carry the lice that cause disease. Vermin and pests are intrinsically inedible and must be eradicated because of the harmful and destructive effect they exercise on nature.

Leach proposes that we move away from polarised notions of pollution and taboo. It is not sufficient to have a discrimination of me/it, we/they; we also need a graduated comparative continuum of close/far, more-like-me, less-like-me. Leach links the origin of taboo to sex and food as the same rules applying to near and far in order to establish boundaries and marginality. Bauman (1973, p. 124), however, finds Leach's work on continuum problematic: Bauman does not see the term taboo applying to the existence of *non-things* because they are unproblematic, excluded from sight anyway, and do not cause disruption. So why would taboo prohibition be an appropriate method for dealing with their nonthreatening existence?

I suggest that this inconsistency is resolved through analysing taboo as a form of establishing a core *group identity* by eliminating all 'non-things,' which I discuss in the rest of this chapter.

Miscegenation taboo, outsiders, vermin, and dirt

Every culture, whether micro and macro, establishes boundaries between what is considered clean/dirty and pure/impure. This differentiation has implications in daily cleansing rituals, their frequency, and form, which classifies between higher and lower status. Social groups are categories of people that require their identity and meaning in contrast to other social or cultural groups (Speltini and Passini, 2016, pp. 165–169). Social groups develop their descriptive and evaluative properties in relation to out-groups, whereby cleanliness is normatively attached to innocence, and dirt laden with disgust, guilt, shame, and sinfulness. Taboo, in this case, is used as a concept to classify and identify certain kinds of transgressions considered contagious to society and used to ostracise marginal or ambiguous social positions.

What characteristics do I share with a sex, clan, or group that make me part of that group and give me a feeling of belonging, containment, and structure? Colour of skin and hair is a visible manifestation of demarcation between groups whereby people of black or darker shade of skin colour have been labelled as inferior and less racially pure. In both cases, Leach's fourth and fifth categories fall under taboo. Such a taboo may apply to people of different world cultures, races, and different skin colour. Dark colours emanating from the margin (skin) is particularly dangerous and tabooed, linked to fear of unknown 'shadow' aspects of dirt, chaos, and death, which emanate across the margins between same and different. Such blackness has travelled from the inside to the outside and can be classified as 'outsider dirt.'

An anthropological history of dehumanisation illustrates how differences become regarded as signs of a lack of full humanity (Johoda, 2014, pp. 13–31). Engaging in positive interactions with others engenders feelings of social connectedness and the sense of belonging. When people are made to feel that they do not belong, are different as an out-group, are not equal to others, or do not deserve to be treated with respect, such dehumanising interactions undermine the humanity of both parties. Such differences were not necessarily physical. During the Middle Ages, the dividing between us and them were usually religious: Christian versus Pagan and subsequently Christians versus Muslims. A black Christian was accepted as fully human while a white Pagan (for example, Scandinavian) was not. White Pagan Europeans, notably Slavs, were regarded as lesser humans who could be enslaved, hence the term slavery.

During the Renaissance, Spanish conquerors treated indigenous Americans as subhuman, as talking soulless parrots in human guise. The seventeenth century scientific revolution engendered orderly 'lawful' principles to human differences and these developed into scientific racism during the eighteenth and nineteenth centuries. Soemmering (1784) examined the cranial capacity and the supposed thickness of nerves that led him to conclude that Moors are closer to apes than to Europeans. The French naturalist, Cuvier (1800–1805) focussed on the protruding chin of a black person as a sign of animality. The attribute of animality to Africans was welcomed by American slave owners to justify their inhumane practices. Virey (1801) emphasised the sexual voracity of blacks, particularly black women. Vogt, a Swiss German naturalist, (1864) put forward the theory of the missing link between a black person and the ape, namely, the human 'idiot.' Much like Curvier, Vogt listed comparisons between ape and black physicality: the neck resembled the gorilla and the teeth the American monkey. Vogt confined his theories mainly to men while LeBon's (1881, Vol. 2. p. 157) misogynistic cultural theories emphasised that adult women were the most inferior form of human being, being closer to children, animals, and indigenous peoples than men.

The latter part of the nineteenth century saw large scale European colonisation, which led to an interest in indigenous psychology as a convenient rationalisation of colonial paternalism. Schultze, German professor of philosophy and pedagogy, stressed (1900) that indigenous peoples have a less well-developed brain and thus lesser capacity for thought. Their lack of logic means they remain at the associative level found in animals, children, and women: they remain childish, imitative, and nonreflective. As children, they need the proper protection and guidance from mature white adult males in their paternal and educative function. Von den Veldon (1906/1907, p. 112) suggested that black children develop normally, but then regressed at puberty because the primitive 'falls into a slough of sensuality' (Miller, 1928, p. 164). Günter (1927) a Nazi expert eulogising the Nordic ideal, was highly influential even after the World War II. Racial ideologies were not just academic theories, but ideas put into practice and reflected the discriminatory, inhumane laws causing untold human misery.

Bergner (2005, p. xiii) uses the work of Du Bois (1903) to describe the state of identity particular to African Americans living in a culture that does not see them as equal. He equates this form of identity as 'double consciousness, this sense of always looking at one's self through the eyes of others…this sense measuring one soul that looks on in amused contempt and pity.' Similarly, Fanon (1952, p. 83) emphasises that when he meets the white man's eyes, 'the man of colour encounters difficulties of his bodily schema. Consciousness of the body is a solely negating activity. It is a third person consciousness.' Fanon (ibid, p. 87) describes further the abject position of the colonised black person in the gaze of the white person: 'I move slowly in the world… I progress by crawling… And already being dissected under white eyes, the only real eyes. I am fixed. Having adjusted their microtomes, they objectively cut away slices of my reality. I am laid bare. …I see in those white faces that it is not a new man who has come in, but a new kind of man, a new genus. Why, it's a Negro.'

Fanon (1952, p. 85) states that blacks are treated as animals without human rights. He underscores the overemphasis of black sexuality and athleticism as projected as a performative threat to white people of both sexes. To prevent interbreeding, unlike the Jews who were initially sterilised, blacks were castrated like farm animals, underlining that the black person is a phobogenic, tabooed object used as stimulus for anxiety of pathological proportions.

Africa was classified as the Dark Continent as early as the middle of the sixteenth century. The fateful meeting of both Africans and apes by white Europeans in the sixteenth century set in motion the conviction in the similarity if not identity of Africans and apes in the European mind, unintentionally supported later in the nineteenth century by Darwin's *Origin of the Species* (1859). This conviction was bolstered by reports of Africans and orangutans mating, giving the notion of the animal-like and excessive libidinous nature of Africans that simultaneously reinforced the sense of propriety of slavery: Africans were slave-apes and God had given European man dominion over the animals (Brickman, 2003, p. 27). Gobineau (1816–1882) propounded the racial theory (1853–55) that each race receives from nature the particular biological gifts that characterise them. The 'white' race and, in particular, the Aryan race is superior in the hierarchy as the highest civilisation. The 'black' race is assumed to be the one least capable of civilisation. The 'yellow' race stands between the two. Such a hierarchy of races appealed to the fixist concept of biology and society. Haeckel (1834–1919) thought that there are greater mental differences between the higher human races and the lower ones than between the latter and anthropoid apes (Haeckel, 1876). Büchner (1824–1899) suggested a closer anatomy of the black person and the ape than that of the European white person. In his view, the black person serves as a transition between man and animal (Büchner, 1870, pp. 257–258). Vogt (1879) speculated that black were congenitally physically and mentally handicapped and halted at a developmental stage that white people have left behind. The origin of the miscegenation taboo is not simply an aversion of a 'superior' race mixing with an 'inferior' because interbreeding alters both races. As anomalies, biracial people have no proper place.

For cultural theorists, Gobineau, Haeckel, and Lapouge, the highest human species was the *Mediterrese,* divided into first, the preferred dolichocephalic (long-headed) blond, blued eyed, adventurous, risk-taking Northern Protestants (Anglo-Saxons) and the less-preferred brachycephalic (round headed) dark-haired, southern European, frugal, passive Catholics (Pichot, pp. 271–272); second, the Semitic with Jews and Moors; third and fourth, Caucasians and the Basque. For Haekel and Lapouge, the Jews were not considered racially inferior that initially characterised people of colour (black, brown, or less dark brown and yellow). Biological antisemitism followed a different route from the racism of an evolutionary racial hierarchy and referred to social, economic, and religious factors, although all three French anthropologists agreed that Jewish cultural 'degeneracy' resulted from interbreeding. Lapouge tried to give the Jews an origin as the blond dolichocephalic but, it was argued that their long history of interbreeding with southern people, including blacks, eliminated that claim.

According to Davenport (1917), interbreeding results in disharmonic products such as the disproportion of various organs, functional difficulties between the organs, and psychological problems incurred by split identities. Davenport suggests that a person from a given race formed a coherent whole and interbreeding risked producing a child who is combined in a disharmonic fashion, made from elements that might not be mutually compatible as they derive from two distinct totalities. In his view, precocious death, madness, and criminality could be explained in terms of interbreeding as well as the cause of the decline of great civilisations in the past (Pichot, pp. 265–257). According to Lapouge (1896), the black person is inferior to the white but was nevertheless harmonic, whereas the black and white half-breed, because of this disharmony, was inferior not only to the white but also to the black. He claimed that mixed raced women had an asymmetrical uterus which rendered them sterile.

The one drop rule

In the US, judicial laws have required individuals of mixed blood to be classified as black, a regulation known as the 'one drop' rule originating in colonial times and accepted by 1915 throughout the nation (Bergner, 2005, p. 55). Extra-legal practices such as lynching, rape, and other terrorist activities helped to enforce segregation laws. Before and after abolition, scientific discourse of anthropology, medicine, eugenics, and psychiatry all corroborated the myth of biological racial difference and its correlative, white supremacy. The one drop rule, still legal in 2000, did not curtail interracial sex but organised its outcome. While effectively minimising sex through racial taboos between white women and black men, it facilitated mixing between white men and black women by ensuring that children of such a union could not inherit the social, legal, or symbolic legacy that is ordinarily derived from the father. In this way, white men could enjoy sex with white and black women and father children from black women without having to assume legal paternal or marital responsibility nor have to finance their offspring's upbringing. The one drop rule did not curtail interracial sex, but effectively encouraged it while protecting and limiting its outcome in favour of white males.

The miscegenation taboo operates to facilitate certain combinations of racial mixing while contradicting the fantasy of racial purity. The taboo constructs racial categories, regulates sex, and organises kinship to determine legitimacy, descent, and inheritance. Biracial or multiracial people who have crossed over the margin/border that structures experience fall into an in-between state of two or more cultures. Their sense of identity becomes sinister, unstable, and uncanny (Bergner, 2005, p. 65). The same disorientation is found with people who have left their known cultures and entered into a new one with completely different sets of rules and belief systems. The mixing of two cultures can have a destabilizing effect, of crossing over one cultural border from the known and into becoming the tabooed 'outsider' as the other.

Nazi Germany, purity, danger and filth

The miscegenation taboo became particularly defined and enforced during the twentieth century in Nazi Germany in their drive to secure a white Aryan ethnic purity. It was legitimised through the mixture of racial theory, Social

Darwinism, eugenics, and medicalisation through genetic research of these ideas and practices that led to indefinite internment, sterilization, and mass extermination of outsider groups. Repressive policies such as enforced sterilization were undertaken in other countries as well, notably Britain, Sweden, and the US during the interwar years. Eugenics became an academic science; breeding out unhealthy groups promised to save money on welfare and rid society of an apparent burden. Germany was perceived as a living organism based on the concept that a nation is susceptible to the invasive contagion of disease that must be rooted out. The source of the disease is found in a particular class of persons, as carriers of filth and disease, as malignant internal objects who must be exterminated quickly and thoroughly to prevent the contagious spread of such diseased impurity (Koenigsberg, 2011, pp. 12–19). The sterilisation law introduced in Germany in 1934 permitted the public health service to collect exhaustive and intrusive data on the intergenerational racial health and propagation fitness of the nation. Registration, institutionalisation, compulsory sterilisation, marriage prohibition, and government propaganda about racial fitness enabled the mass programme of euthanasia of handicapped adults and children (Friedlander, 2001, pp. 150–151) known as T4 killings, which extended to the mass murder of habitual criminals, Jews, and Roma people.

However, it was only in Germany that mass killing became a state policy under the umbrella of racial hygiene beginning with the mentally and physically handicapped in 1939 and leading to the mass extermination of the Roma people and Jews. The rationale behind the mass killings was the genetic unfitness of these impure people to propagate. It that sense, they coincide with Leach's fifth category, of vermin and pests that must be exterminated and not allowed to breed and lead to the plague.and cultural degeneracy. The Nazi ideal of a 'communality of the people' tapped into German traditions that lauded social harmony over conflict and difference. Groups were targeted and subsequently eliminated that did not fit into the white Aryan German ascetic racial ideal. In early 1933, the Communists were the first group attacked. The Nazis viewed political convictions in social and semibiological terms that generated disgust, making it easier to exclude and dehumanise outsiders. Such outsiders were conceived as rotten, diseased elements in the German body who needed eradicating. For example, communists were recognised by their deformed head shapes and the twisted facial features (Gellately and Stoltzfus, 2001, p. 5). The extermination of Roma people during the Third Reich was not based solely on their supposed racial inferiority, but because they were of mixed breeds from the lowest and dirtiest antisocial elements (Pichot, 2001, p. 305).

According to Nazi ideology (Naimark, 2001, pp. 58–59), the Jews were seen increasingly as embodiments of contagious diseases carrying lice, vermin, bedbugs, and flees that had to be exterminated lest they infected the healthy blood and bodies of German citizens; they were also seen as tumours that had to be cut out or depicted as racial tuberculosis that had to be isolated and removed as an urgent and necessary clinical task. Considered both immoral and impure, Jewish men were thought to seduce and actively impregnate innocent German girls, gravitate toward pimping and pornography, spreading syphilis, and other sexually transmitted diseases in their wake. Jewish women were no better placed, accused of seducing pure German men into their depraved and degenerate subculture.

In addition to the ubiquitous biological imagery of Jews as tabooed defilement, Nazi ideology blamed the Jews for the defeat in World War I and the severe burden of reparations and territorial sacrifices codified in the Versailles Treaty, 1914. Behind the unjust accusations and persecutions of the Jews during the 1930s hid the strong economic desire to acquire their financial assets during the interwar depression that had had less effect on German Jews (Bajohr, 2001, p. 48). After 1933, Jewish retailers and middleclass businessmen were subject to the strongest coercive measures such as anti-Jewish boycott activities and expulsion actions directed at their businesses. The November pogrom of 1938 and the legally enforced Aryanisation of Jewish businesses brought an end to Jewish ownership of commercial enterprise in Germany. Jewish daily life became enveloped by lawlessness, ostracism, and loss of human rights. One of the chief objectives of the Nazis had been to foster emigration, but emigration proved extremely difficult due to individual and corrupt officials, gestapo agents, civil servants, and even foreign consulates who demanded bribes and tributes at every stage. One major resistance to the Third Reich's antisemitism were intermarried Jews. Some Aryan partners despite strong ostracism, refused to divorce and remained loyal to their Jewish spouses. This evidence reveals that intimate relationships between people can help develop humane qualities toward the 'other' because persons are seen close up rather than as stereotyped categories designed to dehumanise out groups (Bain, Vaes, & Leyens, 2014, p. 7).

Exclusion was applied to many groups of 'outsiders' but it was the most consistent against those considered 'alien' or 'degenerate.' In Germany, it meant primarily Jews and Roma people, but applied to a small group of non-Caucasians, usually illegitimate children whose fathers were mostly French black soldiers from North Africa, especially Morocco. During the 1930s these coloured children, known disparagingly as 'Rhineland bastards,' were illegally sterilised.

The force of the miscegenation taboo is felt particularly when a culture is uncertain of its own identity and needs an out-group to punish as the 'non-belonging.' The US is a nation of immigrants; Germany became a unified state as late as 1871. The need to scapegoat others who do not meet the ascetic standard of collective purity and sameness, which includes the treatment of physically and mentally handicapped, is indicative of intolerance toward anomalies as indeterminate, in-between states. These in-between states incur as a double taboo: not only have they stepped outside order as 'difference,' they have also overstepped that margin designed to contain sameness/purity and actively carry that transit as risky/filth.

Descriptions of Jews as 'rats' and black people as 'apes' (cf. Leach's fifth category) are designed as mechanisms of *dehumanisation* to take away their human rights and deny them access to humanness. Recent research into dehumanisation (Hodson, Macinnis, Costello, 2014, pp. 88–105) shows that dehumanising metaphors typically communicate that an outsider group as unlikeable, lower in ability and morals, is either subhuman or inhuman, with the level of offensiveness determined by whether a particular animal or object is liked and revered or feared and averted. Research (Hodson, et.al. ibid, p. 101) shows that the dehumanisation process is highly fluid depending on the perceived threat in a given situation/context. For example, if a white person regards a black person as beneath whites, i.e. lower in value, but lower in ability to harm or alter the group status, blacks may be likened to *non-human* primates (apes) as subhumans. In contrast, the same social perceiver may metaphorically map Muslims and Arabs onto terrorists as an *inhuman* representation in the light of the perceived danger of pollution, a malignant contagion of filth, and the likelihood of harming the in-group lifestyle and belief systems. Muslims might similarly map white people into terrorists and see them as inhuman, thus making extermination easier.

Conclusion

This chapter has outlined the genesis of the miscegenation taboo by examining the development of totemism in early indigenous peoples dating back to Neolithic times. During that time, the emphasis was on the close evolutionary, beneficial intertwining, substituting nature of animals and humans. Animals were regarded as positive influences, there to protect and inspire courage in the face of death, a fate all animals, including humans, share. Animal totems as shown by Levi-Strauss contributed to symbol formation and mental agility.

The relationship between animals and human changed with the introduction of monotheism and the development of the first-born male heir's divine right through primogeniture to subjugate all animals and women as inferior, rationalised through the Genesis myth c. 3000 BCE. Instead of the classification of the miscegenation taboo within totems to demarcate and encourage positive exogamy, animals became degraded and classified as edible/inedible, their sole purpose being to prohibit contagion as a negative rather than meaningful taboo. Taboo has become a dehumanising metaphor for 'outsider' groups. Animals lose their sacred taboo kin significance as totem spirit ancestral mediators between animal and human souls and become negative tools in modern dehumanising practices.

The present revival of the totemism by evoking the spirit animal ancestor through indigenous shamanic ritual, however, does allow the *ousted other* to positively enter the psyche. Found in indirect, associative, symbolic thinking of dreams, art, and active imagination in modern clinical practice, such nomadic, imaginative thinking attempts to correct the imbalance in the psyche since the Genesis myth (c. 3000 BCE) introduced primogeniture with its hierarchical, territorial thinking. Serious analysis is given to the unjust projection of tabooed, disassociated, shadow, subordinated, surplus filth onto the 'other' as the psyche-left-behind (cf. Jung, 1961; paras, 578–606; Bernstein, 2017). I discuss the therapeutic aspects of resurrecting taboo ritual in indigenous shamanic practices in chapters 6, 7, and 8 to remedy this split.

Notes

1. This indigenous view of totem ancestors and their sacred animal function differs greatly with the religious aspects of patrilineal inheritance introduced c. 3000 BCE through the Genesis myth, which imagines a hierarchical single male god who produces his first-born son and heir without sexual contact with a woman. All women and animals are subjugated under his rule. Male humans are differentiated from women and animals in that women or animal do not possess a soul. I discuss aspects of patrilineal primogeniture in detail in chapter 5.
2. Levi-Strauss' definition of the polarisation of the opposites in totemism to enhance thinking is similar to Jung's description of holding the tension of the opposites to facilitate symbol formation. See chapter 1 for Jung's definition of symbol formation (Jung, 1921, paras. 814–829).
3. Levi-Strauss' concept of *associationism* bears distinct resemblance to Jung's definition of *indirect* associative thinking (1911–12/1952, paras. 4–55) which I discuss in chapters 1 and 2.

References

Bain, P.B., Vaes, J., and Leyens, J-P. (2014). Advances in Understanding Humanness and Dehumanization. In Bain, P.G., Vaes, J., and Leyens, J-P. (eds.) *Humanness and Dehumanisation*. New York and London: Routledge, pp. 1–9.

Bain, P.B., Vaes, J., and Leyens, J-P. (eds.) (2014). *Humanness and Dehumanisation*. New York and London: Routledge.

Bajour, F. (2001). No 'Volksgenossen:' Jewish Entrepreneurs in the Third Reich. In Gellately, R. and Stoltzfus, N. (eds.) *Social Outsiders in Nazi Germany*. Princeton and Oxford: Princeton University Press, pp. 45–65.

Bauman, Z. (1973). *Culture as Praxis*. London and Boston: Routledge and Kegan Paul.

Bergner, G. (2005). *Taboo Subjects: Race, Sex and Psychoanalysis*. Minneapolis and London: University of Minnesota Press.

Bernstein, J.S. (2017). Border*land* Consciousness. Re-establishing Dialogue Between the Western Psyche and the Psyche-left-Behind. In Brodersen, E. and Glockm M. (eds.) *Jungian Perspectives on Rebirth and Renewal: Phoenix Rising*. London and New York: Routledge.

Brickman, C. (2003). *Aboriginal Populations in the Mind; Race and Primitivity in Psychoanalysis*. New York: Columbia University Press.

Brodersen, E. and Glock, M. (eds.) (2017). *Jungian Perspectives on Rebirth and Renewal: Phoenix Rising*. London and New York: Routledge.

Büchner, L. (1870). *L'Homme selon la science.* Paris: Reinholt.
Clottes, J. (2009). Sticking Bones into Cracks in the Upper Palaeolithic. In Renfrew, C. and Morley, I. (eds.) *Becoming Human, Innovations in Prehistoric Material and Spiritual Culture.* Cambridge, UK and New York: Cambridge University Press, pp. 195–211.
Cuvier, C. (1800-1805). *Lecons d'Anatomie Comparee.* Vols. 1–5. Paris: Baudouin.
Darwin, C. (1859). *The Origin of Species.* London and New York: Penguin, 1958.
Davenport, C.B. (1917). The Effects of Race Intermingling. *Proceedings of the American Philosophical Society* 56, 364–368.
Deloria, V., Deloria P., & Bernstein J.S. (2009). *C.G. Jung and the Sioux Traditions: Dreams, Visions, Nature and the Primitive.* New Orleans: Spring Journal.
Douglas, M. (1966). *Purity and Danger.* Abingdon, Oxon and New York: Routledge, 2002.
Du Bois, W.E.B. (1903). *The Souls of Black folk.* New York: Penguin, 1989.
Dunbar, R., Knight, C. and Power, P. (eds.) (1999). *The Evolution of Culture, An Interdisciplinary View.* Edinburgh: Edinburgh University Press.
Durkheim, E. (1915). The Elementary Forms of Religious Life. In (1979) Lessa, W.A. Vogt, E.Z. (eds.) *Reader in Comparative Religion. An Anthropological Approach,* 4th edn. New York: Harper Collins, pp. 27–35.
Duschinsky, R.S., Schnall, S. and Weiss, D.H. (eds.) (2014). *Purity and Danger Now, New Perspectives.* London and New York: Routledge.
Eliade, M. (1958). *Rites and Symbols of Initiation.* Woodstock, CT: Spring Publication, 1995.
Fanon, F. (1952). *Black Skin, White Masks.* Trans. Markmann, C.L. London: Pluto Press.
Firth, R. (1930-31) Totemism in Polynesia. *Oceania,* 1(3), 291–321; (4), 378–398.
Fortes, M. (1945). *The Dynamics of Clanship Among the Tallensi.* London and New York: Oxford University Press.
Fraser, J.G. (1910). *Totemism and Exogamy, a Treatise on Certain Forms of Superstition and Society.* London: Macmillan.
Freud, S. (1912-13). Totem and Taboo. In *The Origins of Religion, Collected Works,* Vol. 13. London: Penguin Books, 1990.
Friedlander, H. (2001). The Exclusion and Murder of the Disabled. In Gellately, R. and Stoltzfus, N. (eds.) *Social Outsiders in Nazi Germany.* Princeton and Oxford: Princeton University Press, pp. 145–164.
Gellately, R. and Stoltzfus, N. (2001). Social Outsiders and the Construction of the Community of the People. In Gellately, R. and Stoltzfus, N. (eds.) *Social Outsiders in Nazi Germany.* Princeton and Oxford: Princeton University Press, pp. 3–19.
Gellately, R. and Stoltzfus, N. (eds.) (2001). *Social Outsiders in Nazi Germany.* Princeton and Oxford: Princeton University Press.
de Gobineau, A. (1855). *Essay sur l'inegalite des races humaines.* Paris: Belfond, 1967.
Haeckel, E. (1876). *The Evolution of Man* (Vols. 1 & 2). London: Watts.
Hedman, B. (2018). Archetypal Images in Haida Art. *International Journal of Jungian Studies* 10(1), 16–33.
Hodson, G., Macinnis, C.A., and Costello, K. (2014). (Over)Valuing 'Humanness' as an Aggravator of Intergroup Prejudices and Discrimination. In Bain, P.G., Vaes, J., and Leyens, J-P. (eds.) *Humanness and Dehumanisation.* New York and London: Routledge, pp. 86–110.
Jahoda, G. (2014). An Anthropological History of Dehumanisation from Late-18th to Mid-20th Centuries. In Bain, P.G., Vaes, J., and Leyens, J-P. (eds.) *Humanness and Dehumanisation.* New York and London: Routledge, pp. 13–33.

Jung, C.G. (1911–12/1952). Two Kinds of Thinking. In *Collected Works*, Vol. 5 *Symbols of Transformation,* 2nd edn. London: Routledge and Kegan Paul, 1995.

Jung, C.G. (1921). Definitions. In *Collected Works*, Vol. 6. *Psychological Types,* 2nd edn. London: Routledge and Kegan Paul, 1989.

Jung, C.G. (1961). Healing the Split. In *Collected Works*, Vol. 18. *The Symbolic Life*, 2nd edn. London: Routledge and Kegan Paul, 1993.

Königsberg, R.A. (2011). *The Psychoanalysis of Racism, Revolution and Nationalism.* New York: The Library of Social Science.

Kroeber, A.L. (1920). Totem and Taboo: An Ethnological Psychoanalysis. In (1979) Lessa, W.A., and Vogt, E.Z. (eds.) *Reader in Comparative Religion. An Anthropological Approach*, 4th edn. New York: Harper Collins, pp. 19–24.

Lacourt, J. (2010). My father was a Bear: Human–Animal Transformations in Native American Teachings. In *Minding the Animal Psyche*, Vol. 83. New Orleans: Spring Journal, pp. 79–98.

Lacourt, J. (2017). Seeing the Wood for the Trees: Birthing Symbolic Life. In Brodersen, E. and Glock, M. (eds.) *Jungian Perspectives on Rebirth and Renewal: Phoenix Rising.* London and New York: Routledge, pp. 43–55.

Leach, E.R. (1964). Anthropological Aspects of Language: Animal Categories and Verbal Abuse. In (1979) Lessa, W.A. and Vogt, E.Z. (eds.) *Reader in Comparative Religion. An Anthropological Approach*, 4th edn. New York: Harper Collins, pp. 155–166.

LeBon, G. (1881). *L'Homme et les Societies*, Vols. 1 & 2. Paris: Rothschild.

Lessa, W.A., and Vogt, E.Z. (eds.) (1979). *Reader in Comparative Religion. An Anthropological Approach*, 4th edn. New York: Harper Collins.

Levy-Bruhl, (1935). *Primitive Mythology. The Mythic World of the Australian and Papuan Natives.* Trans. Elliott, B. St. Lucia and London: University of Queensland Press, 1983.

Levi-Strauss, C. (1962). *Totemism.* London: Merlin Press.

Lewis-Williams, D. (2002). *The Mind in the Cave.* London: Thames and Hudson.

Lewis-Williams, D. and Pearce, D. (2005). *Inside the Neolithic Mind.* London: Thames and Hudson.

Miller, N. (1928). *The child in primitive society.* London: Kegan Paul.

Mithen, S. (1999). Symbolism and the Supernatural. In (1999) Dunbar, R., Knight, C., and Power, C. (eds.) *The Evolution of Culture. An Interdisciplinary View.* Edinburgh: Edinburgh University Press, pp. 147–169.

Mithen, S. (2009). Out of Mind: Material Culture and the Supernatural. In Refrew, C. and Morley, I. (eds.) *Becoming Human. Innovation in Prehistoric Material and Spiritual Culture.* Cambridge and New York: Cambridge University Press, pp. 123–134.

Morgan, L.H. (1877). *Ancient Society.* New Brunswick, N.J: Transaction Publisher, 2000.

Naimark, N.M. (2001). *Fires of Hatred, Ethnic Cleansing in Twentieth-Century Europe.* Cambridge, Mass and London: Harvard University Press.

Reed, E. (1975). *Woman's Evolution.* New York and London: Pathfinder Press.

Radcliffe-Brown, A.R. (1952). Taboo. In *Structure and Function in Primitive Society. Essays and Addresses.* Glencoe, Ill: The Free Press. pp. 133–152.

Pichot, A. (2001). *The Pure Society from Darwin to Hitler.* London and New York: Verso, 2009.

Renfrew, C., and Morley, I. (eds.) (2009). *Becoming Human, Innovations in Prehistoric Material and Spiritual Culture.* Cambridge, UK and New York: Cambridge University Press.

Retzius, A. (1842–1846). Memoire sur les forms du crane dews habitants du Nord. In *Annales des Sciences Naturelles*, Serie 3, Zoologie, 6. pp. 133–172.

Schultze, F. (1900). *Psychologie der Naturvölker.* Leipzig: Veit.

Soemmering, S.T. (1784). *Über die körperliche Verschiedenheit des Negers, von Europäer.* Stuttgart: Fischer Verlag, 1998.

Speltini, G. and Passini, S. (2014). Cleanliness Issues: From Individual Practices to Collective Visions. In Duschinsky, R., Schnall, S., and Weiss, D.H. (eds.) *Purity and Danger Now, New Perspectives.* London and New York: Routledge, pp. 162–177.

Tylor, E.B. (1873) Animism. In (1979) Lessa, W.A. and Vogt, E.Z. (eds.) *Reader in Comparative Religion. An Anthropological Approach*, 4th edn. New York: Harper Collins, pp. 9–19.

Virey, J.J. (1824). *Historie naturelle du genre humain.* 3 vols. Brussels: Wahlen.

von den Veldon, E. (1906–1907) Zur Psychologie der Negerrase. *Politisch-anthropologische Revue*, iv, pp. 11–12.

Vogt, C. (1864). *Lectures on Man.* London: Longman.

Von Franz, M-L (2000) *Puer Aeternus.* Vol. 87. Toronto: Inner City Books.

Webster, H. (1942). *Taboo: a Sociological Study.* New York: Octagon Books, 1973.

Chapter 5

The origin and positioning of incest taboo

Introduction

Of all the taboos, incest taboo creates the most debate and ongoing fascination. The origin and positioning of this taboo has generated much controversy within anthropology, cultural theory, and psychoanalytical theory. This chapter attempts to unravel the complex issues surrounding and underpinning this taboo and is organised into three sections: the first section examines the origins of incest taboo versus the origins of sex avoidance, analysing when incest prohibition manifests itself as a taboo and the psychosocial conditions behind it; I question the premise that incest taboo is a universal phenomenon dating back to Palaeolithic-Neolithic times. The second section examines psychoanalytical and psychosocial interpretations of the Oedipus complex, one of the main cornerstones of psychoanalytical incest wish theory. The last section explores incest taboo violation and the resultant symptomatology arising from it.

Origins of incest taboo versus sex avoidance

Interest in incest taboo has normally focussed on the explanation of the supposed universality of the incest taboo, that is, sexual intercourse with near kin. A man is forbidden to have sexual intercourse with or marry his mother and sisters. A woman is forbidden to have sexual intercourse with or marry her father and brothers. Such intermarriage of close blood relatives is thought not only immoral but injurious to the species as the progeny of such a union may have congenital defects. While not universal, this taboo is widespread. Even in the absence of a specific taboo, incestuous liaisons are not common. Incest is commonly avoided even without a specific taboo prohibition. One explanation offered is that incestuous relationships between close family members—mother-son, father-daughter, brother-sister—are biologically dangerous as they raise the possibility of deleterious homozygosity. Turner and Maryanski (2005, pp. 35–36) give examples of studies (Adams and Neel, 1967; Seemanova, 1971) that show the injurious effects of interbreeding resulting in mental retardation, seizures, dystrophy, dwarfism, polydactyly, harelip, and cleft palate. However, as Fox (1994, p. 30) argues, it is by no means clear whether the fear of malformed offspring is the reason for incest taboo as for many animals it has a desired effect of increasing the strength of the stock. One argument is that the only secure advantage lies in genetic variation, which is advantageous in a changing environment. Studies of animal and even plant populations have shown that a close interbreeding on a heavy scale is avoided but that inbreeding in the close cousin range is often preferred as it maximises the benefits of concentrating related genes while reducing the danger of too-close inbreeding. In that case, brother-sister, father-daughter incest is avoided but first and second cousins encouraged. For the most part of human history, one of the mechanisms used to avoid incest was dispersion. Problems arose when the sexually mature young remain in their groups, available to each other and their parents. The rate of possible incest, however, must have remained low given short life spans, infant mortality, wide birth spacing, girls marrying out at puberty, and the separation of the sexes when boys left their mothers' care at puberty, as was the case in most early indigenous nomadic clan cultures.

Another factor militated against the innateness of the inbreeding/incest theory was the ignorance of primitive people about the scientific basis of biological processes. During the seventeenth century, Swammerdam first discovered that contact of spermatic fluid with the female ovum was a necessary condition of generation. The male sperm cell was discovered in 1785 and the fertilisation process adequately demonstrated by Fol in 1879 (Briffault, 1931, pp. 443–444). Westermarck (1891) and Hobhouse (see Hobson and Ginsberg, 1931) were the foremost proponents that incest avoidance arose from an innate revulsion of sexual intercourse with family members (cf. Fox, 1994, pp. 32–35 on the evolution of incest prohibition). But if there was an innate revulsion, why was there the need for a specific taboo?

Morgan (1877) ascertained that the maternal gens preceded the family in history where the community was categorised according to sex, age, and their totem. Under the laws of exogamy, no person could have sexual relationship with a member of the same totem kin group. In matrilineal clan structures, motherhood was a social function whereby the individual mother was submerged into the collective of women who were sisters to one another. Clansman had many mothers and sisters, and obliged to keep a distance from these forbidden, tabooed females. In indigenous clan groups, adult males lived in their own quarters; adult women and children lived together in their own quarters. At puberty, or even earlier, young males were removed from the residences of their mothers and sisters to reside with their adult male kinsman, usually the mother's brother. Lang and Atkinson (1903, p. 217) note that the word 'sister' was identical with taboo, but that the term 'sister' comprised a far wider group of women other than one's own biological sisters (ibid, p. 100). As such, incest taboo did not exist; sex avoidance is a more accurate term of the sexual relationships between clan members.

Taboo against spilt blood rather than incest

Crawley (1902, pp. 84–85) suggests that the most widespread and most stringent sex taboo had nothing to do with sexual functions but the prohibition against eating together. Reed (1975) suggests that food segregation was part of a wider segregation between male hunters, mothers, and children based on the taboo of *spilt blood*. Reed (ibid, p. 129) argues that behind the general sex avoidance was fear of women's menstruation blood or indeed any freshly spilt blood. Premodern peoples were ignorant of the cause of menstruation. They considered it as the flow of blood from an internal wound, the cause usually attributed to animal, bird, or snake attack. These imaginary totem attackers concealed male fears that a man found in the vicinity of a menstruating woman could be accused as the possible attacker.

The Maoris, the Indians of Nootka South in British Columbia, and the indigenous peoples in South Africa before and during hunting or warring expeditions have no physical contact with women. The explanation given by the aborigines for strict avoidance of woman during specific times, such as hunting and wartime, were vaguely formulated and open to misinterpretation. It was not due to the supposed weakening, contaminating effect of women upon men as Fraser initially thought, but more the reverse belief that the hunters themselves had a contaminating and dangerous influence on the wellbeing of the women. Hunters and warriors were obliged to go through strict purification rituals to clean themselves of the impurities acquitted through their blood-filled occupation. Any shedder of blood was regarded as taboo. There are numerous descriptions of the purification rituals men had to pass through after a hunt or battle. While in quarantine and isolated in cabins, men would be only gradually released from their fast (Webster, 1942, pp. 210–211). It is more than a sexual avoidance; it was a total taboo on women and children becoming contaminated with the deadly influence of *nuru,* the black spirit of the slain that enacts revenge. Hunters and warriors must perform these purification rites to protect their clan members. Strict taboos were also imposed on what meat men could eat and under what conditions. These food laws were inculcated into young males at puberty during initiation rites at the time of their transfer and separation from the female to the male sector of the community. Durkheim (1915, pp. 33–35) also thought that premodern people were in awe of blood and refused to cohabit with females of their respective clans since their totemic gods were thought to inhabit their clan's blood, and mixing of sacred blood was taboo. The nature of the sacred was transmitted through bloodlines.

Crawley (1902, p. 207) points out that only male animal flesh may be eaten. This ancient segregation of the sexes survives in the separation of milk from meat foods. Although hunters and warriors did not look on women as the contaminating sex, they were considered dangerous if their taboos and rules of avoidance were violated. Not just menstruation blood, but any blood of a woman is held in awe and horror. The process of pregnancy and childbirth, which can kill both the mother and child, is held with great emotional fear of potential loss and attaches itself as a taboo in order to be contained. Men distanced themselves from women particularly during childbirth in case they are held responsible for any death. Newborn babies were similarly tabooed until they reached the age where they safely survived the ordeal of childbirth. Since women's blood was tabooed, the colour red and daubing with blood became the symbol and mark of taboo. Red ochre gradually substituted blood and the sign of taboo (Chapple and Coon, 1942, p. 597; Hocart, 1933, p. 143; Reed, 1975, pp. 129–131, 170–171). Women painted themselves and/or their infant red as a public sign that the rule of avoidance, that is no touching, was in effect. Among the people and objects placed under taboo, protection by being daubed, painted, or sprinkled with blood or red paint were corpses, warriors, war-chiefs, brides, sacred trees, and stones. While some twentieth century anthropologists through the lens of patrilineal inheritance misinterpret that women's blood is held impure and loathsome, the actual meaning of taboo for premodern indigenous people has the opposite meaning: sacred, pure, holy, and not to be touched. Ignorance of the exact cause of women's blood increased with the magnitude of its dread.

Repression of women as negatively tabooed subjects

Morgan (1877, pp. 477–478) suggests that the family with the father as head and the first-born son as the exclusive heir was a late arrival dating from the onset of civilisation c. 3000 BCE. Primogeniture legitimised and rationalised the exclusive inherited right of the first-born male to protect property from diminution and simultaneously distribute surplus resources hierarchically. Earlier Palaeolithic-Neolithic matrilineal clan kin forms, although egalitarian, had led to the dissipation of accumulative goods over time. As only first-born males could inherit, preferred 'masculine' traits were enhanced to support the overseeing and protection of property, such as active brute force, warrior courage, and tactical thinking to reflect their territorial status. 'Feminine' specificity, including her propagation value, became defined as second-class passive domesticity, subjugation, and nurture, losing all its ascendant, inheritable creativity (Brodersen, 2016, pp. 1–2). Before the changeover to patrilineal inheritance and monotheisms, however, women were considered mentally authoritative and physically active in their kin communities, a view shared by Bachofen (1871) and Briffault (1931). Briffault credits women with initiating the humanisation and socialisation of culture who developed their intellect through cooperative multitasking. He notes that in some cases (1931, p. 177) indigenous women are intellectually and physically superior to males, show more courage and ferocity in combat (pp. 162–163) and greater shrewdness in arbitration (p. 178). Goldenweiser (1937, p. 365) argues in his study of the Iroquois tribe that women as counsel of matrons have equal influence in the election of chiefs and in curtailing aggressive tribal behaviour.

After the introduction of primogeniture rationalised by the Genesis myth, and supported by monotheisms, women's menstrual blood became negatively tabooed and cursed. Not only are women's bodies held in contempt as sinful and 'lacking' compared to male bodies (cf. Nye, 2004, on German aesthetic philosophers, including Kant, on the defiling effect of contact with the female body), the colour red became associated with sinful sexuality. Women's intellect underwent the same negative taboo and degradation (cf. Daly, 1973, 1978; Butler, 1997, 1999, 2004). Women became subjugated, dependent surplus as men's property, their emotional voices marginalised, tabooed, and silenced[1] (cf. Cater, ed. 2014, Brodersen, 2016).

There is nothing innate or universal about incest taboo as opposed to sex avoidance. As Engels expressed it (1884, p. 95) the changeover from matrilineal to patrilineal inheritance during the late Neolithic era was a decisive blow for women rights to inherit through the mother. Feminist anthropologists, Coontz and Henderson (1986, pp. 121–131) suggest that the changeover to patrilineal inheritance led to patrilocal residences, which increased control over 'marrying in' wives from other clans. Such women lost their natal lineage claims and became surplus outsiders, subordinated producers within patrilocal, patrilineal kin groups where they were no longer property inheritors and thus had far less to say about the allocation of consumption versus redistribution. Their economic contribution became negatively tabooed.

Psychoanalytical and psychosocial interpretations of incest taboo

Freud (1938) uses the fate of Oedipus portrayed in the play by Sophocles, *Oedipus Rex,* (c. 430–420 BCE) to illustrate the supposed creationist universality of the Oedipus complex. Briefly, Sophocles' play *Oedipus Rex* posits a young man, abandoned at birth, who unwittingly kills his father, Laius, King of Thebes, at a crossroads. As there is not enough space for both to pass each other, Oedipus is forced to respond to the older man's initial aggression of the drawn sword and kill him. Oedipus unknowingly enters his father's kingdom, becomes king, marries his mother, Jocasta, the widowed queen, and has four offspring, two girls and twin boys. A plague breaks out in Thebes, supposedly because the old king's murderer remains unfound. Oedipus offers his services to find the murderer without realising that he himself has unwittingly committed the deed. Once the truth is revealed, Jocasta hangs herself; Oedipus blinds himself and is exiled from Thebes, leaving the kingship divided between his twin sons. Oedipus' tragedy is interpreted by Freud as the outcome of an unconscious incest wish fantasy/fulfilment whereby Oedipus kills his father in jealous competition in order to have sex and propagate with his mother, which only results in tragedy.

Freud (1938, pp. 324–325) postulates the following creationist principle of incest taboo:

> The essential part... I am about to describe occurred to *all* primitive men that is to *all our ancestors*... The strong male was lord and father of the entire horde and unrestricted in his power, which he exercised with violence. *All* the females were his *property-wives* and daughters of his own horde and some...robbed from other hordes. The lot of his sons was a hard one; if they roused his father's jealousy they were killed or castrated or driven out. (my italics).

Freud bases his main theory of psychosexual development on the fear of castration, expulsion, or death enacted by a powerful father on any son(s) who challenge, threaten, or seize his inherited property (including his wife and daughters). Freud mythologises and universalises this narrative as the Oedipus complex. Freud's premise is based on the position of the father as the sole owner of property including wives, daughters and slaves, but, as I have already argued, the father's position only developed after the introduction of primogeniture at the onset of civilisation c. 3000 BCE rationalised by the Genesis myth. The Genesis myth replaced earlier Palaeolithic-Neolithic creation myths that emphasised animals and women as creators, as we witnessed in the development of animal totems in chapter 4. Based on the premise of patrilineal descent, sons compete and plot within themselves and against their father to overthrow him to gain access to all his resources and property, including the women in the horde, and suffer the corresponding guilt and remorse at the father's actual demise.

Freud incorporates the resolution of Oedipus complex as a psychosexual developmental stage, which apparently both sexes experience between three to six years of age. According to Freud, the disillusionment felt by the child that he or she cannot overthrow the opposing mother or father and have a conjugal relationship with the remaining parent results in the corresponding gender role adjustment and societal binary identification. Freud's interest in incest developed out of his preoccupation with the ego in its personal struggle for independence in the first half of life. Freud (1923) postulates this struggle as a necessary heroic strengthening of the ego to withstand and overcome the pull of incest and primal unity to make his/her own way in the world. For Freud, the process begins with the child's *actual* tabooed, sexualised parental relationship. Freud's emphasis on child genital sexuality and the resolution of the Oedipus complex stultifies imaginative cross-gender fertilisation and forecloses alternative definitions of psychic growth such as put forward on attachment theory (Bowlby, 1973; Fonagy, 2001); for example, a child does not innately wish for genital relations with a parent but needs love, closeness, and bodily warmth, which allow separation impulses to develop (Winnicott, 1965). The overwhelming evidence of past and present adult acts of paedophilia against children, which Freud initially accepted but later rejected, falsely puts the guilt *and* the responsibility of incestuous impulses on the child, causing untold harm, which I discuss later in this chapter.

Jung's interpretation of incest emphasises its *symbolic* nature. Jung uses incest as a metaphor for fusion with unconscious creative processes whereby fusion with the contra-sexual other brings forward a rebirth of potential, rather than acts as a concrete sexualised outer relationship. Jung uses (1911–12/1952, paras. 351–354) the Egyptian myth of Osiris as the incestuous sun king, who undergoes death, dismemberment, and resurrection, as analogous with the individuation process. Symbolic incest takes place between the ego/day (Osiris) and the unconscious/night (twin brother Seth, in the form of a snake) resulting in a revitalisation of the ego as the emergent self. Jung (1933, para. 410; 1945, paras. 453–456) describes analysis as working imaginatively and incestuously within a *symbolic* uterus, stressing the transformative efficacy of incest libido in giving birth to the whole person (cf. Brodersen, 2016, p. 174). Through the placental connection, tabooed waste products can be recycled and transformed.

This distinct approach differs from Freud who *literalises* incest as regressive developmental phenomena to be overcome rather than seen as a legitimate drive to become independent through questioning and overturning the authority of the father. Freud sees rebellion and dissent in the service of independent thinking negatively as antilife (1923, pp. 380–388). Incest is, therefore, structured as a tabooed rebellious sexual instinct in the unconscious and handled as such. For Jung, incest is interpreted as a wider symbolic desire to unite with, as yet, unrealised aspects of unconscious potential of the 'other' in service of the individuation process, which facilitates affect regulation, free will, and independent thinking, rather than as viewed as a tabooed sexual instinct to be overcome in order to facilitate a collective gendered alignment.

Cultural theorist, Girard (2004) sees that the son's urges derive from the father in his role as model. However, unlike Freud, Girard cut Oedipus loose from an incestuous primordial relationship object, the mother, and endows him with an abstract mimetic desire, that is open-ended and capable of remoulding itself to fit the mediator of the moment. Oedipus may enter into rivalry with the father for an object other than the mother, and so too take the mother as object in imitation of a mediator other than the father.

Jung (1912, paras. 405–406) takes a similarly independent stand from Freud; he interprets regression as a temporary stage needing repetition to overcome old obstacles that hindered psychological development and independence in childhood, and later in life, hold the person captive and overly obedient to old parental authoritarian blocking mechanisms that need to be outgrown.

Hillman (1987, p. 120) suggests that Oedipus, Laius as father, and Freud all share a literalist psychology. None reflects on the hidden meaning behind the oracle. Oedipus interprets the sphinx's utterances intellectually, unable to grasp their ambiguous, symbolic inferences. His father, likewise, literalised his own prophesy concerning his son without grasping that all sons are born to usurp their father in an act of regeneration that requires a healthy psychological distancing, not a literal killing of the bond between them. Hillman's emphasis of infanticide within the Oedipus myth puts the onus on Oedipus' early history when he is abandoned by his parents, rather than later when Oedipus unwittingly kills his father and marries his mother. Oedipus' overly unconscious attachment to his mother is *because* Laius disinherited him. Oedipus blinds himself by Jocasta's broach seeing and realising that attachment too late.

Hillman suggests (ibid, pp. 126–128) that the attempted infanticide is explained by Laius' previous history through Aeschylus' play *Laius* (c. 467 BCE) and Euripides' *Laius* (c. 411–409 BCE). Both plays depict how Laius fell in love with Chrysippos, the beautiful son of King Pelops and abducted him to be his lover. As punishment for the abduction, the oracle at Pelops cursed Laius to be killed by his own son. When Laius is cursed for pederasty, he only interprets the taboo as a prohibition against Eros. He dare not love his own son as the son would need to be loved, because this son will replace him as father. This knowledge nurtures the infanticide instinct and facilitates the displacement of his desire onto a less harmful, other man's son.

Using other sources concerning Oedipus' heritage, Kerenyi (1990, p. 71) notes that Jocasta as granddaughter of Echion, the snake-man or dragon-sowing, is the rightful indigenous Theban heir, not Laius. Kerenyi suggests that Jocasta is the main source of royal power and interprets Jocasta's incest as in line with older matrilineal fertility rites when mother earth performed symbolic/literal incest with her son/sun to regenerate the land through this ancient blood fusion.

Walker (1983, pp. 429–430) underscores Kenenyi's perspective, interpreting Oedipus' mother-marrying and father-killing as part of the ancient matrilineal ritual whereby the goddess mother is supplied with new virile bride-grooms as 'sons' who embody the same blood line. Oedipus' family position stresses his complex, multiple symbolic roles: he is the son of his mother and the oldest brother among her children. His age category makes him also a mother's brother to her other four children as well as the father of the four offspring. Oedipus is, thus, simultaneously, father and son, and a mother's brother, incorporating both matrilineal and patrilineal modes of production in his kinship/kingship intergenerational make-up.

Oedipus' position at the crossroads between patrilineal and matrilineal inheritance

Reed (1975, pp. 525–539) argues that the tragedy of Oedipus has nothing to do with incest between mother and son, nor fears about inbreeding between close family members. All four of Oedipus' offspring had neither physical nor mental deformities as a result of interbreeding. Oedipus did, however, unwittingly breach of the old law of exogamy. Far overshadowing this breach, however, was patricide, considered the worst crime under patrilineal inheritance. Reed (1975) and Hamilton (1940) suggest that remnants of matrilineal kin clan forms are present within patrilineal structures in the tragedy of Oedipus and that he and his family are caught in the crossroads between two inheritance forms: matrilineal and patrilineal, which have nothing to do with incest. In line with other royal matrilineal families who kept vestiges of matrilineal inheritance after the introduction of patrilineal primogeniture, the House of Thebes is a divided family. The undissolvable unit is the sister-brother pair; the husband is king only through his marriage to the queen. Queen Jocasta stands between two men, her brother Creon and her husband, Oedipus. They are her male corulers. The brother-sister relationship is not incestuous, but based on exogamous matrilineal rules: the queen's brother is the permanent ruler by right of birth; the husband is king only through his marriage and sexual alliance to the queen for procreation, and then only until her death or his disposition. The tense overlapping relationship between the two men, Oedipus and Creon, Jocasta's brother, has been overlooked, compared to the scandal caused by the incest relationship between Jocasta and Oedipus.

The ambivalent crossover between matrilineal and patrilineal inheritance continues, however, with Oedipus' daughter Antigone, in Sophocles' play *Antigone* (c. 441 BCE). King Creon forbids the official burial of one of Antigone's brothers, Polynices, which means that with no official mourning ritual, his soul will wander without rest, his decomposing body inviting the plague. Although Antigone is betrothed to Creon's son, Haemon, she refuses to submit to the edict, disobeys the King, builds a pyre for his body, and scatters earth to release his soul for divine blessing. She is caught in the act of defiance, admits it, thus signing her own death warrant of being entombed alive. Butler (2000, pp. 78–79) contends that, although Antigone is betrothed to Haemon, Creon's son, she does not choose this heterosexual closure to her mourning. Antigone's insistence on a public, rather than private, recognition of her grief threatens Creon's sovereignty because she asserts her own kin matrilineal brother-sister relationship over the relationship to his son. I interpret Antigone's public grief for her brother as particularly threatening to Creon because a public/conscious grieving of loss of primary matrilineal kinship ties prevents it from being privately/unconsciously transferred intact through projection onto his son, thereby weakening Creon's own lesser kinship matrilineal claim under patrilineal primogeniture that he hoped to strengthen through his son's marriage.

Freud (1917, pp. 251–268) suggests that mourning is successfully worked through when the libido originally invested in the lost object is transferred onto a new one. Freud's handling of the supposed incest disappointment and loss that sons and daughters experience when they realise that they cannot seduce their parent as a sexualised love object and surmount the competition, does not sufficiently digest intrapsychic matrilineal kinship transference libido through a public mourning. In psychoanalytical practice, matrilineal kin loss is simply repressed as regressive and its libido foreclosed onto a heterosexual patrilineal partner. The work of recollecting the animus/anima kin endogamous projection from brother or father for a female patient as one's own vitality is left undone, as the transference is handled as a tabooed sexuality and used as a tool to foreclose matrilineal empowerment. Until recent history in Western Europe, and still practiced in other cultures world-wide, kinship libido is transferred in marriage as the husband's exclusive possession and entitlement. Post Freudian psychoanalytical methods, for example, Mann's (ed.) (2002) clinical perspectives on 'love and hate,' or Caldwell (ed.) (2005) on 'sex and sexuality,' do not revive this imaginative flexibility of working with incest either, because they literalise 'incest' frustration as sexual rather than freeing up its regressive, dissenting, tabooed, frustrated content as an endogamous kin potential. The psychic muscles of this potential have been wasted because primogeniture has disinherited and subordinated matrilineal energy into a fixed binary heterosexual closure (Brodersen, 2016, p. 176). Butler (2000, pp. 78–79) movingly portrays the plight of mourners whose relationship with the other is denied legitimacy because it remains taboo, hanged or buried alive, in a liminal, transitional realm between life and death, outside the symbolic realm of the father as patrilineal inheritance.

I thus argue that the Oedipus complex is not innate, as it belongs to interpretations and resolution of drives attributed to patrilineal primogeniture. Primogeniture reversed the earlier Palaeolithic-Neolithic eras when inheritance passed through the female gens and the initiation of mother's sons was given to the mother's brother (Engels, 1884, p. 95; c.f. Brodersen, 2016, pp. 38–59). Incest taboo based on the position and property of the father could not have taken place as no one knew who the biological father was. During Palaeolithic and Neolithic times, biological information about the role of male sperm in reproductive processes was unknown.

Early premodern peoples thought that women gave birth spontaneously through their magical powers or something they had ingested (Reed, 1975, pp. 405–407). Incest taboo became enforced later through primogeniture and the growth of the nuclear family. During the development of the privatised nuclear family supported by the Catholic Church, children left home past puberty and posed more threat to intergenerational sexual abuse. In premodern indigenous cultures, puberty rites of passage ensured that boys left their mothers around age 12 to live with their male clan kin. Girls entering puberty were subject to strict taboo and seclusion to protect them in some measure from unwanted pregnancies before their marriage ceremony.

Other psychosocial-anthropological interpretive paradigms

Turner and Maryanski (2005) explore the origins of incest taboo with an overview of anthropological material. Using Westermarck's classic work (1891), they argue incest aversion protected the injurious effects of inbreeding and incestuous desire was seldom felt between siblings in close contact. They would be 'inedible.' Westermarck's argument has been substantiated by Spiro's 1958 data from children being raised in a Kibbutz in Israel. These children who lived, worked, and prayed together did not form sexual ties at puberty. However the natural propensities of avoidance were insufficient to prevent all incestuous acts.

Parsons' (1954) view on the development of incest taboo adopts Freud's argument that incestuous desires, especially boys for their mother, must be repressed for the sake of emotional growth of children and the ability of children to assume extrafamilial roles in the wider society. Levi-Strauss (1949, pp. 12–25) admits to the problem of categorising incest taboo. He argues that the incest taboo is an essential part of the exchange system between different kin units. Incest taboo forces individuals to seek partners outside their immediate kin. Turner and Maryanski (2005, pp. 185–200) conclude that the origin of incest taboo developed because hominids, as evolved apes, inherited the mother-son avoidance pattern as the last common ancestor from present-day chimpanzees to the hominoid line culminating in humans. From the beginning, they argue, a hardwired avoidance of sexual relations existed between mother and son. Female transfer at puberty represented another behavioural propensity in apes and hominoid. These innate behavioural programmers along with the Westermarck effect reduced the likelihood that closely related kin would have sex.

I have argued, however, in this chapter that sex avoidance had little to do with incest taboo. Turner and Maryanski maintain that incest taboo developed during the time of *Homo erectus*, despite anthropological evidence to show that matrilineal clan kinship structures reveal that sex avoidance was in reality a blood taboo that protected both sexes from incest. There was no nuclear family as such. When fitness became enhanced through patrilineal primogeniture c. 3000 BCE, selection began to work at cross purposes.

Male ownership of property, which included women, increased the development of emotions associated with exclusive entitlement so that the propensity to transfer fertile females into other clans was delayed.

Through the late nineteenth century and well into the twentieth century, anthropologists have hotly contested incest taboo within the origin of totemism and exogamy without questioning its actual validity. Levi-Strauss and Fox debate on the place of incest taboo as a bridge between nature and culture. According to Levi-Strauss (1949) the incest taboo is part of nature because it is found in all cultures; but defined differently between cultures. Some define mating between cousins as incestuous; some do not. In essence, the definition of incest taboo is a definition of the margins and spaces within culture itself. Fox (1994, pp. 29–38) sees a continuity of evolution between nonhuman and human kinship, arguing that the rudiments of human kinship are found among nonhuman primates with its roots in matrilineal descent. Reed (1975, pp. 21–42) analysing the implication of matrilineal descent in relation to incest taboo arrives at the following conclusions: in premodern clan systems, the rule of avoidance was wider and involved the physical separation of the sexes. Adult men lived in their own quarters or houses separate from women and children who lived together in their own quarters. At puberty or earlier, young males were removed from the mothers' and sisters' residences to reside with their adult kinsmen. The term mother was not a family term but a functional clan term. Females of every age belonging to a male's own clan were tabooed. As I have mentioned, Lang and Atkinson (1903, p. 217) point out that that in some languages the term 'sister' is identical with taboo and 'not to be touched.' They regard the rule of avoidance as a primordial law dating back into prehistory and ordained a barrier between mother and son, brother and sister (ibid, p. 219). Toward the end of the nineteenth century, questions were raised about the harmfulness of inbreeding. Briffault (1931, pp. 204–40), for example, states that there is no fear of incest among animals and that inbreeding can actually enhance the value of animals such as prize breeding bulls matched with their daughter offspring.

Scientific knowledge about genetics barely grasped in our time could hardly have influenced premodern peoples. It has been argued that humans must have erected an instinctual barrier against incest, but if that were so, why would it be necessary to legislate against something that everyone passionately wishes to avoid? Psychologists have taken a diametrically different position: they proceed from the basis of natural attraction rather than instinctual aversion. Freud, for example, disclosed the widespread character of secret incestuous desires among members of the same family. Freud's error was to think that such desires had existed through all human existence. In Western societies, kinship stems from biological or genetic relationships founded on the individual family. Primitive kinship systems were not based on individual families but expressed a social relationship founded upon kin clan systems embracing the whole community. A sex prohibition that forbids members of the same totem from mating cannot be called an incest taboo. The terms sex taboo and incest taboo have been joined to create a serious misunderstanding. Morgan (1877) by discovering matrilineal clan forms, noted the classificatory system of kinship, whereby a child will refer to a number of women as mother and saw motherhood as a social function. Briffault (1931) underscores the importance of the social function attached to motherhood in matrilineal clan structures.

Turner and Maryanski (2005, p. 167) argue that the growth of complex emotions made potential inbreeding among more sexually aroused, frustrated, and passionate humans more likely amongst those who did not have powerful bioprogrammers for sexual avoidance, except for the mother-son and the activation of the Westermarck effect for siblings. If daughters stayed home after puberty instead of being transferred to another community as an essential part of exogamous practices, sexual attraction would become heightened and incest followed.

Evidence of incest taboo violation and harm in families

Turner and Maryanski (2005, pp. 178–184) stress that because incest in families is prohibited, it remains a hidden and secretive act, making it difficult to acquire reliable data. The rate of incest and the psychological effects are important to try to assess so that the tabooed act becomes more transparent. Same-sex incest occurs more frequently than commonly thought: mother-daughter incest is probably more common than mother-son and it is increasingly apparent that sexual abuse of males comes more from fathers than mothers. The incidence of mother-son and father-daughter incest stands in sharp contrast. The former is rare; the latter occurs with some frequencies in most societies. One reason given is that by the time boys mature, mothers have reduced fertility or have entered menopause. It makes little practical sense for a son to mate with his mother at the end of her breeding life whereas fathers have the chance for more offspring with a much younger female. Incidence of incest has increased since the eighteenth and nineteenth century industrial revolutions with the development of close, overcrowded, often isolating family units in towns, cities, and factories.

Personal pathologies of individual nuclear family members such as drug use, drinking, stress, and domestic violence increased with late industrialisation. Rising divorce rates after World War II further eroded the power of kinship norms to control sexual relations, increasing the presence of males in the household whether as stepfathers or lovers who were not biologically related to the children of the household. The result would lead to increased opportunity for sexual abuse of children, particularly when their presence is accompanied by family tension and personal pathologies. Under these conditions, the efficacy of incest avoidance is considerably weaker since the males are not biologically related to the children in their care.

In cases where the mechanisms of automatic avoidance or inhibition situated in the neocortex in hominoid evolution are weakest, the father is obviously exploitative and the mother is afraid to intervene. The majority of men have intact mechanisms for avoiding incest, but are more susceptible to sexual arousal and act out inappropriately due to alcoholism or when the mother is missing either through death, divorce, or separation from her children.

The data collected on the frequency of incest supports the evidence that sibling incest may occur as frequently as father-daughter incest. Turner and Maryanski (ibid, p. 180) doubt that it is more prevalent than stepfather-stepdaughter sexual relations. Both sibling and father-daughter incest is dramatically higher than mother dyads. Research indicates that mother-daughter incest exhibits more serious psychopathologies than daughters in father-daughter incest relationships, suggesting that the mother's violation of bonds of nurturance and trust cause severe emotional problems to both sexes. Mother-son incest is more harmful psychologically than father-daughter or sibling incest. A higher percentage of males suffer severe anxiety disorders and a significant number reveal borderline or psychosis. Virtually no daughters or sisters reveal psychotic symptoms, although they all reveal anxiety disorders and post-traumatic stress syndromes, but not as severe as mother-son. The reason for the difference is that mother-son incest crosses neurological wiring in the brain of the child, activating more intense and destructive emotions as well as defence mechanisms to control the emotional turmoil. Although father-daughter incest is not exposed to the same phylogenetic wiring, this type of incest still has extremely harmful cultural effects. Because a daughter is usually financially dependent on the father, episodes of father-daughter incest violate that bond of trust, upset the daughter's relationship with her mother and prohibit the daughter's bid for financial independence. It places her in sexual competition with her mother, which can cause considerable distress because of role reversal and generational boundaries become blurred.

Daughters suffering from incest develop a mild to severe neurosis, are often unhappy, anxious, depressed, develop problems establishing and maintaining a sexual relationship with their spouses, but rarely need hospitalisation. Father-daughter incest is likely to occur in families with a patriarchal structure and with high levels of wife dependency and passivity. The fathers exhibit an authoritarian personality structure, weak ego control, physical abuse of other family members, and alcoholism (Anderson and Shafer, 1979; Cohen, 1983). Mother-son incest places the son in direct competition with his father, putting the son under enormous guilt and anxiety in patrilineal societies where inheritance is passed through the father. It is also clear that brother-sister incest is a much more common occurrence than previously believed, even five times more frequent than stepfather-stepdaughter incest

(Green, 1984: Smith & Israel, 1987). Brother-sister incest tends to occur in disfunctional families that exhibit high levels of violence, drug and alcohol use, and intergenerational child abuse (Wiehe, 1997). Whatever the exact cause of sibling incest, the Westermarck prohibitive effect clearly is insufficient.

Feminist theorists have argued that the daughter-father, brother-sister incest reflects relations of patriarchy in the nuclear family consistent with the male right to dominate and own social relations, including sexual ones, in the family. Another point emphasised by feminists is that young daughters can be blamed for the incest, branded as little seductresses, and the mothers seen as enablers held partly responsible for the incest taboo violation. This is in a similar vein as Freud's emphasis of incest on the child's seductive drive toward the opposite-sex parent. A similar constellation of the right to dominate without redress is found among male teachers and Catholic priests in their sexual abuse of vulnerable children and teenagers in their care.

Conclusion

It is evident from the material in this chapter, that the origins of incest taboo are open to debate. I have argued that during Palaeolithic-Neolithic eras, no specific incest taboo existed and that sex avoidance was practiced associated with exogamy, food, and blood taboos. Incest taboo emerged with the development of the patrilineal nuclear family that eroded older patterns of sexual avoidance and required culturally based patterns to prevent incest. Turner and Maryanski (pp. 198–200) using Fox's (1994) main arguments similarly argue that incest taboo is an outcome of both biological and sociocultural pressures to safeguard intergenerational distance and allow new impulses for change to enter into family dynamics.

Father-daughter and brother-sister incest tend to reproduce the same familial gender role models based on mother-father interaction rather than open-ended, experiential, fresh generational ones. Incest taboo violation, often interpreted as the original sin, causes guilt-ridden feeling of sin in offspring that dampens and depresses their natural urge for independence and realise their ambition. The desire to outgrow and supersede their parents is interpreted as antagonistic and antilife, rather than as a natural urge to individuate and separate from parental authority. It can be argued that the focus on incest rather than the facilitation of dissent has been used as a social control mechanism to stifle ambition in offspring by blaming them for seduction.

Note

1. Eliade (1958, pp. 15–16) discusses how neophytes in rites of passage are not allowed to speak as if they are dead. I suggest that after the introduction of primogeniture, women in patrilineal, monotheistic cultures have become suspended in an eternal, liminal space, between the margins, without a voice, as if dead.

References

Adams, M.S. and Neel, J.V. (1967). Children of Incest. *Pediatrics* 40, 55–62.

Aeschylus (467 BCE) *Laius: Seven Against Thebes*. Loeb Classical Library. Harvard: Harvard University Press.

Anderson, L.M. and Shafer, G. (1979). The Character Disordered Family: A Community Treatment Model for Family Sexual Abuse. *American Journal of Orthopsychiatry* 49, 436–445.

Bachofen, J.J. (1871). *Myth, Religion and Mother Right*. Princeton: Princeton University Press.

Bowlby, J. (1973). *Attachment, Separation and Loss*. 3 vols. London: Pimlico, 1998.

Briffault, R. (1931). *The Mothers, The Matriarchal Theory of Social Origins*. New York: Macmillan.

Brodersen, E. (2016). *The Laws of Inheritance. A post-Jungian Study of Twins and the Relationship Between the First and the Other(s)*. London and New York: Routledge.

Butler, J. (1997). *The Psychic Life of Power. Theories of Subjection*. Stanford, California: Stanford University Press.

Butler, J. (1999). *Gender Trouble*. New York and London: Routledge.

Butler, J. (2000). *Antigone's Claim. Kinship Between Life and Death*. New York and Chichester, UK: Columbia University Press.

Butler, J. (2004). *Undoing Gender*. New York and London: Routledge.

Caldwell, L. (ed.) (2005). *Sex and Sexuality, Winnicottian Perspectives*. London and New York: Karnac.

Cater, N. (ed.) (2014). *Women's Voices*, Spring 91. New Orleans: Spring Journal.

Chapple, E.D. and Coon, C.S. (1942). *Principles of Anthropology*. New York: Holt.

Cohen, T. (1983). The Incestuous Family Revisited. *Social Casework* 64, 154–161.

Coontz, S. and Henderson, P. (1986). Property Forms, Political Power and Female Labour in the Origins of Class and State Societies. In Coontz, S. and Henderson, P. (eds.) *Women's Work, Men's Property, The Origins of Gender and Class*. London: Verso, pp. 108–155.

Coontz, S. and Henderson, P. (eds.) (1986). *Women's Work, Men's Property, The Origins of Gender and Class*. London: Verso.

Crawley, E. (1902). *The Mystic Rose* (2 vols. in 1). New York: Meridian, 1960.

Daly, M. (1973). *Beyond God the Father. Towards a Philosophy of Women's Liberation*. London: The Women's Press, 1995.

Daly, M. (1978). *Gyn/Ecology, The Metaethics of Radical Feminism*. Boston: Beacon Press.

Durkheim, E. (1915). The Elementary Forms of Religious Life. In (1979) Lessa, W.A. and Vogt, E.Z. (eds.) *Reader in Comparative Religion. An Anthropological Approach*, 4th ed. New York: Harper Collins, pp. 27–35.

Eliade, M. (1958). *Rites and Symbols of Initiation. The Mysteries of Birth and Rebirth*. Woodstock, CT: Spring Publications.

Engels, F. (1884). *The Origins of the Family, Property and the State*. London: Pathfinder, 1972.

Euripides (c. 411–409). *Laius*. Loeb Classical Library. Cambridge: Harvard University Press.

Fonagy, P. (2001). *Attachment Theory and Psychoanalysis*. London and New York: Karnac.

Fox, R. (1994). *The Challenge of Anthropology. Old Encounters and New Excursions*. New Brunswick, NJ and London: Transaction Publisher, 1995.

Freud, S. (1917). Mourning and Melancholia. In *Collected Works*, Vol. 11. *On Metapsychology*. Trans. Reddich, J. London and New York: Penguin, 2003.

Freud, S. (1923). The Ego and the Id. Sections, 1-5. In *Collected Works*, Vol. 11, *On Metapsychology*. Trans. Reddich, J. London and New York: Penguin, 2003.

Freud, S. (1938). Application. In *Moses and Monotheism (III)*. In *Collected Works*, Vol. 13. *The Origins of Religion*. London and New York: Penguin, 1985.

Girard, R. (2004). *Oedipus Unbound*. Stanford, California: Stanford University Press.

Goldenweiser, A. (1937). *Anthropology: An Introduction of Primitive Culture*. New York: Appleton-Century-Crofts.

Green, A.H. (1984). Child Abuse by Siblings. In *Child Abuse and Neglect* 8, 311–317.

Hamilton, E. (1940). *Mythology*. New York: New American Library, 1959.

Hillman, J. (1987). Oedipus Revisited. In Kerenyi, K. and Hillman, J. (eds.) *Oedipus Variations, Studies in Literature and Psychoanalysis*. Woodstock: Spring Publication, 1991.

Hobson J.A. and Ginsberg, M. (1931). *L.T. Hobhouse: His life and Work*. London: Allen & Unwin.

Hocart, A.M. (1933). *The Progress of Man: Short Survey of His Evolution. His Customs, and His works*. London: Methuen.

Jung, C.G. (1911–12/1952). Symbols of the Mother and of Rebirth. In *Collected Works*, Vol. 5, *Symbols of Transformation*, 2nd edn. London: Routledge and Kegan Paul, 1995.

Jung, C.G. (1912). The Theory of Psychoanalysis. In *Collected Works*, Vol. 4. *Freud and Psychoanalysis*, 2nd edn. London: Routledge and Kegan Paul, 1993.

Jung, C.G. (1933). King and Queen. In *Collected Works*, Vol. 16. *The Practice of Psychotherapy*, 2nd edn. London: Routledge and Kegan Paul, 1993.

Jung, C.G. (1945). Immersion in the Bath. In *Collected Works*, Vol. 16. The Practice of Psychotherapy, 2nd edn. London: Routledge and Kegan Paul, 1993.

Kerenyi, K. (1990). Oedipus: Two Essays. In Kerenyi, K. and Hillman, J. (eds.) *Oedipus Variations, Studies in Literature and Psychoanalysis*. Woodstock: Spring Publication, 1991.

Kerenyi, K. and Hillman, J. (1991). *Oedipus Variations, Studies in Literature and Psychoanalysis*. Woodstock: Spring Publication.

Lang, A. and Atkinson, J.J. (1903). *Social Origins: Primal Laws*. London and New York: Longmans, Green and Co.

Leach, E.R. (1964). Anthropological Aspects of Language: Animal Categories and Verbal Abuse. In Lenneberg, E.R. (ed.) *New Directions in the Study of Language* Cambridge Mass: The Massachusetts Institute of Technology.

Lenneberg, E.R. (ed.) (1964). *New Directions in the Study of Language* Cambridge Mass: The Massachusetts Institute of Technology.

Lessa, W.A., and Vogt, E.Z. (eds.) (1979). *Reader in Comparative Religion. An Anthropological Approach*, 4th edn. New York: Harper Collins.

Levi-Strauss, C. (1949). *The Elementary Structures of Kinship*. (revised edn.) Boston: Beacon Press, 1969.

Mann, D. (ed.) (2002). *Love and Hate, Psychoanalytical Perspectives*. Hove and New York: Routledge.

Morgan, L.H. (1877). *Ancient Society*. New Brunswick: Transaction Publisher.

Nye, A. (2004). *Feminism and Modern Philosophy*. London and New York: Routledge.

Parson, T. (1954). The Incest Taboo in Relation to Social Structure and the Socialisation of the Child. *British Journal of Sociology*, 5, 101–117.

Reed, E. (1975). *Women's Evolution. From Matriarchal Clan to Patriarchal Family*. New York and London: Pathfinder Press.

Seemanova, E. (1971). A Study of Children of Incestuous Mating. *Human Heredity* 21, 108–128.

Smith, H. and Israel, E. (1987). Sibling Incest: A Study of the Dynamics of 25 cases. *Child Abuse and Neglect* 1, 101–108.

Sophocles, (c. 441–420 BCE). *The Three Theban Plays, Antigone, Oedipus The King, Oedipus at Colonus*. London: Penguin Classics, 1984.

Turner, J. & Maryanski, A. (2005). *Incest, Origins of the Taboo*. Boulder and London: Paradigm Publishers.

Walker, B. (1983). *The Women's Encyclopaedia of Myths and Secrets*. San Francisco: Harper Collins.

Webster, H. (1973). *Taboo, A Sociological Study*. New York: Octagon Books.

Westermarck, E. (1891). *The History of Human Marriage*. London: Macmillan.

Wiehe, V. (1997). *Sibling Abuse; Hidden Physical, Emotional and Sexual Abuse*, 2nd edn. Thousand Oaks, CA: Sage.

Winnicott, D.W. (1965). *The Maturational Processes and the Facilitating Environment*. London: Karnac, 1990.

Chapter 6

Taboo and emotional ambivalence

Introduction

This chapter examines the correlation between taboo, the development of conscience, and emotional ambivalence. Freud (1912–13) suggests a link between emotional ambivalence and a taboo incest wish (Oedipus complex). In chapter 5, I argue that the Oedipus complex is not innate and developed with the introduction of patrilineal inheritance with the positioning of the father rationalised through the Genesis myth around 3000 BCE; the development of conscience, therefore, in the form of taboo must have happened earlier. Chapter 3 explores Douglas' seminal work on purity and danger (1966) with the positioning of taboo on the margins of the body, and Kristeva's later idea of abjection (1982) to examine tabooed subjectivity on the border between 'me' and 'not-me.' This chapter ties together the emotional components of taboo, how they develop into symptomatology, and is divided into two main aspects: the first questions Freud's overemphasis on incest wish as the basis for symptomatology, such as obsessive compulsions. I stress that the aetiology of such symptoms develop from the need to cross over margins into the freedom of the 'other,' a movement that is prohibited in totalitarian, monistic, hierarchal cultures that interpret the 'other' as risky and sinful. I use Reddish's (2014) new theory of conscience to further question Freud's positioning of a *patrilineal* totem in relation to taboo.

I examine authoritarian dynamics through the work of Stenner's (2005) comparative research methodology, social psychologist Stein (2017), psychoanalyst Miller (1987, 1998), and cultural theorist and psychoanalyst Luci's (2017) in-depth psychosocial perspectives on the relationship between terror, love, and brainwashing, as shown in authoritarian-totalist disorganised attachment mindsets. Using the clinical research, vignettes, and perceptions of Bisagni (2017), Costello (2006), Hillman (1967, 1977), Woodman (1982, 1985), and Ziegler (1983) amongst others, I compare Freudian psychoanalytic perspectives with Jungian archetypal positioning of taboo as *disallowed space* for independent thinking.

The second part of the chapter outlines the conflict between safety/obedience/good and freedom/disobedience/sinful that are played out at the orifices/margins of the body as *illegitimate tabooed subjectivity.* I explore this by using two clinical case studies from German clients (both sexes) from Catholic ethnic-German postwar immigrant backgrounds suffering from obsessive compulsions, such as excessive washing when inadvertently touching body discharges of others (including any leftovers such as food, clothes, tissues) and eating disorders, which relate to taboos on blood, food, and the movement toward independence.

Freud and emotional ambivalence

Freud (1912–13, pp. 124–131) examines taboo and emotional ambivalence using the works of Fraser (1912) and Wundt (1906), seeing it as the origins of conscience and obsessional neurosis. He surmises that taboo conscience is probably an earlier form of conscience whereby the phenomenon of conscience is processed through a taboo prohibition. After a taboo has been breached, a taboo sense of guilt develops as the next stage in the formation of conscience. Freud's (1912–13, pp. 131–139) explanation of the totemic patrilineal primal horde as a male grouping in which sexual rivalry is the main cause of the development of taboo and conscience, ignores the real physical hazards of group survival, fear of death through starvation and the nurturing properties of totemic, archaic, matrilineal relationship to the natural world of animals and vegetation as I explain in chapter 4. Reddish (2014) rightly asserts the benefit of working with patients with *petrified egos*, that is, being dominated by a taboo conscience trapped in an archaic superego structure. Based on annihilation anxiety stemming from early childhood trauma, these patients show extreme emotional ambivalence to life and are caught up in repetitious, compulsive rituals to rid them of the ever present and contagious tabooed tension.

Freud stresses that patients with obsessional neurosis show a strong desire to touch that is promptly met with an external prohibition against carrying out this kind of touching, which finds support in powerful internal forces. The patient looks upon touching as supreme enjoyment, but because s/he cannot perform it hates it as well. Some patients develop amnesia so that the source of the original taboo is disassociated. Freud suggests that 'the character of obsessional neurosis is a scrupulous conscientiousness which is a symptom reacting against the temptation lurking in their unconscious' (ibid, p. 125). The more acute the obsession—for example with dirt that expresses itself as washing compulsion, the inability to touch another person's hand, removing 'dirt' such as hair or a tissue belonging to another, or the inability to use of public toilets—the more acute the sense of guilt arising from the conflict. If wish impulses are repressed, their energetic charge changes into anxiety and equalised through symptom formation. The blocked, foreclosed, tabooed energy is unsayable and, therefore, unable to transform into more life enhancing energetic structures. Freud stresses that taboo is also an agent of social control as the superego that causes extreme anxiety and dread if it remains unquestioned.

Reddish (2014), however, asserts that the primary task of the infant and therefore the origin of morality and conscience is *safety*. Although Reddish adheres to the Oedipal superego mechanism, she places a primary, archaic stage of morality in the forefront, stating that the Oedipal superego only comes into being once the embryonic ego challenges the archaic superego. The archaic superego is the structure that enables this (ibid, p. 5). Reddish notices that a patient's description of themselves as *bad* originates only on one moral plane almost entirely by identifying with a controlling archaic superego that would be impossible to challenge because it would feel like killing themselves.

Reddish (2014, p. 67) takes the status of helplessness and dependency in babies that gives a sense of an annihilation anxiety with any deviation from this primary model of safety. Knowledge of the constant threat of starvation, disease, and violence is defended against by identification with the ever-safe/constant object and its attendant idealisation, giving rise to the first incarnation of an ego ideal. At this stage, the embryonic ego and the ego ideal are undifferentiated with a high degree of correspondence between reality-testing and anxiety mastering as archaic superego functions. The infant fully identifies with what is *safe*, and, therefore, *good*. However, this safe space is also both a rigid and a narrow mental space with little room for exploration, psychic growth, and development. Where taboo prohibitions dominate, Reddish suggests that curiosity and exploration are disallowed with the ego ideal withholding the permission to know and think for oneself.

A new type of anxiety, therefore, arises about a world beyond safety. This awareness engenders both anxiety *and* aggression, leading to fear of the unknown being tolerated with a decatharsis from the ego ideal and a decrease in pressure for the ego to attain the same status as its ideal. As absolute thinking dissolves, aspirations become a choice rather than a habitual compulsion. Through this process, the ego learns to regulate its own instincts. The archaic superego can still serve as a 'safe place' during times of stress, but the fact that the ego has challenged it and survived the confrontation, *strengthens* the ego with the knowledge that its destruction does not lead to annihilation.

To illustrate the power of the archaic super ego that has been insufficiently challenged, Reddish draws on the experience of working with clients whose early relationship did not provide sufficient safety and containment for annihilation anxiety if they moved forward into the freedom of making their own judgments. Most of her patients judged themselves as 'bad,' caught in a double bind of 'damned if I do and damned if I don't' (ibid, p. 78). Their petrified egos are holding on with a white-knuckled grip to the archaic super ego function as an unthinkable betrayal of the mother, irrespective of her actual attributes as mother. The need to live up to an unyielding, dominant, perfectionist, archaic super ego leaves her patients emotionally exhausted whereby their internal objects could only be managed but never satisfied. This very structure imprisons them because they perceive themselves as having damaging wishes rather than having been damaged. Above all, the need to separate and differentiate from the mother is considered taboo. Reddish's patients are caught in an archaic, rigid system of psychosocial beliefs that increasingly restrict their thinking and behaviour to maintain an unyielding but nevertheless safe presence.

Reddish (pp. 96–97) notes that the space between archaic and ego negotiated morality effects social attitude to independent thinking. She points out (p. 80) that the unthinkable betrayal could also refer to a race of people who have been ethnically cleansed. She suggests that any situation where individuals are caught up in the culture *of totemisation* lose touch with their humanity because they are not psychologically individuals with free will to think about and choose their responses. Rather, they are enthralled in a state of mind in which psychic independence is itself tabooed. She sees an important link between authoritarian dynamics and *totemisation* in religious dogma, cults, and political parties where racial or religious groups are massacred entirely on the basis of difference from an unquestioned norm.

Although I agree with many of Reddish's well-articulated thoughts on the archaic super ego structure, her handling of *totemisation* does not sufficiently take into account their subtlety and contribution to dialectical thinking, which I outline in chapter 4. My own clinical experience of working with female patients with obsessive compulsions and eating disorders shows that the original, independent, instinctual energy and vitality of the totem animal has been devalued and disassociated. Through working with dreams of depressed and anxious patients of both sexes, where strong totem animals suddenly appear in the form of tigresses, bears, lionesses, elephant matriarchs, and beavers, instinctual energy and vitality return as patients suddenly align themselves with a root instinct that had been disempowered through patrilineal inheritance (see Brodersen, 2016, pp. 175–187). One could argue that the archaic superego has become rigid over time because the original vital, independent energy invested in maternal warmth and nurture has become devalued. Through dream work, the vitality of certain totem animals and plants, such as trees, are resurrected and liberated.

Authoritarianism: taboo on dissent and independent thinking

Freud (1912–13) assumes that the desire for incest is the main taboo and uncovering the aetiology of distress leads inevitability to an incomplete resolution of the Oedipus wish. He does not interpret a child's love for the parent as a need to be held and supported in the need for containment and separation dynamics. The failure of the parent in either of these two functions leads to disillusionment and depression. Disappointment stems from not coming to terms with the guilt of an unfulfilled disappointed, incest wish, and is thus expelled through ritual cleansing. I suggest that for Freud, the impulse toward dissent and independent thinking is a blind spot in his view of psychosocial development: Freud himself had an authoritarian mindset in keeping with the central European climate of his time. Crews (2017, pp. 653–655) and Farrell (1998, pp. 231–232) comment on Freud's insistence of complete obedience amongst his psychoanalytical circle to *his* sexual interpretation of the aetiology of mental illness, bullying and ridiculing those who questioned his methods, stifling debate, scheming, and rewarding faithful adherers with gold rings as a symbol of their oath of unswerving allegiance to *his* dogma. The main instrument of Freud's terror tactics was a Stalinist type secret committee formed in 1912 until 1936 that authoritatively imposed censorship behind the scenes to attack, belittle, and blacklist gifted defectors, particularly Jung, Ferenczi, and Adler. This closed, punitive atmosphere is, according to Holt (1992, pp. 21–22), still duplicated at psychoanalytical training institutions with their supercilious, authoritarian infantilizing of training candidates and nonteaching members.

Political psychologist Stenner (2005, p. 239), through her extensive research into the authoritarian personality structure, outlines several main characteristics; the main aspect being that 'authoritarianism is a fundamental predisposition concerned with minimizing difference, and constraining the individual freedom that tends to surround and confront us with different people, beliefs and behaviours.' She contrasts libertarian with authoritarian mindsets and notes that when confronted by diversity, the former become excited and engaged, the latter become frightened and unhinged by differences (ibid, p. 217). Fear tends to diminish performance on a wide array of cognitive tasks, leading to a decrease in complex thinking, increased rigidity, and a premature closure to alternative solutions. The rigid mindset of *one true people* and *one right way* influences education. In authoritarian families, value is placed on traditional family values, such as obedience, hygiene, respect for parental authority, and adherence to collective rules, compared to libertarian families where value is placed on the importance of dissent, independent thinking, and an experiential exploration of new vistas when thinking about culture, race, and gender. We witnessed such traits in chapters 4 and 5.

Stenner maintains that disagreement, dissent, and disobedience, plus the determination of the common good by debate between competing world views, are anathema to the authoritarian-totalist mindset. Authoritarians are alarmed by the departure of moral and cultural absolutisms and seek an unquestioning allegiance and conformity to an external authority, as Adorno (1950) and Arendt (1958/1973) noted previously, which paves the way to the dangers and perfection of totalitarian logic. Arendt (ibid, p. 458) insists that totalitarianism does not exist simply as a lust for power but from an ideological drive to make the world consistent and safe (Rose, 2016, p. 213). As feminist cultural critic, Rose (ibid, p. 216) eloquently points out that the drive for totalist thinking effectively blocks out any space for reflection and creativity as compulsive thinking obliges one to falsify thoughts. Rose suggests that real mental freedom consists in the freedom to think nothing, or to think of a thousand different things at the same time. This is very different from the pressure to conform to the Order of the World as an unchangeable, static mindset mobilised to prohibit independent thought and the value of subjectivity in the service of social justice and change.

Psychoanalyst and cultural critic Miller (1987; 1998; 2006), in her extensive work on *poisonous pedagogy* still practiced worldwide in authoritarian, monistic cultures, notes the parallels between Freud's drive theory and the authoritarian mindset. Miller (1987, pp. 59–60) outlines the basic tenets of poisonous pedagogy from parenting manuals still in use: adults are the masters, not the servant of the dependent child, and determine in a godlike fashion what is right and wrong; the child is held responsible for his/her anger and parents must always be shielded from it by breaking the child's will as soon as possible so that no spontaneity exists. Other tenets include: obedience makes a child strong; a high degree of self-esteem is harmful; tenderness and responding to children's needs is risky; severity and coldness prepare a child for life's hardships; the body is something dirty and disgusting; strong feelings are harmful and parents are always right. Miller suggests (1998, pp. 212–213) that Freud's drive theory is an offspring of poisonous pedagogy because it entails a denial of the reality of parental sexual abuse and wide-spread paedophilia, an insensitivity to childhood suffering, a refusal to give credence to the patient's past and present grievances, and a misunderstanding and denial of the roots of neurosis that lie in the enforced repression—not of the child's instinctual drive—but of his/her awareness of having been traumatised through maltreatment and the prohibition (taboo) against articulating this. Cruelty on the part of the parent is interpreted as the product of the child's drive fantasies generated by the child's own aggressiveness and obstinacy. Religious dogma particularly endorses the notion of original sin and the need to break the will of children through abuse into an unquestioning obedience in order to cleanse them of dangerous impurities. Miller's views underscore my own clinical observations drawn from clients of German postwar Catholic backgrounds on the aetiology of symptoms stemming from *disorganised* attachment models, discussed in the second part of this chapter.

The anomalies of attachment theory; *disorganised* attachment in totalist thinking

Social psychologist, Stein (2017) in her study of attachment and its abuse in modern-day religious cults and totalist systems, endorses much of views expressed by Arendt, Rose, Stenner, Miller, and others. A survivor herself of a totalist cult, Stein brings insider knowledge to the present existing practices within these ideological systems that are based on the exploitation of the underlying attachment and safety needs of its members. Using research of Lorenz (1935) on the imprinting behaviour of geese and Harlow's discovery that baby monkeys clung to a comforting cloth even though no food was available, opened up thinking about child attachment that was more complex than the mother simply being the source of food. Attachment theorist and child psychiatrist Bowlby (1969) argues that the attachment theory is based on an independent instinct separate from the needs for food, shelter, or sex. Attachment to others serves as a protection, a safe haven; attachment behaviour is most evident under conditions of fear or signals indicating changes in the environment or in one's vulnerability to it (such as fatigue, illness, war) that requires increased vigilance (Stein, ibid, p. 29). Bowlby and child psychiatrists Winnicott (1965; 1971) and Stern (1984) see attachment as a homeostatic control system with proximity-seeking behaviour alternating with exploratory behaviours in a transitional and playful environment. Its effectiveness of providing a facilitating environment for containment and separation impulses, as in *secure* attachment, is impaired when caretakers cannot empathetically respond to these dual dynamics with the result that *preoccupied* or *dismissing* attachment behaviours develop. In *preoccupied* attachment, the child's exploratory behaviour is limited because of the uncertainty of a parent's positive response to freedom within a transitional space. In the *dismissing* attachment, children remain unattached, unable to depend upon or trust significant others. They tend to display aggressive traits such as bullying, when aroused, and are unable to seek comfort.

A fourth type of attachment dynamic, *disorganised* attachment, however, occurs when a child has been in a situation of *fright without solution*, where comfort and threat are presented by the same person as caretaker. Usually the child stays close to the frightening caretaker because there is no choice when, internally, both their withdrawal and approach systems are simultaneously activated and in conflict. Attachment *disorganisation* in infancy predicts a variety of outcomes: future controlling behaviour and dissociative symptoms when one is no longer able or allowed to think about what is felt or happened regarding the frightening relationship. Panic is followed by giving up independent thinking and emotional independence. Stein, similar in some aspects to Reddish's description of the archaic super-ego, maintains that a totalist ideology is based on a *disorganised* attachment that isolates, engulfs, and creates ongoing stress in order to keep their followers in a state of fright without an escape or a solution. It allows for no alternative views and, once accepted, provides a *cognitive* lock; the prohibition or taboo through isolation of alternative attachment models provides the *emotional* lock.

Stein sees an attachment status as malleable in that attachment experiences continue to adapt and can be manipulated in a negative way. For example, persons from reasonably secure and good-enough attachment structures may still become prey to a totalist system if they have moved and lost their previous attachment ties. Being away from home and having the need to belong to a group with a charismatic leader promising love, security and personal growth, may be enough to ignore the warning signs of an unquestioning obedience and loyalty attached to a totalist dogma. Stein points out (2017, p. 109) that totalist leaders manipulate their followers through a combination of terror and (apparent) love and are exploitatively dependent and power-oriented. Such persons are offspring of domineering fathers and punitive or passive mothers with an upbringing that involved threats, coercion, and the withdrawal of love as a mean to induce obedience. In this view, totalist leaders are anxious and insecure requiring constant reassurances, lacking flexibility in thinking, perceiving only their own perspectives and lacking in empathy. They offer their followers an emotional component as a collusive glue to offset their own fear of abandonment and choose scapegoats to punish and channel their rage.

Stein (2017, ibid, p. 111) stresses that such leaders with disorganised attachment are mirrored in the structure offered by totalist ideologies, that is, the dissociative barrier to critical thought that reflects their own internal chaos. Thinking is separated from feeling; totalist thinking disengages central route thinking and replaces it by peripheral modes of perception used to detract from focussed attention. Such distractions include fear arousal, rapid delivery through propaganda slogan, blanket statements, and collective overgeneralisations that seem sound but do not stand up to the scrutiny of a critical, fact-focussed analysis of any given situation. Stein (pp. 150–155) shows how the disassociation of right and left brain functioning, achieved by overarching abstract ideologies, lack any concrete substance, further mystifying and trampling upon central route thinking so that the creation of a segregated self sits on top of the real thinking self in a kind of *doubling* act. As an example, Stein quotes Arendt's (2003, p. 159) description of Adolf Eichmann's personality in his organisation of transporting and killing of Jews during the Third Reich as stemming from a *curious, quite authentic inability to think*.

A psychoanalyst and human rights expert, Luci (2017, p. 139) similarly observes that a performed pattern of knowledge exists within monolithic authoritarian social structures that practice torture, demand unquestioning obedience, organise and construct their thinking around a catastrophic threat, and offer an omnipotent power to protect against a dangerous and hidden enemy. Luci (ibid, p. 165) links state terror to deprivations in early childhood attachment that cause an inability to separate from the maternal object. The resulting fused self/object of the self gives rise to catastrophic annihilation anxieties. This nameless dread and terror closes *in-between, liminal spaces* among multiple positions and damages the reflective ability to hold in mind three poles: Me, You and Other (ibid, p. 161). Luci describes the massive use of states of *two-ness* as a result of the splintering of the *Reflective Triangle.* Once the self is deprived of the space to find meaning and forced to adhere to meanings provided by authority, reality can be manipulated at will through a massive denial and splitting. History is continually rewritten through a day-to-day falsification of the past based on *doublethinking,* similar in concept to Stein's *doubling act* mentioned above.

Clinical applications

Freud (1912–13, pp. 128–129) differentiates between taboo and obsessional neurosis: the punishment of the violation of the taboo threatens to fall upon those who have violated it. In the latter case, the punishment will fall on someone else, which accounts for the contagion in taboo violation and the nobility expressed by the obsessional neurotic who sacrifices his/her happiness for someone else: mother, father, etc. The original wish that the loved person may die is displaced by that very fear. However, I think that the sacrifice of happiness is a real punishment in itself whether it is clothed as altruism or not. In my clinical experience with patients with obsessive compulsions, severe obsessional neurosis, such as compulsive body washing (three hours a day) or an extreme avoidance of spittle, hair strands, or ear wax belonging to other persons, is not attached to an unfulfilled, forbidden incest wish of the child, but from a generalised, protectionist, societal taboo on disobedience, expressions of subjectivity, assertiveness, and the bid for autonomy and independent thinking freed up from parental control. The extent to which bodily fluids particularly belonging to others are repellent reveals the internal structural insecurity of risk and of assimilating and overstepping external margins into new experiences contained by the other as not-me (see chapter 3 on purity and danger). This repressive dynamic happens particularly in authoritarian, patrilineal, monotheistic cultures, with its concept of original sin tied to punishment and purification, where independent thinking is not encouraged nor are boundaries traversed outside their monotheistic gendered procreation dogmas, which remain static, tortuous, and overprotected. The appropriate rite of passage into separation and risk has become stuck in the border/margin between dependency and separation and projected out as untouchable, marginalised body defilements attached to others. Differentiating the emotion of anxiety and the intense dread imbued within the projected taboo, particularly through dream and art work helps to alleviate their severity.

Jungian perspectives

Freud's blind spot is not shared by Jung (1955a, para 237–242) who stresses the importance of the nutritive function in childhood to promote a sense of self. Similar to Bowlby, Winnicott, and Stern, Jung does not see the tension for food, shelter, and warmth, and its release through gratification, as a psychosexual process. Jung defines the drive toward independent thinking as primary, not secondary, and not a result of an incest wish disappointment (Jung, 1955b, paras. 265–266). Jung (1955c, 303–311) suggests that a retardation of psychic, energetic processes in children and adults lies in *parental complexes* that are transferred unconsciously to their offspring, causing dissociative states, blocked vitality, and stagnant growth. Working with unconscious intergenerational parental complexes, particularly disturbed attachment and the fear of abandonment, is crucial to gain sufficient contact at the archetypal core of the complex, parental and societal that is causing painful symptomatology in the present as *unfinished business*.

A Jungian analyst and child psychiatrist, Bisagni (2017) suggests that the obsessional use of overvalued ideas that prohibit mental freedom and constrain intersubjective space is presented in most cases of obsessional neurosis. Through his empathetic work with patients, Bisagni (ibid, pp. 67–121) outlines how moving patients from stereotypic thoughts and action toward experience of unsaturated archetypal patterns offers a vision of a reparative reconstruction of the psyche. For the mind to grow, a space in which it can be thought about is needed. This in-between space has been missing in the lives of his patients with authoritarian, disorganised, intergenerational, traumatised parental attachment dynamics. The closed, transitional space is clogged with *bad* smells, anal stench, and faeces (pp. 185–193) because no fresh outlet for inner impulses is allowed nor sufficiently regulated to partake in the outside world. The body becomes trapped and immobile within its own overloaded debris.

Abramowitz, Taylor, and McKay (2009) note that obsessive compulsions are generally symptomatically heterogeneous conditions and outline their five main dimensions: first, feeling responsibly for causing or failing to prevent harm leading to checking compulsions and reassurance seeking; second, symmetry obsessions, and ordering and counting rituals; third, contamination obsessions, and washing and cleaning rituals; fourth, repugnant obsessions concerning sex, violence or religion; and, fifth, hoarding, that is obsessions about acquiring and retaining objects. Compulsions are repetitive behaviours that the individual feels compelled to perform in response to an obsession, such as cleaning, continual handwashing, checking, ordering and arranging, hoarding, and asking for reassurance. They are aimed at preventing or reducing distress. The compulsion is not pleasurable (Veale and Roberts, 2014), which differentiates it from compulsive acts of immediate gratification, such as shopping and gambling. Compulsions seem to act as an immediate punishment for a wrongdoing, such as a thought or an intense fear of a sudden taboo emotion that erupts unexpectedly, needing an act of atonement and urgent purification.

Avoidance of situations is an integral part of obsessive compulsion when faced with events that trigger an emotional ambivalent involvement, particularly tabooed anger about personal attributes that have been wasted and projected onto their waste products, and those of others, particularly the elimination of faeces. Specific actions may include avoiding touching toilet seats, door handles, or taps used by other people, and hiding potentially harmful objects, such as knives. Avoidance is dynamically linked to phobias when the content of obsessive thoughts contains repressed aggressive impulses and their corresponding feared violent actions, which are displaced on to others as *their* excrement.

Jungian archetypal perspectives of Hillman (1977) and others such as Starr Costello (2006) and Ziegler (1983) give important in-depth analyses of the symptomatology of patients caught between developmental stages, unable to cross over. Hillman (1979) and von Franz (2000) personify this painful blockage as the *puer aeternus* archetype (the eternal child within the male adult). I use the archetypal perspective of the *puer* in my presentation of the first case study, as this perspective widens the case parameters by including the objective, archetypal patterns, as well as the personal aetiology. For the second case study involving anorexia nervosa, I refer mainly to Ziegler (1983) and Woodman (1982; 1985) using their in-depth analytical perceptions of the pressure to confirm within a rigid patrilineal ascetic perfectionism that has its archetypal root in the *puella* (the eternal child within the female adult).

Hillman (1967, pp. 7–8) correctly asserts the importance of archetypal factoring in understanding patient aetiologies in analytical practice. He suggests that nothing is revealed through reading about current events in newspapers unless the essence can be grasped from within through an archetypal pattern. The archetype provides the basis of uniting the *incommensurables* and are organised to disclose essential psychological meanings. Hillman (p. 7) remarks that:

> The archetypal orderings of historical facts are the eternally recurring mythemes of history and of our individual souls. Through these meanings history affects our psyche, while at the same time, history is the stage on which we enact the mythemes of our soul.

An archetypal understanding of events helps cure the compulsive fascination with one's case history by presenting it through the dimensions of a wider and deeper myth that transcends definitions of finite/profane time. Memory returns to its reminiscence of primordial creation by uncovering patterns in the entwined ancestral roots that regenerate history, in an act of a cleansing and baptising ritual.

Case Study 1

The patient whom I will call Alfred[1] aged 62, started analysis because of symptoms of tiredness, compulsive washing, extreme fear of contact with bodily fluids from others, plus the inability to sustain interest in work or hobbies. He has been unemployed since 2005. Alfred takes medication and has psychiatric support on a monthly basis to discuss his physical health, blood pressure, and the effectiveness of his antipsychotic medication. He has undergone behavioural therapies, including hypnosis, but none have rid him of his intense dread and disgust when in contact with bodily fluids of others, which results in compulsive washing and avoidance of anxiety arousal.

Establishing timelines about biographical details was initially difficult because Alfred could not remember dates and was fuzzy on detail. Dream work has improved his concentration because his dissociated unconscious emotions with past events have become more integrated. On the onset of therapy, I found Alfred well read, lively, and intelligent, highly interested in politics, religion, and in world affairs. In appearance, he is of middle stature, with a rotund figure and balding grey hair. He normally wears T-shirts, jeans, and a straw hat in summer, carrying a rucksack. Alfred has a pleasant, direct, and open countenance and describes himself as sunny beach-boy who has never grown up. At first, although Alfred's mind was quick, his thought processes were very rigid, as he was overly concerned about processing information in the *right* way. He had a great fear of making mistakes. As my German is fluent but not perfect, he started correcting it; we discussed his need for perfection, correctness and getting it *right*. I noticed that just by opening the space to discuss perfectionism had the almost immediate effect of calming this trait within the analysis.

Alfred is the third child born in 1955 with two older siblings, a brother and a sister. His father was a German refugee from Silesia, his mother a German refugee from Sudetenland. They both arrived in Germany carrying one suitcase each. Historian Naimark (2001, pp. 108–138) describes in graphic detail the brutal treatment ethnic Germans in Poland and Czechoslovakia suffered after 1945. Branded as traitors in both countries, blamed and scapegoated for Nazi atrocities, the majority of ethnic German families were forced to leave their employment, land, and property behind, often given as little as 15 minutes to pack the possessions they could carry by hand. German women and young girls were brutally raped, gang-raped, and considerable numbers of both sexes committed suicide by wrist slitting. Families committed wholesale suicide under the prospect of a future with no hope.

Alfred's parents met in Hessen, 1947, in the American occupation zone and married in 1949. Their first home was a one-bedroom flat where they raised three children in quick succession. Alfred was raised as a Roman Catholic with a great fear of disobedience and original sin. The parents grew up during the Second World War under Nazi propaganda, which banned independent thinking as treason. The father was authoritarian and treated Alfred, the youngest child, with scorn and brutality. Around the age of four, Alfred developed problems with toilet training, manipulating, and letting go of his faeces when he left small lumps on the living room carpet. Alfred said he enjoyed retaining his faeces, building up the pressure, and then releasing them in small lumps. He said it satisfied a feeling of rebellion that he could not openly express. He was openly bullied by his older brother and not protected from it by other family members. He remembers not wanting to touch the toilet chain handle when he went to the toilet for fear of contamination but he could pull the chain to flush waste away.

Alfred's mother seems to have been caring toward her children in a passive, dutiful way. She feared physical contact with poorer neighbours whom she described as *dirty* and was overly submissive to her husband. She warned her children about using public toilets and of mixing with people of lower social standing. She was overly protective and intrusive toward Alfred, washing his private parts until he was at least 11 and did not encourage his independence.

Alfred's mother confided in him when he was six years of age that she had not wanted a third child, because she disliked sex with Alfred's father, but was pleased when he was born. His father did want a third child, but Alfred disappointed him and his father rejected him around the age of seven because he could not concentrate on his school work and was hyperactive. At first, his father did all the school homework himself without showing Alfred how to do it himself; then he suddenly stopped. Alfred felt both emotionally and intellectually abandoned by his father. Alfred's mother was unable to help him with his school work past the 5th grade. She warned him that a black man would take him away if he asked too many questions. His mother reported Alfred's misdemeanours to his father who exercised brutal corporeal punishment. Alfred felt betrayed by his mother but could not speak out as she was his only tie to security and some form of nurturance. This is an example of Stein's *fright without solution*.

Alfred was not encouraged to become independent, perform jobs around the house, or make his own bed. Homework was difficult, as the only table was in the living room where the mother had the television on during the day. Any venture outside the home environment was considered risky and better not attempted. His mother did not work outside the home; she accompanied Alfred to school until he was nine, fearing that something would happen to Alfred and she would be left alone. As a child, his mother had long periods in hospital without visits from her family. His parents divorced when Alfred was 17. He has affectionate memories of his extended family, grandmother, aunts, and uncles where he spent summer holidays at his grandmother's home. All his extended family suffered in varying degrees from washing compulsions and idiosyncratic intrusive habits such as spying on each other through key holes, particularly bathroom keyholes. He described his family members as passive but critical, often self-righteous onlookers. They watched each other and the lives of other's without being genuinely constructive, active, or adventurous themselves. I would say this depiction accurately describes Alfred's own partial personality in his critique of others.

Alfred's parental marital relationship was not a positive one. The mother had planned to marry someone else, but the grandmother forbade it because he had contracted TB and she was afraid that the illness could be inherited.

The father was a disappointment to Alfred's mother as he was not her original choice and had not earned sufficient money to buy a house. Buying a house was particularly important to Alfred's mother and grandmother because they had lost their home, their property, and their original status as German immigrants. Alfred's parents, particularly the mother, had great hopes for all their children but could not help them achieve them beyond the level they had reached themselves. Alfred's older brother did not take *Abitur*[2] and entered the same office job as his father; the sister did take Abitur and studied law for a year then stopped because of anxiety attacks. His older brother left home in his twenties, married, and has four children. His sister left home at 40 with difficulty and now lives with a boyfriend. She has no children. Alfred left home at the age of 50 with the help of hospitalisation for his compulsions. He stated that he wanted to leave home in his twenties but his mother did not actively encourage him. Alfred has sporadic contact with his sister but no contact with his brother whom he does not trust. He finds him unreliable and untruthful. His father died 1995. Alfred did not attend the funeral because of his washing compulsions. His mother died in 2005. Since then, Alfred lives in a small room in social care housing.

Alfred was bullied at school. When he told his mother that he wanted to take up judo to defend himself, his mother would not allow it saying that it would be too dangerous. At the age of 14, a school boy spat on his shoes and trousers while they were playing soccer. Although his mother washed his shoes and trousers he was unable to touch or wear them again. The shoes, in particular, stood in the corner of his room as tabooed items. Alfred gradually developed an intense dread of any bodily fluids or left-overs belonging to others. If a tissue on the street became attached to his shoe, he was unable to remove the tissue or touch the shoe when he came home. He is unable to use the small public toilet at his lodgings because he is afraid of coming into contact with housemates' sticky bodily fluids from picked noses or smeared ear wax, which would stick to the toilet roll, toilet wall, or the toilet seat.

Although Alfred passed Abitur at age 22, he could not settle on a study course. His mother was keen for him to study medicine, but he developed severe washing compulsions when he began his studies and had to discontinue. He felt he would not succeed and his mother was over ambitious. However, the clerical jobs he undertook left him bored and aggressive with his co-workers. Alfred experienced debilitating attacks of washing compulsions at the workplace after a few months' duration. He developed phobias about touching the fax machine, the toilet seat, or the work telephone if they had been used by his boss or a co-worker who picked his/her nose in public and used saliva to seal down envelopes. Anything that was touched by these persons were instantly taboo. He imagined his boss' nasal discharge was glued to any office equipment and this thought fuelled his symptoms. Alfred is intelligent and now realises that his boredom and frustration at work resulted in an unbearable fear of any contact with sticky bodily fluids at the workplace. He felt trapped and glued; the nasal pickings of his boss absorbed his anger and frustration; he admitted he wanted to be boss himself; his body washing relieved him of the unbearable tension and contamination from such ambitious thoughts that he rejected as belonging to himself and displaced them onto his boss' gluey nasal discharge as *bad* thoughts that had *crossed over.*

Alfred considers himself as a carefree child who never grew up. He enjoys having no job or responsibilities, pursues his dream of becoming an artist, never wanting to marry or have children. He said that he did not want to put his children through the type of childhood he experienced as if it would be repeated and unopen to change. Alfred is still looking for a rich young woman who could cater for his needs just as his mother had done, only with better financial resources than his father. She has to look a certain type: young, slim, and attractive. He hardly ever reflects on his own appearance unless I ask him what he could realistically bring into the relationship in terms of getting a job or providing some active contribution to lifestyle situations. The woman would take care of him and pay for everything as his due.

This description of Alfred fits with von Franz's (2000) description of the *puer aeternus,* in his attachment to women as mother replacement, his grandiosity, the inability to work, his artistic temperament, and evasion of responsibility. The original *puer aeternus* is the child-god of antiquity, the divine youth, god of vegetation and resurrection (von Franz, ibid, p. 7). Von Franz sees the main problem of this type as too greatly dependent on the mother, as the only beloved object. However, I see Alfred's main problem as fear of paternal abuse, which left him stranded with his mother. His father's ridicule and demand for strict obedience left Alfred without a father who would support him during the painful rites of separation from mother at puberty as practiced by indigenous peoples that I elucidate in chapter 7. Alfred has remained in a liminal state between boyhood and adulthood, neither a child nor an adult.

Course of therapy

We have discovered a mutual interest in history, psychology, the origins of religion, art, and the aetiology of his symptoms. Since our first meeting, we meet on a weekly basis for two hours where Alfred brings his dreams and his artwork. He understood fairly quickly that behind his symptoms were difficult tabooed emotions that needed proper acceptance and airing. I encourage Alfred to read psychology and he finds the work of Verena Kast (2003) on anxiety and parental relationship, plus Alice Miller (1980; 1981) on totalitarian upbringing and pedagogy, particularly helpful. Alfred is intelligent and competitive, but finds it difficult to translate his gained knowledge about his symptoms into practice. He still prefers not to take risks toward more independence. He has, however, been able to fit his symptoms into a wider historical archetypal framework, which has helped him gain distance and reduce his compulsions.

Alfred's washing compulsion has now abated to normal proportions of short twice a day washing periods (morning and evening) apart from taking showers twice a week. He understands that his earlier washing compulsions were caused by certain taboo emotions that swelled up that he needed to wash off quickly in a ritual of cleansing and purification. Since we now discuss all his subjectivity: rage, anger, loss, jealousy, and particularly the strong ambivalent feelings toward his very restrictive, anxious mother and the hatred toward his father's beatings and neglect, his washing compulsions have dramatically receded. He is now able to keep his room cleaner and sort out his clothes. However, Alfred is still unable to use the toilet at lodgings. Instead he goes to the toilet in his room wrapping up his faeces in plastic bags and disposing of them in the communal dustbin. He rationalises his disposal methods by comparing them to those of astronauts and mountaineers who wrapped their faeces and take them with them. We have discussed various ways of him being able to let go into the toilet, which would be far less strenuous. Although Alfred is now able to use the toilet in my praxis and at the public library, he cannot yet use the small communal toilets where he lives.

We discuss 'letting go' and he finds that very difficult, particularly in confined spaces where he feels a life-threatening danger of suffocation and being stuck with gluey discharges belonging to others. We examine his father's discharges of anger and the fear of catching them and sticking to him like glue as his, and how that has affected his washing compulsions.

Obstacles remain as well with finding work. Alfred states that being around people, for example, working as a waiter would be problematic, as he cannot touch food leftovers. Alfred has a lively personality and we discussed him working as a gardener or walking dogs, but these idea have not really taken root as he finds staying bed in his room still easier. As a child, he was put to bed for *bad* behaviour where he sometimes stayed all day. It is his safe haven, which still acts as his prison particularly when he is faced with the freedom of working through the restrictions of his symptoms that have kept him safe, childlike, and dependent.

We have discussed the too close emotional and physical contact with his family members as a child due to cramped poor living conditions. As the youngest child and 'baby' of the family, he slept between his parents in their bed until the age of five, which he loved. There was very little transitional space to develop independence as this space was blocked by Alfred's parents' own unconscious need for a family scapegoat who could carry the weight of their own traumas. Through his washing compulsions, Alfred has effectively sacrificed his life so that his mother would be safe and cleansed from the atrocities that she had witnessed growing up during the Third Reich, and later being shunned as an emigrant in postwar Germany.

Dream work

At the beginning of therapy, dream work involved the appearance of various animals such as tigers, lions, and sharks that embodied his tabooed instincts, vitality and aggression. Rats[3] featured, for example, in one dream where he discovers his mother in the bathroom being watched by her own mother through the bathroom keyhole. His mother goes to the toilet and produces a rat as faeces. Alfred associates the rat with betrayal and that his mother used to 'rat' on him to his father when he came home from work. His mother received the same treatment from her own mother and lack of privacy as a form of intergenerational child abuse in the form of verbal abuse and beatings. He admits he likes watching people as well. As a teenager, he used binoculars to spy on an attractive woman neighbour through the window into the apartment opposite from theirs. He enjoyed the secret voyeurism.

In another dream, Alfred finds a way into an apartment next door, which is forbidden by his sister, but that he accesses anyway by climbing through a hole under a wardrobe to reach the other apartment. Once there, he opens another wardrobe to find a child inside and three or four women trapped as sex slaves. Alfred remembers that he was never told what was going on in his family; information was kept from him. It was as if his energy was trapped in the unconscious in the 'other' flat. We talked about the reality of sex trafficking and how women are kept prisoner without human rights. Alfred could relate to the sadomasochistic fantasies involved in imprisonment as a punishment for rebellious thoughts, translated as sexual.

One final dream shows Alfred with his social worker trying to cross a street to the other side. He cannot manage to cross because there are too many stationary cars blocking the way. He sees a blue Ferrari, which belongs to him, but the social worker turns it upside down so it blocks the passage to the other side even more. Alfred admits to grandiose wishes (blue Ferrari), but prefers not to have some dreams turned upside down. He would like to afford pleasures that cost money, but he does not want to work to pay for them. We discuss how Alfred could move past all the cars that are standing stationary by looking at part-time job possibilities, but none are 'good enough' for him to contemplate. The blockage reminds him of his childhood: he had so many dreams, mainly those of his mother, but no-one helped him in the task of crossing the street to the other side, so he has remained stuck and unable to cross over.

Therapeutic Reflections

Reading Freud's useful work on the connection between taboo and obsessive compulsions, as well as Bisagni's (2017) research on blocked developmental processes, I note that a repressed, tabooed sexual fantasy of wanting to sleep with his mother is not the case. Alfred had a normal sexual relationship with a woman in his early twenties, but they argued and the relationship ended. She went to university to study law and left him behind. He expects women to serve his needs as his mother had, but gender roles have moved on.

I would suggest that Alfred's main developmental problem was/is entering the rites of passage that facilitate independence because they were severely blocked. The idea of separating from his mother felt like a real—instead of symbolic—death because there was no help from the other side in traversing the borders between safety and risk to develop an independent life. His considerable energy and intelligence felt like a sin and a betrayal. Energy became trapped and is still symbolised in his wrapped up faeces whereby he carefully controls their expulsion.

Douglas' 1966 research (see chapter 3) examines how bodily fluids emanating from the margins constellate anxiety because they have traversed the margins between 'me' as no 'longer me.' In Alfred's case, his fixation with bodily fluids emanating from orifices/margins as taboo that need purification and cleansing reveals his fear of contagion about moving beyond the safe authoritarian dogma of Catholicism and German collective asceticism about purity and sameness into a different mindset that incorporates subjectivity and dissent as the other (not me) as acceptable. Alfred's fragile sense of self is compounded by both his parents' refugee status after the Second World War in 1947 when they arrived as unwelcomed, second-class ethnic German citizens who were expelled from their homes and livelihood. These migratory border-crossings may have intensified Alfred's washing compulsion and the handling and letting go of his waste as his discharge in a collective space, as there is no inner safe container.

Stein (2017) and Luci's (2017) pertinent work on the abuse of human rights shows how totalitarian or totalist thinking, for example, during the Third Reich, blocks the ability to reflect and think independently. Total ideology disengages central route thinking in favour of peripheral processing. Undoing this intergenerational mindset takes time. During therapy, Alfred learns to reflect rather than make blanket statements. He used to blame the Americans for every negative international event, but now takes time to reflect on such easy black and white polarisations of good and evil. This has reduced the anxiety and terror about the right or wrongness of his statements and has led to a reduction of his symptoms. It may take a while longer for Alfred to realise that he is caught in an outdated time warp of ideas about purity.

Puer elements in the transference-countertransference dynamics

There has been considerable improvement in Alfred's outward appearance, his general agency, and self-cohesion. The transference-countertransference relational dynamics offer Alfred a much needed transitional space to work with his blocked energy within a different type of developmental maternal container than he experienced as a child. As I come from a working-class, Protestant, nonconformist background, with a different conscious and unconscious relationship to independent thinking and the value of work, the differences within our two cultural complexes has helped Alfred to work more constructively and relationally with his fear of the foreign 'other' (me/not me), which he has projected out as 'shadow' tabooed filth emanating from the orifices of 'others.' This fear of the unknown is gradually abating along with his symptoms. The governing idea that he will be *saved* simply by being childlike, innocent, and obedient is in line with Catholicism and authoritarian dogma; of not having to work as a result, apart from tragically sacrificing his life for his mother, is becoming more apparent and open to discussion. Behind his sacrifice, Alfred admits that he dislikes responsibility and wants to be free from it. His compulsions give him the opportunity to avoid people he dislikes or work in jobs that he feels are beneath him. But they also reveal how intolerant, perfectionist, and indifferent he is to the real suffering of others, in line with his totalitarian family background. Alfred keeps himself free from all forms of contamination emanating from the orifices of others, and in doing so, reveals that he has not yet crossed over his own intrapsychic borders into the humanity of others. The border still remains a *risky* unknown domain that collects and stores the wasted properties of others as symbolic filth.

Alfred's father was too brutal to inspire sufficient trust in positive animus qualities, such as realising ambition, passing exams, and moving into the future. The necessary, painful initiatory separation from his mother during puberty and later in life was not accomplished because Alfred had no outside support, except for the help and support of a male psychiatrist in a psychiatric clinic at the age of 50 when he could finally leave home. As Oliver (2002, p. 57) elucidates, lack of social support from peers or family members leads to feelings of exhaustion and alienation caused by the inability to find the social space to express one's own body and meaning. Alfred is, however, developing a *peur-senex* consciousness as elucidated by Hillman (ibid, pp. 30–31). His father's inflexible, authoritarian mindset is reflected now in Alfred's own static lifestyle. He reflects that he has become an old man (his father) straight from childhood without experiencing life in between. As a child, Alfred took on the burden of his family history, unconsciously pressed and glued upon him by *carrying the pack of history on his back* (p. 10). Thus, one could argue that Arthur began as a *puer senilis,* both older than his age and struggling heroically to retrieve his youth as it recedes before him.

Case Study 2

This case study involves a German woman called Laura, aged 54, born into an authoritarian, Roman Catholic household consisting of a maternal grandmother, parents, and younger brother; the father came from Silesia, as a postwar youth carrying all his valuables in one suitcase, looking after his mother and younger siblings on the journey into postwar Germany. His father had been killed during the war. As first-born daughter, Laura grew up with high expectations of both parents to be successful and socially adapted. She has a younger brother who committed suicide in his early twenties because his artistic abilities were not accepted as viable marketable gender traits. At school, Laura performed well and studied politics and philosophy at University. She achieved separation by moving out of the parental home into a flat with a boyfriend before Abitur, so she could study in peace. After university, she became a journalist, political editor, and radio commentator with a successful career as moderator.

She came to analysis because she felt that no one saw her at work. When she passed in the corridor, her colleagues used to avert their gaze as if she did not exist. Laura felt that she had disappeared. Now in her early fifties, she was concerned that she would be passed over for younger women in her job. Much of her conversation centred on her job performance, her intense irritation and disdain of her colleagues, and her immediate boss.

When Laura came to analysis initially, she was, indeed, in the process of disappearing. She was small in stature, with dyed dark hair, a sweet made-up face, and skeleton thin as if she were wasting away. Her clothes and make-up, however, were colourful and stylish as if to ward off the impression that she was dying inside. We discussed her skeletonlike form, which really concerned me. I could understand why her colleagues would look the other way when she passed in the corridor. Her extreme thinness showed an intense misery that contradicted her brave, colourful appearance. She told me that she has undergone abdominal operations that left her stomach unnaturally bloated when she ate food. She had also undergone treatment for a thyroid imbalance. She said she had always been very thin with little time to waste on food and disliked eating. She recounted as a child she was forced-fed butter milk by her mother every morning and vomited afterward because she could not bear the taste. The idea of eating certain foods, particularly buttery products, still makes her feel nauseous. Laura's revulsion to food resonates with Kristeva's theory of *abjection* discussed in chapter 3.

The *abject* represents the hidden, tabooed, unacknowledged, and feared parts of self-identity against which normalcy is defined. Bodily fluids and emissions from the pores and orifices, such as milk and blood, signify the abject without boundaries that threaten the illusion of the contained, rational subject and threatens stability and social unity. Gross (1990, pp. 80–103) argues that the female form with its creases and curves, seepages and secretions, as well as its changing boundaries during pregnancy and menopause, signifies association with the animal world of birth and mortality in contrast with the clean, contained, proper body, unspoiled by fecundity. The female body is not intrinsically abject or polluted, but it has been positioned as such by patrilineal ascetics with its inherent connotation of deviance and danger.

Laura related her unremitting social life with numerous friends that she squeezed in with her demanding full-time job. She goes regularly to the gym and wonders why the instructor does not see or applaud her ascetic shape. He avoids eye contact. She admitted that her hectic life style left little room for reflection or to examine the reason why she felt she was disappearing. She travels internationally for her job as journalist and enjoys analysing other cultures with blanket statements, but carefully avoids criticism of her own German cultural history, as if it had been placed in a tabooed locked cupboard. Although Laura is well-educated and well-read, she is also authoritarian and likes to dominate conversation with her world views. She was surprised and threatened when I contributed a different viewpoint. I stressed that I was merely opening up the topic for discussion, not trying to force her to accept my viewpoint. She realised that her rigid thinking stemmed from her authoritarian upbringing based on *only one right answer is allowed.* Laura subsequently liked the idea of our work together as offering a third liminal, in between space, neither right nor wrong.

We carefully looked at her family background where an in between creative space had been missing or flattened out (Oliver, 2002, p. 63). She related how passively her mother and grandmother subjugated themselves under the authority of her father without a fight. She had learned to copy her father's authoritarian manner rather than transform and outgrow it. She realised that her authoritarian manner and impatience sabotaged her effectiveness at the workplace, deadening creative interaction and making her co-workers want her to disappear. Laura related how her father carefully cut her hair uniformly in a basin form and generally interfered with her appearance as a young girl. Corporeal punishment was meted out for poor grades at school, so Laura avoided that physical abuse through hard work and study.

Laura's father was pleased with her ascetic boy-like appearance, diligence, and intelligence which, she said, made her mother jealous. She, in turn, became her father's favourite offspring basking in his preference for her above everyone else in the family. Her mother preferred her brother who was less ambitious and whom she protected from the father's scorn and the corporeal punishment of his sensitive, artistic nature. Laura felt that she had filled the place of the first-born son as her brother was unable to realise their father's ambition for a clever, hard, dynamic person, unburdened from caring for weaker, unworthy 'others.' She admits to feeling intense guilt and remorse that she colluded in her father's ridicule and punishment of her brother. Her brother committed suicide by cutting his wrists and bleeding to death in his artist studio. He had succumbed to the tragic consequences of *fright without solution,* as portrayed by Stein mentioned earlier in this chapter. He may have also acted out the suicidal aspects of his father's trauma when his family was evicted and hounded from their home in Silesia after the Second World War. No family member discussed Germany's Nazi past; it was a taboo subject described so well by Miller (1998, pp. 173–184) in her discussion of nonsexual taboos among German patients. Miller notes that German psychoanalysts are reluctant to breach that taboo and that her comments are usually met with a collective stony silence.

Suicides by wrist cutting were numerous on the road to Germany for expelled ethnic Germans as well as wholescale family suicides (Naimark, 2001). Laura says that with her brother's death, an important part of her also died, namely, an active compassion for others. She wanted to resurrect that dead, sensitive, creative, relational part of herself so she could begin to *live* again. Pictures of Laura and her brother as teenagers show them both to fit into the German collective ascetic images of fair hair, slimness, regular facial features, and modest dress.

Laura decided early not to have to have children. Her menstrual cycle was so infrequent that she did not notice when she entered menopause. Laura's mother is still alive, living a small village community. Her father died five years ago from a heart attack. When Laura visits her mother, now in her mid-eighties, she makes sure that she wears non colourful clothes so as not to embarrass her mother before her friends. By developing her intellect, Laura could not fit in with her mother's passive, nonquestioning feminine identification; nor did she wish to.

Course of therapy

Laura's life has been so dominated by fixed ideas of asceticism and perfectionism that she is oblivious to how little she eats and how thin she looks: her leg and arms are like sticks poking out from under her clothes. When Laura began therapy, she said that she was hopeless at drawing; that had been her brother's creative talent. I encouraged her to draw freely without wondering whether it was *good* art to be rewarded with a good grade. During the course of analysis, through dream work, Laura contacted her disassociated instinctual animal nature in form of large elephants appearing in dreams walking slowly down one side of busy streets, and of rats that appeared, previously hidden under her floorboards. Laura's hectic life rhythm slowed down as she felt the betrayals she had hidden in the unconscious. She rekindled her love of music and has joined a group of musicians who offer music therapy to deprived children in hospices. To compensate for the conscious derision she felt toward her fellow workers, Laura dreamed that she helped colleagues find keys to their lockers and find their missing cutlery at the canteen. As she uncovered those missing aspects of herself she had locked away, her appetite improved. After several months, she dreamt that she placed a bigger reading lamp on her desk at work, as if she had gained more relational insight into the negative emotions she projected on to others and began expanding her competencies in a natural rather than in a purely competitive way. Laura now feels more seen and liked at work and has less fear of disappearing. She has rekindled a former sexual relationship.

Roots of asceticism and taboo on food

Jungian analysts Ziegler (1983, pp. 91–100) and Woodman (1982, pp. 47–57) have studied the root cause of anorexia nervosa, found in the ascetic instinct, the addiction to perfection, and the *taboo on food*. Ziegler points out that the image of the feminine has changed over time. The term *ascetic* originally meant *exercise*, the preparation by moderation in lifestyle and physical training of Greek athletics for competition. With the onset of civilisation patrilineal inheritance c. 3000 BCE, a person's sense of self became increasingly discordant. The body as animal nature became an object of disgust. Freeing oneself from its 'prison of slime or mud' was regarded as the highest virtue. This attitude was adapted by several schools of philosophy, the Pythagoreans, the Stoics, and Cynics, and permeated the history of Christian Europe. This was in sharp contrast to the shape of the original mother image during Palaeolithic-Neolithic times, unsurpassed in weight and corpulence, signifying fecundity and unashamed sexuality (Gimbutas, 1989; Neumann, 1955). All of these manifestations of unbridled female biological instincts, such as breastfeeding and childbirth, incorporated in these Neolithic feminine cult figures became objects of taboo and their potency vanished with the spread of an ascetic body image: hairless, flat chested, flat bellied, and hipless, like Laura's.

Ziegler (ibid, p. 95) comments that the drive for activity is strong in anorexics: they avoid laziness, not primarily to lose weight, but to avoid the gravity of all earthly biological drives, such as childbirth, and the physical suffering that it involves. Their avoidance of food belongs to a societal unresolved tension between instinct and asceticism, still prevalent in postwar Germany where surprisingly strong unchanged collective gender norms govern and prevail, perpetuated through the present German educational system (Brodersen, 2016, pp. 148–155).

Under National Socialism, German women served solely the will of the nation (see Haste, 2001, pp. 73–99 on the description of the ideal Nazi woman). Himmler enlarged on the ideal Nazi total woman: she is a slender, beloved child to be scolded and punished when foolish, but also protected and cherished because of her frailty and weakness. Her obedient tenderness and pure, childlike sanctity gives a man his strength to endure hardship. Emancipated, intellectual women were seen as agents of degeneracy, a tool of Bolshevik-Jewish conspiracy, luring women in rational thinking, unrestrained individualism, and an unhealthy preoccupation with sex. We saw in chapter 4 on taboo and kinship structures that a difference or deviation from the norm of Aryan perfectionism and collective obedience during the Third Reich, particularly in physical appearance and mindset, was punishable by death. Despite the modest, conservative gains achieved by German women during 1900–1920s (see Lefko, 1997, pp. 129–144; Albisetti, 1988, pp. 170–172), any movement toward liberating women's education and definition of work was severely squashed under National Socialism and mixed with misogynist remarks about female cultural identity in connection with cleverness (Brodersen, 2016, pp. 107–111). The fear of difference, disobedience, and need to conform to a collective mindset that precludes independent thinking still exists in modern postwar Germany, showing itself in the half-day state educational system as part of a deep cultural complex about the fear of independent thinking and overstepping the authority of the father.

Woodman (1982, p. 73) stresses that the dilemma of the anorexic woman in modern hierarchical, patrilineal cultures world-wide is that she is locked into a one-sided authoritarian masculine principle that destroys her body with its rigid and fixed standpoint. The anorexic is fighting her battle for consciousness through the rejection of food. The task her own mother failed to perform in terms of differentiating herself as a woman, she performs alone in shamanic rites of passage, being reduced to skin and bone in the process. I would add that refusing food is a form of rebellion because human rights have been violated. British suffragettes used hunger strikes to protest about gender inequality and advocate the right for women to vote. Laura's hunger strike is a form of somatic protest because her independent rights were ignored about expressing the sort of nurture she required from both parents.

Added to the above considerations about human rights for women and starvation, there also exists a strong connection between menstrual blood and food taboos, particularly red meat. In some indigenous cultures, menstrual blood and blood from animals should not mix and be kept separate as a strict food taboo. Menstrual blood attracts the strongest taboo because it facilitates regeneration. Its profound creative substance must be kept free from contamination, whether animal or human. In indigenous cultures, as I explain in chapter 2, menstruating women are protected from contact with hunters who kill animals for food. They are regulated under strict food taboos that protect their blood from mixing with the blood of animals (see chapters 2, 3 and 4). These ancient food taboos could still unconsciously deter modern women from eating meat and be anxious about the reproductive process connected to their animal nature and menstrual blood in general, often regarded negatively and expressed as a *curse* (cf. chapter 2 on Delaney, Lupton, and Toth, 1988; Buckley and Gottlieb, 1988).

Woodman eloquently explains (1983, p. 135) that the *puella* (the child in the women) having accepted her father's anima projection from infancy, has lived to please him, to share his intellectual pursuits, and meet his standard of authoritarian perfectionism. In the dynamics of such a relationship, the mother is either absent or a rival, as in the case of Laura. The father's daughter walks a tightrope in a precarious balance between *not living* at all and living a *living death*. Similar to the *puer aeterus*, the *puella* is caught in an in-between liminal space as a *fright without solution* because no deeper ritual meaning has been found for her blood sacrifice and for the crossing of the internal-external border from childhood to womanhood.

Woodman (1985, pp. 13–31) movingly describes the chrysalis/cocoon stage that is tragically missed or incomplete when girls have no visible container to transform into women.

One of Laura's most poignant revelations was discovering the power she exercised over her father when, as an adult, she rebuked him. He cried like a little boy and she thus forgave him for trespassing her boundaries because she realised he was looking for a mother. Behind the authoritarian, patrilineal perfectionism he demanded from her was a lost boy who needed mothering and who, therefore, could never support her request for genuine independence.

Puella elements in the transference/countertransference dynamic

On one side of Laura's paternal roots were Roma people who her father's family had disowned. Laura lived this nomadic side of her heritage through her appearance of dyed dark hair, makeup, vibrant colours in her clothing, and frequent travelling. During analysis and the *puella* transference-countertransference dynamics between us, she became conscious of her need to play, to express her need for intellectual freedom from fixed, territorial, hierarchical thinking that had governed her conscious life. As I am dark-haired and originally from Wales, UK, I could perhaps personify Laura's nomadic, nonconformist shadow 'other' as someone who has already crossed her borders and entered into new terrain without the fear of punishment and reprisal. Laura was able to discuss her family's past because I am unaffected by the intergenerational taboo of speaking about Nazi atrocities. As I come from a different culture but now live in Germany, I could open that door without the same fear of guilt and reprisal and offer a shared communality as the 'other.'

I would like to finish this section on the two clinical cases with a dream I had while working in analysis with them. I dreamt that I was walking to the end of a street in Frankfurt at night carrying a large watering can filled with water. At the end of the road stood a large collective metal dustbin with a lid on it in, which I imagined must carry a lot of the garbage of the city. I was curious to know what kind of rubbish was inside, so I took the lid off and peered into the darkness. To my surprise, instead of dirty rubbish being stored in the dustbin, it was filled instead with rich, dark earth. I noticed that bulbs were growing through the earth and some had already sprouted green shoots. I took my watering can and watered the bulbs in the dark.

This dream showed the unconscious analytical work that was taking place in the collective unconscious with my clients' and my own tabooed left over bits and pieces that were being recycled into new growth. I supplied the water to aid the process. The rubbish was being transformed in the darkness into rich *prima materia,* capable of sustaining new growth. The container as dustbin showed that transformation took place in the refuse that we throw away.

I interpret the creative process of nighttime dream work as providing the black nurturing container found in the personal and the collective unconscious that transforms dirt and waste products into new growth that I describe fully in chapters 7 and 8.

Conclusion

In this chapter, I have attempted to trace the origin of conscience and emotional ambivalence by linking the two with a taboo against independent thinking and food. I trace Freud's definition of a repressed incest wish to illustrating the dynamics of patrilineal, authoritarian thinking, which disallows any form of dissent and difference both intrapsychically and interpersonally. The two case reports (Alfred and Laura) show how taboo on independent thinking manifests itself in symptomatology attached to obsessive compulsions and anorexia nervosa. I support my findings mainly through the in-depth works of Miller (1987; 1998; 2005), Stenner (2005), Stein (2017), Luci (2017), Bisagni, 2017, Douglas (1966), and Kristeva (1982) into the abusive, fixed, patrilineal mindset structure, using the archetypal framework of Hillman (1967), von Franz (2000), Woodman (1982; 1985), and Ziegler (1983) to deepen psychosocial understanding of parental complexes reflected within wider cultural taboos.

The postwar effect of Nazi totalist fixed thinking is still evident in German clients suffering from obsessive compulsions who were born in the 1950s and early 1960s. Their parents suffered from *disorganised* attachment that ensured safety, obedience, and loyalty to rigid collective rules. In both client cases, their symptomatology reveals differing aspects of taboos placed upon expressing subjectivity, independent thinking, and dissent, as well as having to contain and absorb conscious and unconscious aspects of their respective parental traumatised fears of crossing borders, intrapsychically and interpersonally, experienced first-hand by ethnic Germans after their expulsion from their homes in 1945; genuine creativity is caught in a *liminal* space between developmental borders, personified by the *puer/puella* archetype. Both clients have sacrificed their right to propagate and pass their inheritance on to the next generation, perhaps in an act of unconscious despair about themselves as viable future models. They benefitted from dream work and from entering into that tabooed terrain to legitimise their hitherto disallowed subjectivity and promote genuine independent thinking.

Notes

1. I use false names to protect the identity and anonymity of the clients in case studies 1 and 2.
2. *Abitur* is the German academic school leaving certificate, taken usually at 18 years of age and used primarily for entry into higher education.

3. Rats as a composite dream image appearing in the dreams of both client cases 1 and 2, offer a wide spectrum of emotionality as a symbol: first, rats are unwitting carriers of disease and dirt through the fleas they carry in their fur; second, they are intelligent, curious, and dexterous; third, rats are able to adapt and thrive in dark, dank places such as prisons, often historically, as a valued source of protein; fourth, they are associated in India as the steed of the elephant god, Ganesha, the overcomer of obstacles (cf. Cooper, 1978, p. 137; Chevalier and Gheerbrant, 1994, pp. 788–789). In Eastern cultures, such as China as well as India, rats are revered for their fecund, nocturnal, matrilineal, regenerative connection to goddesses. Rats appearing as faeces or hidden under floorboards could well point to such composite attributes that have been *eliminated, wasted,* or *betrayed.*

References

Abramowitz, J. Taylor, S. & McKay, D. (2009). Obsessive-compulsive Disorder. *The Lancet*, 374, pp. 491–499.

Adorno, T.W., Frenkel-Brunswick, E., Levinson D.J., et.al. (1950). *The Authoritarian Personality.* New York: Wiley.

Albisetti, J.C. (1988). *Schooling German Girls and Women: Secondary and Higher Education in the Nineteenth Century.* Princeton, N.J: Princeton University Press.

Arendt, H. (1951). *The Origins of Totalitarianism.* London and New York: Penguin Classics, 2017.

Bisagni, F. (2017). *Obsessions; The Twisted Cruelty.* London: Karnac Books.

Bowlby, J. (1969). Attachment and Loss, Vol. 1 *Attachment.* London: Pimlico.

Brodersen, E. (2016). *Laws of Inheritance. A post-Jungian Study of Twins and the Relationship Between the First and Other(s).* London and New York: Routledge.

Buckley, T. and Gottlieb, A. (1988) (eds.) *Blood Magic: The Anthropology of Menstruation.* Oakland: University of California Press.

Chevalier, J. and Gheerbrant, A. (1994). (Trans. Buchanan-Brown, J.) *Dictionary of Symbols.* London and New York: Penguin Books, 1996.

Cooper, J.C. (1978). *An Illustrated Encyclopaedia of Traditional Symbols.* London: Thames & Hudson.

Costello, M.S. (2006). *Imagination, Illness and Injury: Jungian Psychology and the Somatic Dimensions of Perception.* London and New York: Routledge.

Crews, F. (2017). *Freud, The Making of an Illusion.* London: Profile Books.

Delaney, J., Lupton, M.J., and Toth, E. (eds.) (1976). *The Curse, A Cultural History of Menstruation.* Urbano and Chicago: University of Illinois Press, expanded ed. 1988.

Douglas, M. (1966). *Purity and Danger.* New edition. London and New York Routledge Classics, 2002.

Farrell, J. (1998). Paranoia Methodized. In (1998) Crews, F. (ed.) *Unauthorised Freud, Doubters Confront a Legend.* New York and London: Penguin Books, pp. 228–245.

Ffytche, M. and Pick, D. (eds.) (2017). *Psychoanalysis in the Age of Totalitarianism.* London and New York: Routledge. pp. 207–220.

Fletcher, J. and Benjamin, A. (eds.) (2012). *Abjection, Melancholia and Love. The Work of Julia Kristeva.* Abingdon and New York: Routledge.

Fraser, J. (1912). Spirits of Corn and of the Wild. In *The Golden Bough*, Part V, Vol. II. Mishawaka, IN: Adamant Media Corporation, 2000.

Freud, S. (1912-13). Taboo and Emotional Ambivalence. In *Collected Works*, Vol. 13. *The Origins of Religion.* Trans. Strachey, J. London and New York: Penguin books, 1990.

Gross, E. (1990). The Body of Signification. In (2012) Fletcher, J. and Benjamin, A. (eds.) *Abjection, Melancholia and Love. The Work of Julia Kristeva.* Abingdon and New York: Routledge, pp. 80–103.

Haste, C. (2001). *Nazi Women, Hitler's Seduction of a Nation.* London: Chanel 4 Books: Macmillan.

Herminghouse, P. and Mueller, M. (eds.) (1997). *Gender and Germanness, Cultural Productions of Nation.* Modern German Studies, Vol. 4. Providence and Oxford: Berghahn Books.

Hillman, J. (1967). Senex and Puer: An Aspect of the Historical and Psychological Present. In (1979) Hillman, J. (ed.) *Puer Papers.* Dallas, Texas. Spring Publishers, pp. 3–53.

Hillman, J. (1977). Puer Wounds and Ulysses' Scar. In (1979) Hillman, J. (ed.) *Puer Papers.* Dallas, Texas, Spring Publishers. pp. 100–127.

Hillman, J. (ed.) (1979). *Puer Papers.* Dallas, Texas. Spring Publishers.

Holt, R.H. (1992). Freud's Parental Identifications. In Gelfand, T., and Kerr, J. (eds.) *Freud and the History of Psychoanalysis.* Hillsdale, N.J.: Analytic, pp. 1–28.

Jung, C.G. (1955a). The Theory of Infantile Sexuality. In *Collected Works*, Vol. 4 *Freud and Psychoanalysis*, 2nd edn. London: Routledge and Kegan Paul, 1993.

Jung, C.G. (1955b). The Concept of the Libido. In *Collected Works*, Vol. 4. *Freud and Psychoanalysis*, 2nd edn. London: Routledge and Kegan Paul, 1993.

Jung, C.G. (1955c). Neurosis and Aetiological Factors in Childhood. In *Collected Works*, Vol. 4. *Freud and Psychoanalysis*, 2nd edn. London: Routledge and Kegan Paul, 1993.

Kast, V. (2003). *Abschied von der Opferrolle.* Freiberg: Herder Verlag.

Kristeva, J. (1982). *Powers of Horror: An Essay in Abjection.* Trans. Rondiez, L.S. New York: Columbia University Press.

Leach, E.R. (1964). Anthropological Aspects of Language: Animal Categories and Verbal Abuse. In (1979) Lessa, W.A. and Vogt, E.Z. (eds.) *Reader in Comparative Religion. An Anthropological Approach*, 4th edn. New York: Harper Collins, pp. 153–166.

Lefko, S. (1997). *Truly Womanly* and *Truly German.* Women's Rights and National Identity in Die Frau. In Herminghouse, P. and Mueller, M. (eds.) *Gender and Germanness, Cultural Productions of Nation.* Modern German Studies, Vol. 4. Providence and Oxford: Berghahn Books.

Lorenz, K.Z. (1935). Schiller, C.H. (ed.) *Instinctive Behaviour.* New York: International Universities Press, 1957.

Luci, M. (2017). *Torture, Psychanalysis & Human Rights.* London and New York: Routledge.

Miller, A. (1980). *Am Anfang war Erziehung.* Frankfurt: Suhrkamp Verlag.

Miller, A. (1981). *Du Sollst nicht Merken.* Frankfurt: Suhrkamp Verlag.

Miller, A. (1987). *For Your Own Good, The Roots of Violence in Child-rearing.* London: Virago.

Miller, A. (1998). *Thou Shalt Not be Aware; Society's Betrayal of the Child.* New York: Farrar, Straus and Giroux.

Miller, A. (2006). *The Body Never Lies. The Lingering Effects of Hurtful Parenting.* New York and London: Norton Publisher.

Naimark, N.M. (2001). *Fires of Hatred, Ethnic Cleansing in Twentieth-Century Europe.* Cambridge, MA and London: Harvard University Press.

Oliver, K. (2002). Psychic Space and Social Melancholy. In Oliver, K. and Edwin, S. (eds.) *Between the Psyche and the Social, Psychoanalytic Social Theory*, New York and Oxford: Bowman & Littlefield Publishers, pp. 49–65.

Oliver, K. and Edwin, S. (eds.) (2002). *Between the Psyche and the Social, Psychoanalytic Social Theory.* New York and Oxford: Bowman & Littlefield Publishers.

Reddish, E. (2014). *The Petrified Ego. A New Theory of Conscience.* London: Karnac.

Rose, J. (2016). Total Belief, Delirium in the West. In Ffytche, M. and Pick, D. (eds.) *Psychoanalysis in the Age of Totalitarianism.* London and New York: Routledge. pp. 207–220.

Stenner, K. (2005). *The Authoritarian Dynamic. Cambridge Studies in Public Opinion and Political Psychology.* Cambridge and New York: Cambridge University Press.

Stein, A. (2017). *Terror, Love & Brainwashing. Attachment in Cults and Totalitarian Systems.* London and New York: Routledge.

Stern, D. (1984). *The Interpersonal World of the Infant. A View of Psychoanalysis and Developmental Psychology.* London: Karnac Books, 1998.

Veale, D. & Roberts, A. (2014). Obsessive-compulsive Disorder. *British Medical Journal* 348, g2183.

Von Franz, M-L. (2000). *The Problem of the Puer Aeternus.* Toronto: Inner City Books.

Winnicott, W. (1965) *The Maturational Processes and the Facilitating Environment.* London: Karnac Books, 1990.

Winnicott, W. (1971). *Playing and Reality.* London and New York: Routledge Classics, 2005.

Woodman, M. (1982). *Addiction to Perfection, The Still Unravished Bride.* Toronto: Inner City Books.

Woodman, M. (1985). *The Pregnant Virgin. A Process of Psychological Transformation.* Toronto, Canada: Inner City Books.

Ziegler, A.J. (1983). *Archetypal Medicine.* Woodstock, Connecticut: Spring Publications.

Chapter 7

Taboo, rites of passage, and indeterminate states

Introduction

This chapter examines the rites of passage as period of margin or liminality as an interstructural phenomenon subject to taboo. In chapter 6, I present two clinical case studies that outline severe symptomatology when borders are not allowed to be crossed. The taboo against crossing over to a different perspective or a different opinion is seen as dangerous. Monistic, authoritarian structures that do not allow differences inculcate their populace with an intense fear of overstepping margins and entering into new territory. The motivation needed for entering transitional, developmental stages is neither encouraged nor accompanied.

Meade (1995) suggests that the radical dismantling of institutions, boundaries, and belief systems in the twentieth and twenty-first centuries, through two world wars and interregional upheavals that terrorise their populous, leave cultures bereft of the capacity to handle death and embrace life fully. Without some spiritual vision and ritual structure, helplessness in face of war, change, and separation is covered up by displays of force and greed. Denial arises as a defence against the flood of losses and endings. As we have seen in the previous chapter, when the family offers no rites of passage to offspring to encourage independence at puberty, severe symptomatology can develop on the margins between childhood and adulthood. Meade argues that the cost of mass denial is found in the increase of random violence, drug abuse, and confusion about personal, gender, and national identities. Without conscious ritual of loss and renewal, individuals lose their capacity to experience the sorrows and joys essential to feel fully human. Without a ritual to inform the psychic and physical wounds that occur at separation, pain and suffering increase but without a meaningful container and structure to aid such difficult passages. Where drops of blood once symbolised life trying to change, pools of blood stain the city streets without renewing the spirit of life. Carefully prepared puberty rites are replaced by gangs of youths hurling their wounds into bloody street sacrifices. Unguided by ritual elders and genuine spiritual aims, disorientated groups become simple gangs. When the death side of life is ignored, regeneration becomes obscured by lack of orientation.

Definition of rites

This chapter defines rites as *rites of passage* assessing the works of van Gennep (1960), Eliade (1958), Turner (1964, 1969), Bell (1992), McCauley and Lawson (2002), and Goodwyn (2016) in their emphases on the importance of ritual processes in the transition period, which Turner (1964, pp. 4–20) describes as *betwixt and between,* an interstructural indigenous phenomenon to describe and constitute transitions between states. By 'state,' Turner means a more inclusive meaning than status or office and refers to any type of stable or recurrent condition that is culturally recognised. He regards the transitional state as a *liminal* process that has the capacity to transform properties. Turner differentiates between a *ceremony* as a confirmatory process within social states where politicolegal institutions have importance and a *ritual* which transforms them. Goodwyn (2016, p. 204) underscores the importance of rituals as a 'the central element in a dense interactivity of mind, culture, and body…they have the ability to cure both mind and body; in the case of the body, they can help cure physical ailments. In the case of the mind, they can cure anomie, rootlessness, emptiness and role confusion.' In the absence of transition ritual, there is no separation ritual that marks the physical and mental courage to fulfil new life responsibilities (ibid, pp. 155–156).

The efficacy of rites lies in their providing a focusing, structuring mechanism (Douglas, 1966, pp. 78–81). The frame of the ritual supplies a marked off time or place and alerts a special type of expectancy. It enlivens memory and links the present with the relevant past. Rites are also creative at the level of performance as they aid perception through mnemonic action. Rites control experience by offering social rules through taboo prohibitions that offer containment and security during the difficult rites of passage into new developmental roles.

Bell (1992, p. 19) suggests that ritual is generally perceived as action (what is done) as opposed to the conceptual aspects of religion such as beliefs (what is thought). Bell (ibid. pp. 206–298) posits ritual as a strategy for cementing power relations that appear to be instinctive and involves two dimensions: the first, as the dynamic of the social body, its projection, and embodiment of a structured environment. Rituals work below the level of discourse. It produces and objectifies constructions of power that the neophyte as social agent then re-embodies. Participants do not realise that the rites they re-embody have been orchestrated so that their patterns of dominance and subordination generate a sense of integrated totality and group cohesion. The second involves the actual limits of rites as a means of domination and control because rites also empower those who may at first appear to be controlled by them. Integral to the process of objectification and control are concomitant variables of resistance and internal discrimination. Bell assesses ritual as an embodiment of both dimensions and experienced as a negotiated compromise between action and thought.

Earlier, Radcliffe-Brown (1952, pp. 154–159) stresses that rites can be interpreted as regulated symbolic intergenerational expressions of certain sentiments or values upon which a society depends for its cohesion and social solidarity. Rites and their rationalising beliefs develop together as part of a coherent whole. Similar to Bell, Radcliffe-Brown places emphasis on action or the need for action that controls or determines belief, and not the other way around.

During the rite of passage between two states of being, the person is ambiguous and taboo. The subject of passage ritual in the liminal period is structurally, if not physically, *invisible.* Van Gennep (1960, pp. 10–11) characterises a class of rituals with three successive and distinct moments in ritual time: separation, margin and reaggregation. This characteristic belongs to specific, affective, structural aspects of status change and the attendant risks attached to moving into unknown territory that typically occurs during the occasion of birth, puberty, marriage, midlife, old age, and death. The second characterisation of preliminal, liminal, and postliminal is concerned with units of space and time where behaviour is freed from the norms and values of structural forms. It is important to note that during the intervening liminal state, the subject is marginal and taboo: he/she passes through an indeterminate stage that has few characteristics of the attributes of the past or the future.

Van Gennep (1960) states that rites of passage are not only linked to specific maturation periods, but also cover times of war, the passage from scarcity to plenty, and even the entry into political office. This chapter, however, concentrates on rites of passage connected to separation, liminality, and margin, but also takes into account war trauma, which complicates the process of rites of passage. In such initiation rites, a person is structurally defined as a *transitional being* and called a neophyte; she/he has a physical, but not a social reality, hence they are hidden. They have no status, rank, personal clothing, or kinship position to demarcate them structurally. In so far as they are no longer classifiable, the symbols that represent them are drawn from the biology of death, decomposition, and other physical bodily taboos.

Separation

The first phase of separation is *childbirth* when the offspring leaves the safety of the mother's womb and enters into the outside world. In many indigenous cultures, pregnancy and childbirth are governed by taboos that stress the culture's intense fear of involvement with the powerful birth process, which is associated with dread. Fraser (1922, pp. 250–251) observes that Australian aborigine women are secluded at childbirth. In some practices, the newborn child is separated from his/her mother for a few days, which according to van Gennep (1960, pp. 50–51) is not connected to the arrival of the mother's milk. Van Gennep notes that the newborn is first a stranger who must be separated from his/her previous environment before being accepted into the community. The baby is given to another woman for the first few days to aid that separation. In the Punjab, even the cutting of the umbilical cord has symbolic ceremonial significance. Through the choice of instrument (a knife for a boy and a spindle for a girl) deemed appropriate for future gender activity, the baby is initiated into the outside world.

During this period, mothers themselves are in a dangerous, tabooed position that could infect any person or anything they touch; hence they are put into quarantine until that danger has passed. In Tahiti, women after childbirth are secluded for a fortnight in a temporary hut erected on sacred ground and barred from touching provisions, needing to be fed by another person. In some tribes, no one is allowed to touch postpartum women and they are fed on food reached to them on sticks. In some Bantu tribes, a miscarriage is viewed with particular dread, particularly when it is not revealed. The blood from a hidden miscarriage is particularly threatening because that blood has not yet formed into a child. Medicine men perform special purification rituals so that the misfortune does not spread. Babies are not allowed to be touched by the husband for the first three months after birth for fear of contamination.

The second separation at *puberty* maps the transition from child into adulthood and attracts more extreme rites of passage performed under strict taboo. Van Gennep (1960, p. 65) stresses that these rites are concerned with reaching *social* puberty and less with physiological puberty. In their classless and sexless state, the transitional being or liminal person is defined by a name and by a set of symbols. For example among the Ndembu of Zambia, the name *mwadi* may mean many things: it may stand for a boy in circumcision rites or a chief designate undergoing his installation rites. The symbols attached and surrounding the liminal person are complex and governed by taboo and in some ceremonies s/he is treated as a corpse. Neophytes may be buried, forced to lie motionless in a burial posture, and painted black or white. Neophytes in some tribes isolated in the bush are assimilated as ghosts. They cannot take food with their hands only directly through their mouths, as the dead are supposed to do. Sometimes they are painted white, a sign that they have become ghosts (Eliade, 1969, p. 114).

On the other hand, symbols can also be modelled on processes of gestation and parturition. In these cases, the neophytes are likened to and treated as embryos, newborn infants, or suckling. Douglas (1968) suggests that in such states, neophytes are particularly polluting since they are neither one thing nor another, and thus fall outside classification. Bettelheim (1954) notes that neophyte lack of specific sex, which gives them a kind of *prima materia* that denotes androgyny and sexlessness. Crossing one type of border allows the opening up of transgender possibilities as well. Turner (1969, p. 95) differentiates between states that have been ambiguously or contradictorily defined, and those that derive from ritualised transitions between states. In the latter case, we are not dealing with structural contradictions but with essentially nonstatic, unstructured, and often unbounded phenomenon experienced as in a sacred *other* space. Liminal entities as threshold people are neither here nor there; they are *betwixt and between,* in the positions assigned to them by laws, regulations, and customs.

Eliade emphasises (1958, p. 3) that puberty initiation represents the revelation of the sacred and access to the whole body of the cultural mythology and traditions. The initiate passes beyond the natural mode into cultural values. In such undifferentiated states, neophytes are forced to think about the cosmos, their clan lives, and their interrelationship. Undoing, dissolution, parturition, and decomposition are accompanied by processes of growth, transformation and the reformulation of old elements into new patterns (Turner, 1964, p. 248).

Initiation for boys

Symbolic usage of structural forms conveys many meanings; huts and tunnels are simultaneously tombs and wombs, lunar symbolism for the same moon waxing above, as well as snakes symbolising indeterminate *sexuality,* appearing to die but are shedding their skins. Courage is evoked by confrontation with fearful animal-monster hybrids as embodying indeterminate states during initiation processes. Since initiation ceremonies were founded by the Divine Being or the mythical ancestors, primordial time is reinstated in the *here and now* whenever they are performed. That is why a rite has such efficacy: it participates in the completeness of the sacred primordial time. Their periodical reiteration in puberty rites regenerates the entire psychic life of the community. Separation from the mother takes place dramatically and brutally. Among the *Yuin* in Australia, the novice is put under the charge of two guardians who prepare his food and instruct him into the traditional myths and legends and his duties to the tribe. A huge fire is built and the novices are 'roasted' for 10 minutes as part of the painful, symbolic, death-rebirth initiation to become adult (Eliade, 1958, pp. 7–8). From that moment on, the boys share only life with male clan members. The mothers mourn their departure as if they were dead.

Separation from the mother is the violent break from the world of childhood blissful state of irresponsibility and ignorance. In the case of nearly all Australian tribes, the mothers are convinced that the boys are killed and eaten by a hostile and mysterious divinity whose voice they have heard through the terrifying sound of the bullroarers. They are assured that this divinity will resuscitate the novices in the form of grown men. In that sense, the novices die to childhood and are seized by unknown, often masked men, carried from their familiar surroundings, laid on the ground and covered with branches. The experience of darkness and the fear of death at the hands of terrifying Divine Beings is repeated and expanded throughout the initiation. Passing from the maternal, profane world to the sacred, one must courageously 'die' to childhood to gain access to the painful burden of maturity and responsibility.

Some initiation rites demand the extraction of an incisor, other puberty initiations usually include circumcision followed after some time by subincision. Circumcision is wide spread among most indigenous premodern people in Austral-Asia, Africa, North and South America, and believed to be performed by divine or demonic beings, whether called the Great Spirit *Twanyirrika* or *Gnabaia* who swallows the novices and then disgorges them as initiates. Divine beings performing circumcision are often imagined as beasts of prey: lions and leopards in Africa, jaguars in South America, crocodiles and marine monsters in the Pacific islands, underlining the connection to archaic hunter gatherer cultures. Soon after circumcision, the novices themselves are dressed in leopard or lion skins, that is, they assimilate the divine totem essence of the initiatory animal and hence restored to life within it.

Eliade (1958, p. 23) notes the following four mythical-ritual distinctions: first, mythical *beings* manifest themselves through bullroarers to kill, eat, swallow, or burn the novice; second, they resuscitate the notice, but have changed into a new person; third, these *beings* often manifest themselves in animal form and are closely connected with an animal mythology; fourth, the animals' fate is identical with that of the initiate—when they lived on earth, they were killed and resuscitated and by their resurrection, established a new mode of existence. These *beings* reveal to the initiates the sacred mysteries of life, death, and rebirth through first-hand experience of tension, conflicts, drama, aggression, suffering, and death. The painful operation of circumcision is an expression of the initiatory death aligned with the psychic suffering experienced with separation from the mother. The strong emotions and the physical suffering aroused in puberty ordeals is likened to being swallowed and digested by a monster. The enclosed and isolated cabin where the boys are kept during the initiation rites often represents the body or the open maw of a water monster, crocodile, or snake.

In New Guinea, for example, a special house is built for the circumcision of boys (cf. Gillison, 2002, p. 118). It takes the form of the Monster Barlun, who is believed to swallow the novices, through its large mouth at one end and its smaller tail at the other. Eliade (1958, p. 36) suggests that the cabin not only represents the womb but also the return to an embryonic state in cosmological terms. It is not only a repetition of gestation of the carnal birth but a temporary return to the precosmic mode (symbolised by night and enclosed darkness) followed by a rebirth that can be homologised with the creation of the world in those great cosmic moments re-enacted to revitalise culture. The symbols of initiatory death and rebirth are complementary because the dead are supposed to know more than the living. Having gone through the death process, the dead possess arcane knowledge, giving rise to the gradual movement from Supreme Beings in initiation rites to the importance of mythological ancestors.

In parts of Australia, Melanasia, Africa, and Indonesia, circumcision is followed by *subincision*. The interval between the two operations varies from five to six weeks among the Arunta, to two to three years among the Karadjeri. According to some ethnologists (Winthuis, 1907; Roth, 1897) the purpose of subincision is to symbolically give the neophyte a female sex organ. The subincised member represents both male and female organs in a divine totality. In Africa among the Masai, the Nandi, the Nuba, and other tribes, the novices are dressed as girls, while in other tribes, girl novices are dressed as boys. In some tribes, androgyny is considered superior to both sexes because it incarnates totality and the return to primordial wholeness.

However, in Australia, one of the main purposes of subincision is to obtain fresh blood. Blood is a symbol of vitality, fertility, and strength. In some puberty rites, boys are given male blood to drink because the blood hitherto in his veins is entirely from his mother and, thus, female. Subincision supplies him with male blood and a way to get rid of maternal blood so the novice can enter manhood. Among the tribes, maternal blood is removed by perforating the nose, an operation that has the same symbolical effect as further mutilation of the genitals, in order to release the mother's blood that has accumulated since he was in the womb.

Another explanation offered by Eliade, (1958, p. 27) is that men observe women's menstruation and try to imitate their fertility by inflicting a genital wound making the penis similar to that of the vulva. It is, thus, not merely a need to separate from mother's blood but the wish to regenerate that blood by periodically eliminating it by imitating menstruation. Subincision makes it possible for a man to obtain a certain amount of regenerative blood by periodically opening their wounds. The novice is thus initiated into the mystery of blood. He is taught about the connection that exists between himself and his mother and how he can release that connection and become a man. Since female blood is the maternal product of feeding, the male novice is subjected to numerous dietary taboos after circumcision and subincision as extra protections during the transitional period between boy and manhood. As already mentioned in chapter 2, another ritual is performed by swallowing long strands of flexible cane in order to vomit up the last traces of their mother's milk still thought to reside in their intestines (Gillison, 2002, p. 128).

Initiation for girls

Outsider knowledge of girls' initiations has been less accessible than that of boys' because they are individual, based on the onset of menstruation, whereas for boys, initiation is a group process (Eliade, 1958, p. 41). Female initiation begins with the first menstruation, but progresses further into pregnancy, birth, postpartum, and menopause, making girls' rites more complex; their association with different kinds of blood emanating from the orifices and margins (free flowing, clotting, dark red, bright red, cessation) make them subject to different taboos. The onset of menstruation compels a separation from the community: the girl is immediately segregated as an individual who undergoes this initiation alone. The length of individual segregation varies from three days (Australia and India) to twenty months (New Zealand) or even several years (Cambodia). Not mentioned by Eliade (1958) or by Fraser (1922) in their accounts of girls' puberty rites, but mentioned in some detail by van Gennep, in most indigenous cultures (particularly in parts of Africa, India, the Middle East, and Asia), girls undergo genital mutilation in the same painful way as boys are circumcised. The reasons why female genital mutilations (FGM) are performed vary from one region to another as well as over time, and include a mix of sociocultural factors within families and communities.

The most commonly cited reasons for the practice are: FGM is considered a necessary part of raising a girl, and a way to prepare her for adulthood and marriage. FGM is often motivated by beliefs about what is considered acceptable sexual behaviour. It aims to ensure premarital virginity and marital fidelity. In many communities, FGM is believed to reduce a woman's libido and therefore believed to help her resist extramarital sexual acts. When a vaginal opening is covered or narrowed, the fear of the pain of opening it, and the fear that this will be found out, is expected to further discourage extramarital sexual intercourse among women with this type of FGM. Where it is believed that being cut increases marriageability, FGM is more likely to be carried out. FGM is associated with cultural ascetic ideals of femininity and modesty, which include the notion that girls are clean and beautiful only after removal of body parts that are considered unclean, unfeminine or male. Although no religious scripts prescribe the practice, practitioners often believe the practice has religious support.

Religious leaders take varying positions with regard to FGM: some promote it; some consider it irrelevant to religion, while others contribute to its elimination (cf. Daly, 1978: Walker, 1983; Hernlund and Shell-Duncan, 2007). I suggest that such practices developed after the Neolithic period when patrilineal inheritance became enhanced under civilisation c. 3000 BCE and women's procreation power had to be physically as well as symbolically controlled and curtailed (see chapters 4 & 5). Such practices may also have been developed by women during the Palaeolithic-Neolithic era to protect themselves from unwanted sexual advances and to keep their *sacred* menstrual blood from spilling out and being wasted. Among matrilineal societies, the initiation of girls includes festivities that manifest public joy at their puberty.

The great mother archetype

During these initiation rituals, girls do eventually form a secluded group and their initiation is performed under the direction of older female relatives. These rites were governed by older postmenopausal women due to the ancient belief that these women are the wisest mortals because they permanently retain their wise blood. They are filled with magical power because their menstrual blood remains in their veins (Walker, 1983, p. 641). During the period of seclusion, the novices learn ritual songs and dances and specific skills such as spinning and weaving. The symbolism of these tasks is highly significant as the ancient Goddesses of Destiny are spinners; the moon spins time and weaves human lives, linking the girl novices to the ancient matrilineal Palaeolithic-Neolithic era of the Great Goddess. As these girls are in a transition/liminal/*betwixt and between* state of moving from the state of childhood to sexual maturity, they are invisible and subject to strict taboo: some rites insist that the girls' feet do not touch the floor and they are sometimes sown up in a blanket, shrouded like a corpse suspended from the ceiling (Fraser, 1922, pp. 714–728; pp. 829–836). In this incubation period, the sun must not touch them. Strict dietary rules, which include periods of fasting, are observed as well as sitting positions inside the hot and stifling huts or cages, all of which are symbols of the incubation period inside the womb of the Great Mother. Daughters of chiefs in Borneo undergo particularly rigorous initiation that can last several years, entering seclusion around eight years of age. On attaining sexual maturity, their bodily growth is stunted and their complexion pale and wax like, like that of newborn children or the moon in its new moon phase. Other similarities with the moon exist: among the *Dyaks,* a pubescent girl is isolated in a white cabin, dressed in white, and eats only white food. At the end of her segregation, she drinks blood from a young man's open vein through a bamboo shoot (Eliade, 1958, p. 44) thus ending her separation from men. The meaning of this ritual could mark the end of her temporary androgyny and asexuality, leaving her childhood, the innocent, untouched, reflective moon phase (white/silver) behind, as she moves into life, rebirth, and motherhood (red blood).

As Baring and Cashford elucidate (1991, pp. 162–163), the Great Mother archetype is associated with the moon and its monthly phases of waxing, waning, and disappearing for three days; it provides an image of the idea that death is necessary to renewal. By imitating the moon's apparent separation and death, people themselves assist in restoring the fertilising of the earth. When the cycle of the moon is experienced mythically, death is not final, it is simply one phase of a greater cycle. Perpetually moving, the moon changes form in a way that is always the same (Cashford, 2003, p. 15). It tells one fundamental archetypal story: birth, growth, fullness, decay, death, and rebirth in a form that human life and transformation can be measured, structured, and reflected upon. Before the development of agriculture during the upper Neolithic era, which necessitated the sun to ripen crops, the moon was the chief source of spirituality for the nomadic hunter gatherers centred on the cycles of the Great Mother.

Puberty initiatory ordeals for both sexes thus take place in darkness and enclosed spaces, hidden from daylight. For the boys, symbolic death is ritualised by entering the jaws of a monster, the terrifying and devouring aspect of the Great Mother associated with pain, separation, and death in order to overcome their wish to remain boys tied to the mother, and be reborn as men. Jung (1911–12/1952, para. 332) explains that it is not a desire to enter the mother to cohabit with her, but to be reborn again as separated from her. The effect of incest prohibition stimulates creative imagination, which opens up into new possibilities and new gradients. Neophytes are symbolically either sexless or bisexual and may be regarded as *prima materia*, that is, undifferentiated raw material. In some boys' initiation ceremonies, newly circumcised boys are explicitly likened to menstruating women as if liminality also presupposes transgender status fluidity. Some initiations are individual rather than collective, without instructors; for example, *Omaho* boys of North American tribes venture alone into the wilderness to fast, pray, and await a dream for instruction. If they dream that they receive a woman's menstruation strap, they are compelled henceforth to dress and live as a woman as a *mixago*, that is, in an in-between gender fluid status, which is accepted fully by the tribe.

Death Rituals

Rituals concerning the dead emphasise death as the final separation and are filled with taboos as precautionary, prohibitive measures to ward off and protect against the dangerous state of liminality where the newly dead, with not yet decomposed flesh, can wander off looking for a new soul to inhabit and wreak havoc on the living. The existence of flesh on a corpse is particularly important as a sign that the identity of the dead has not left the margin, but remains in that liminal zone or margin between the living and the dead as '*me but not me.*' S/he is still recognisable as human and thus dangerous in that state (cf. Douglas, 1966, p. 197). According to van Gennep (1960, pp. 146–165), funerals comprise the most dramatic, complex ritual of all, because they include the rites of separation not just for the deceased but also for the mourners of the deceased. During mourning, the living mourners and the deceased constitute a special group situated between the world of the living and the world of the dead. Social life is suspended for all those affected by it and the length of the period increases with the closeness of the ties to the deceased. The separation rites include transporting the corpse in a special way, washing, and purifying the body under special taboos in which the mourners also participate. A safe journey to the land of the dead is facilitated by the behaviour of the mourners.

An anthropologist, Hertz (2009) reviews the practice of *double burial* in a variety of indigenous cultures worldwide, where a newly dead corpse is buried for a time in a special location, then exhumed and buried again elsewhere. The first burial represents a liminal state between the newly dead and the permanent dead. Between the first and second burial, vigil is practiced with the deceased, as the newly dead are thought to be vulnerable to attack and must be helped and protected. For example, many funerary practices include lighting fires to keep demons at bay and warming the souls of the deceased. Lewis-Williams and Pearce (2005, p. 79) stress the emotional importance of the liminal transition period where mourners learn to carry on in new circumstances. The transition period is deemed over when the flesh of the deceased has decomposed and the bones can be buried without further taboo within the confines of house, signalling the reintegration into the community. Boyer, (2001, p. 224) points out that the time between the funeral of separation and the funeral of incorporation allows anxiety and disassociation to subside (Haule, 2011, p. 232). Similar to puberty rituals, the dead are reintegrated into the community with new identities and new roles as ancestors.

The status attached to the dead person has special significance for funerary rites. Children who have not been baptised, named or initiated, the homeless, death by suicide or murder, struck by lightning, or in violation of a taboo, are classified as the *dangerous dead* and are never allowed to enter the world of the dead (van Gennep, 1960, p. 161). Goodwyn (2016, p. 170) adds stillborn children and women who die in labour to this list. They would like to be reincorporated into the world of the living as ancestors, but since they cannot be, they behave like hostile strangers toward the living as vengeful ghosts. In Hindu belief, as in many other cultures, violent and sudden deaths are believed to make the dead vengeful and torment the living in form of nightmares and accidents. Proper rituals based on strict taboos are performed to prevent this happening such as *sharing in the deceased state* of not shaving, washing, wearing of clothes, avoiding hot food, and abstaining from sex in order to appease them.

Land of the dead

The land of the dead is envisaged in various physical forms (van Gennep, 1960, pp. 150–155). The journey to the other world and the entrance to it depend on distance, climate, and topography. The Northern *Ostyaks* locate the land of the dead beyond the mouth of the Ob, in the Arctic Ocean, illuminated only by the light of the moon. For the Irtysh *Ostyak,* the land of the dead is located in the sky, reached by ascending ladders or by climbing up a chain. For the ancient Britons, the other world called *Annwn,* Welsh for *Otherworld,* is under the sea. *Annwn* contains crystal fortresses, rotating portals and glass ships, giving images of a restless watery expanse of sunken treasure, difficult to access in the moving twilight of tidal currents and deep swirling caverns. These images coincide with the movement of the Atlantic Ocean surrounding Wales where the dead are said to reside. Having lived through death, the ancestors communicate courage, psychic roots and tribal wisdom (Brodersen, 2012, p. 143). Other locations suggest citadels surrounded by walls or an underworld abode with bolted doors (the Sheol in Hebrew tradition) or situated high in a mountain or in its interior (Hindu India). Since the deceased must make this voyage, families are careful to equip him/her with the necessary material objects used in life to facilitate a safe passage, such as coins for the ferry man who transports the dead to their final destination. The land of the dead is perceived as a continuation of earthly life where members' status is protected through similar rules. Some funerary rituals emphasise rebirth and renewal, such as the daily revival of the Egyptian sun god, Ra-Osiris, whose sacred importance would be lost if not renewed through resurrection rites (Brodersen, 2012, pp. 139–141). The biblical *NT* death and resurrection of Christ follows along similar lines of overcoming death through resurrection and rebirth.

Bodies that have transgressed social and religious taboos and bear evidence of execution or torture, such as corpses buried in peat bogs to preserve them from decay around 2,600–1,600 years ago, could have been kept in a permanent unresolved liminal state on purpose with their souls never allowed to rest. Taylor (2002, p. 16), an anthropologist, suggests that these bodies could not be burned and sacrificed without offending the gods, but neither could they be properly buried without offending the ancestors or remain unburied for their souls would wander and do harm to the living. The only solution was to keep them permanently marginal, their partially decomposed bodies kept recognisable to keep their souls near them. The bogs themselves were liminal places, watery, raised above dry land. The decomposition process was arrested and time effectively stopped. These ancient bog corpses bring to mind the tragic images of zombies as unforgiven, soulless, liminal beings in a permanent state of transgressed taboo. Composed of half eaten flesh, but still recognisable and therefore most dangerous at the margins of society, they are the outsiders, doomed to wander the earth looking for peace.

Importance of ritual mourning

Goodwyn (2016, pp. 165–183) correctly underlines the importance of death rituals and its relationship to clinical study of mourning and complicated grief. Mourning rituals help participants access, express and process their grief. For example, among the North Cheyenne Native American clan, grieving and weeping is expected to end after four days because death is seen as a release from the hardship of life. The actions and the emotional behaviours are connected to the manner that emphasises the needs of the deceased who require emotional strength—not be hindered by an excess of sorrow—to traverse the liminal passage to the land of the ancestor. Tears would dampen the deceased's imagined wings as a spirit or make the road too slippery to traverse (ibid, p. 169). In some ceremonies, among the Australian aborigines, violent mourning rites are practiced such as the burning of breasts, the slashing of thighs to give space to the painful emotional outpouring of grief within a confined space, transforming the violent scenes later into a jubilant celebration that emphasises that love conquers death. Anthropologists Lifton and

Olson (2009, pp. 32–34), stress that mourning rituals aim toward expressing symbolic immortality, without which everyday living is a challenge, and the capacity to feel at home in the world. These various forms of immortality are expressed through the production of cultural expressions, such as art and music, through theological speculation, communion with nature (as nature carries on independently of death so representing renewal and revitalization), and through altered states of consciousness.

Taylor (2002, p. 279) argues that modern cultures tend to insulate themselves emotionally from the reality of death and have lost connection with indigenous funerary rituals through industrialisation, two world wars, and a growing disconnection with nature. Under the advance of science and medicine, tabooed fears about the human corpse as sacred as well as dangerous have been rationalised and sanitised. Experts, such as funerary undertakers, have taken over the process of mourning as taboo rites about purity, dirt, and danger have been eliminated from the death process along with the active special relationship between the deceased and the mourner. Mannix (2017) equally stresses that actively preparing for death helps ease the transition for the dying and their bereaved families. Since the second half of the twentieth century, the emotional familiarity and intimacy with death rituals has been lost that were once acknowledged and valued. Taboos about death need to be acknowledged with a renewed openness and positive structures that guide the painful process, rather than be met with denial.

The mourning process attached to loss and bereavement is further complicated, prolonged, and tabooed when a deceased close family member carries for the bereaved intense feelings of belonging, homeland, and status attached to cultural roots lost through the trauma of war, forced migration, or the shifting borders of cultural identity (cf. Debs, 2017, pp. 95–113). In such cases, the bereaved need to find ways to confront unprecedented experiences of destruction and loss that include not just the loss of a significant personal relationship, but the loss of cultural roots and identity embedded within that person. Debs (ibid. p. 100) suggests that the mourning process conceptualised by Freud (1914, p. 150) as a repetition compulsion can help master distress caused by overwhelming loss and trauma. Repetitive play, for example, contributes to creating a new liminal space capable of transforming trauma by tempering its negativity by confronting the tabooed emotions associated with death and bereavement. Zeavin, (2017, pp. 1–13) stresses the efficacy of war games and art work to codify, identify, and contain trauma as *an active agency* in the self to comment upon and reinvent memory.

Another aspect of mourning for the dead concerns those whose death cannot be confirmed, because they are missing or forced to disappear by tyrannical force (Debs, 2017, pp. 106–107). When family members disappear without trace, their absence is transformed into a spectral presence that continues to haunt, considerably complicating the work of mourning. In the absence of the corpse or any material sign that gives form to absence, the disappeared becomes incorporated and encrypted within the self, perpetuating identification with the existence of the lost person. Efforts to shed light on the fate of the disappeared are the only ways to make such family losses of loved ones open to grieving (Abraham & Torok, 1972).

Goodwyn (2016, pp. 177–183) notes that the modern revival of mourning rituals in therapeutic practice is a response to loss, melancholy and depression, a view which I support in my own clinical experience. Patients with prolonged and complicated grieving have often lost their homeland, relatives, status, and psychic roots, and find it difficult to transplant their cultural roots into new soil. The advantage of ritual in times of role transition can be well-applied to death ritual and the mourning process. Ritual creates semipermeable boundaries that help the bereaved formulate and express the new difference in status and relationship between the bereaved and the dead loved one. The ritual in the liminal space allows the bereaved time to process their grief and loss and think about it intensively. It also allows for an enactment of the difference in spatial, verbal, and bodily terms and lets the reality of death sink in. The semipermeable boundaries in death rituals between the deceased and the bereaved rituals are transcended but not erased, so that the dead can still communicate with their family after they have symbolically reached their final resting place. The boundary between life and death is not rigid or absolute, but it is not too porous either. The ritual container differentiates grief, so that the bereaved does not carry on indefinitely in a process that saps vital energy from life.

Communication of the *Sacra*

Initiation rites that promote separation, whether collective or individual, puberty or death rituals, impart arcane knowledge or gnosis and change the inner-most nature of the neophyte impressing him/her with the characteristics of his/her new state. This is not merely an acquisition of knowledge but a change in being. According to Harrison (1903) communication of the *sacra* has three main components: exhibition (what is shown); actions (what is done); and instructions (what is said). Exhibitions include evocative instruments or sacred articles such as aboriginal *churingas*, sacred drums, masks, images, or effigies that look simplistic, but their interpretation is complex. Among the instructions received are the names of deities or spirits believed to reside over the initiation rites. Neophytes are taught the outlines of their clan's cosmogony and mythical history that gives them psychic roots and ontological security.

Turner (1964, p. 238) points out three components when considering transmission of the *sacra*: first, their frequent disproportion, second, their monstrousness, and, third, their mystery. When one examines masks, costumes, and figurines displayed in initiation ceremonies as liminal *sacra*, certain features are disproportionate, either too large or too small. Some maintain their customary shape but are portrayed in unusual colours. To enlarge, diminish or discolour is a primary mode of distraction, which makes it into an object of reflection. The same may be said about the appearance and use of monsters as human-animal hybrids in the liminal period. Some earlier anthropologists (McCulloch, 1913) regard such hybrids as an indication that indigenous people draw little distinction between human and animal and transformation from one to other was possible. Turner, however, thinks that such hybrids are created to teach neophytes to distinguish between the difficult factors of reality. From this perspective, much of the grotesqueness is not aimed at terrifying the neophytes into submission but as a way of startling neophytes into thinking about objects, persons and their environment which they had hitherto taken for granted. Liminality breaks down customary thinking and enfranchises speculation. For example, the appearance of a lion headed hybrid provokes thoughts about the characteristics of lions and their relationship, differences, and similarities with humans. An aspect of human physiology with its attendant bodily emissions for example, menstrual blood (red), sperm and milk (white), and faeces (black) is used in abstracted form by the *Ndembu* tribe as a model or template for social, cosmic and religious ideas using the human body as a microcosm of the universe (Turner, 1964, p. 241). Thus, communication of the *sacra* involves three processes: first, the reduction of culture into recognised components, second, their recombination in fantastic or monstrous patterns; third, their recombination that makes sense with regard to the neophyte's new state and status.

Recent research on ritual forms by McCauley and Lawson, (2002 pp. 79–82) stress that such initiation rituals, although painful, simulate memory attached to emotional arousal. Using the research of Damasio (1994, 1999), McCauley and Lawson argue that the extremely heightened emotional arousal during puberty rites helps to mark them as culturally significant events that merit their complete concentration and their recollection for future tribal use. The first element is surprise: the initiation ceremonies begin unexpectedly with senior men waking the initiates in the middle of the night and driving them in the forest. The second is sensory pageantry with its positive and negative sensory stimulation. Hardships and torture and the associated deceptions and surprises are protracted and invariably accompanied by the third element of communicating previously forbidden or taboo knowledge. Narrative consolidation through memory is promoted by increased concentration brought about by emotional arousal.

Studies in posttraumatic stress disorder, when applied to the *Baktamen* neophyte's experiences, indicate that initiation rites do not engender the same type of negative result. The positive regard and pride of initiated adults, the participation of similar age cohorts, and the profound cultural importance accorded to these initiations generally cast these ordeals in a different and more positive light than similar events that elicit posttraumatic stress. Undergoing these initiations is unequivocally considered as a recognised achievement among the *Baktamen* and thus do not generate persistent feelings of fear or shame (McCauley and Lawson, p. 81).

Initiation and regeneration

Initiation rites that foster a rebirth and regeneration are not only experienced at puberty when nakedness and vulnerability receive symbolic significance. For example, during the ritual of the Swazi chief during the *Incwala* ceremony, the chief is identified with the well-being of the nation (Turner, 1964, p. 242). Both require periodic ritual strengthening. Lunar symbolism is prominent such rites with the chief or king personifying the nation. His tabooed seclusion represents the moon in transition between phases, neither waxing nor waning, and both are strengthened through a rite of passage. In this case, it is called the First Fruit ritual, which takes place midsummer when the early crops ripen. During the chief's night and day seclusion, he is painted black and remains in darkness. The chief is unapproachable, dangerous to himself and others. The entire population is temporarily in a state of taboo and seclusion: no touching, no washing, no movement, nor sexual activity. Other symbolic acts are performed that exemplify the darkness and the waxing and waning moon themes including slaughtering of a black ox and the painting of the queen mother with a black mixture until the ritual is over when both the chief and mother are washed. Both the chief and the queen mother are in eclipse until the black paint is washed off with ceremonial water and the ritual subject becomes reborn into lightness and normality (Kuper, 1947, pp. 219–220). The chief during this rite is naked, hidden, and divested of all his outward trappings of status, being reduced to the earth's substance as *prima materia*. In this fruitful darkness, the king and his people are closely identified in a participation mystique. It is only in darkness, silence and in the absence of merriment and movement, that the chief and his people can be united. There is a mystical solidarity between them that starkly contrasts with normal hierarchical status.

Liminality and *Communitas*

Turner points out (1969, pp. 234–237) that the relationship between the neophytes and their instructors during initiation rites is *hierarchical* that demands complete submission to grind them down and fashion them anew, endowed with the additional powers won through the initiation rites to face life's hardships and the challenges ahead. Between the neophytes themselves, however, exist a communal *horizontal* structure. Secular distinctions of rank and status disappear or are homogenized. No special favours are granted to sons and daughters of chiefs. Deep friendships based on familiarity, ease, and mutual outspokenness are encouraged between novices of the same age based on their shared ordeals, which last a lifetime. One can compare these horizontal indigenous structures to the fraternity of university campuses or at the same class in a naval or military academy in the US or Western Europe.

Liminality can be easily recognised by the symbols that cluster around them as the powers of the weak, misfortunate, and down-trodden of low status or position. The court jester operated as a privileged arbiter of morals and was given licence to jibe kings, courtiers, or lords of the manor. Jesters were usually men of low class or impoverished priests driven out of their usual estate. African monarchs were frequently accompanied by dwarfs and other misshapen people (cf. Gluckman, 1965). Shakespeare (c1603) employed the character of the Fool in *King Lear* to point out Lear's foolishness regarding the behaviour toward his three daughters. All these figures representing the poor and the deformed appear to symbolise the moral values of *communitas*.

Turner (1969, p. 96) suggests that initiation rites, through liminality, facilitate a 'moment in and out of time' and 'in and out' of secular social structures, however fleetingly. Through the use of symbols, in the liminal phase, forms are relatively unstructured. Liminality or *communitas* breaks in through the interstices of structure, at its edges and on the margins, from beneath, as inferiority. It is held as sacred or holy because it transgresses or dissolves the norms that govern structured and institutionalised relationships. Through the levelling or stripping of previous identity and status through initiation rites, instinctual energy is released that fills their participants with affect. Liminality, marginality, and structural inferiority are conditions that generate myths, symbols, rituals, philosophical systems, and works of art. These cultural forms provide humans with a set of templates or models that reclassify a person's relationship to society, nature, and culture, as an incitement into action as well as thought. During rites of initiation, positions are changed: they give recognition to an essential and generic human bond without which society cannot exist. Liminality implies that the high could not be high unless the low existed, and he/she who is high must experience what it feels like to be low. The tabooed passage from a lower to a higher status is through the limbo of being statusless. This play of opposites is also experienced through the intersection between matrilineal (communal) and patrilineal (hierarchal) kin clan structures.

In patrilineal clan structures, access to the matrilineal horizontal kin forms is experienced through initiation rites that reconnect the neophytes to the ancient, matrilineal Great Moon Goddess in both her containing (positive) and separating (negative) forms. Neophytes return symbolically to the dark womb, journey through the death process of being buried alive or devoured by water and through contact with the *vagina indenta,* the rapacious bloody side of the animal, a nature goddess identical with the obsidian knife, which cuts and separates at the entry into the womb. As Neumann, (1955, p. 163) expresses it: 'The Great Mother as Terrible Goddess of the earth and of death is herself the earth in which things rot. She is the mistress of the vessel...into which the dead souls enter and out of which they fly up again.'

Along with Fortes (1949, p. 32; p. 325), Turner (1969, pp. 114–118) maintains that the later patrilineal tie is associated with property, status, exclusiveness and particularistic interests, whereas the earlier matrilineal uterine tie is associated with spiritual characteristics, imbued with mutual, inclusive, collateral interest, and concerns.[1] In strong patrilineal clan structures, based on primogeniture and hard descent rules of property and the transmission of authority, it seems appropriate that *communitas* is symbolised by matrilineal ancestors, especially through mother images, since women enter as outsiders, as 'marrying in' wives into patrilineal kin clan forms. During initiation rites, the symbolic mother becomes the neophytes' link to the wider community in a horizontal, ethical distribution of humanness as a necessary quality to acquiring a new status. Its function during initiation rites is to prevent neophytes from using their status for personal aggrandisement and forgetting their unity and compassion for others.

Taking the example of the *Tallensi* tribe based on Fortes (1949) research, Turner (1969, p. 117) stresses that whereas patrilineality is the basis of their social structure, the individual link to other members is through matrilineal descent. By matrilineality, the individual in his/her integral character is emancipated from the segmental status incumbencies determined by patrilineality into a wider life of the community. Among the Nuer of the Sudan, the role of the leopardskin priest links the symbolic value of the mother's brother in patrilineal descent to the attributes of liminality characterised as *rul*, strangers, and not *diel* who own tribal property. Nuer leopardskin priests have attributes of *communitas:* he is a stranger, a mediator, acts for the whole community, represents peace against feud, and unaligned with political segments.

Conclusion

This chapter shows the connection between rite of passage, liminality, and taboo. Liminality breaks through fixed hierarchical structures to promote more freedom of expression. I trace the rites of passage from birth (separation from the mother) through puberty and other initiations rites that are performed to engender courage in the neophytes and to initiate them into adulthood. The physical pain endured during these rites is meant to prepare the initiates for life's hardship and adulthood within the clan structure of myths and stories of their origin.

In the state of *betwixt and between*, fixed ideas of sex biology become gender-fluid; it is as if the crossing of one border in liminal space allows the crossing of another. Indigenous rites show ingenious complexities as they attempt to traverse the passage from childhood into adulthood, opening up and redepositing ideas about cultural forms as they proceed. Goodwyn (2016, pp. 201–202) emphasises the *participatory* nature of rites. Participation fosters a particular state of mind created by ritualised behaviour. From the biological perspective, ritual connects participants by way of a shared imagery, which can alter physiology. From the cognitive view, collective rituals de-emphasise the personal element in order to amplify the participatory mode of collective resonant thinking giving participants a *sense of belonging*.

Psychodynamically, ritual allows ideas, taboo emotions, and aspects of the self to be concretised as material symbols. Projecting aspects of the self into ritual objects and places allows the participants to use nonverbal, imagistic, synchronistic, and emotional channels that allows one's sense of self (also tabooed) to be part of a wider whole within a beneficent collective purpose. Finally, a strong participatory function reinforces grid and group structure by allowing embodied expressions of cultural drama—whether through dance, music, or theatre—to reconnect the spiritual to the physical embodiment of human existence, evoking the courage and cohesive collective elements to face their painful losses, separations, and rebirths.

Note

1. I discuss these two structures as *archetypal:* hierarchal and horizontal as overlapping matrilineal and patrilineal laws of inheritance, which pervade all cultural forms, in Brodersen, 2016, *Laws of Inheritance*.

References

Abraham, N. and Torok, M. (1972). Mourning or Melancholia: Introjection Versus Incorporation. In (1994) Rand, N.T. (ed.) *The Shell and the Kernel*. Chicago: University of Chicago Press, pp. 125–137.

Auestad, L. (ed.). (2017). *Shared Traumas, Silent Loss, Public and Private Mourning*. London: Karnac.

Baring, A. and Cashford, J. (1991). *The Myth of the Goddess, Evolution of an Image*. London and New York: Penguin Books.

Bell, C. (1992). *Ritual Theory, Ritual Practice*. Oxford: Oxford University Press.

Bettelheim, B. (1954). *Symbolic Wounds, Puberty Rites and the Envious Male*. New York: The Free Press.

Brodersen, E. (2012). In the Nature of Twins: a Study of the Archetypal Realm of Universal Duality, Opposition and Imitation Between the 'First' and 'Other' in Creation Myths. *International Journal of Jungian Studies*, 4(2), 133–149.

Brodersen, E. (2016). *Laws of Inheritance: A post-Jungian study of twins and relationship between the first and other(s)*. London and New York: Routledge

Boyer, P. (2001). *Religion Explained: The Evolutionary Origins of Religious Thought*. New York: Basic Books.

Cashford, J. (2003). *The Moon, Myth and Image*. London: Cassell Illustrated.

Daly, M. (1978). *Gyn/Ecology. The Metaethics of Radical Feminism*. London: the Women's Press.

Damasio, A.R. (1994). *Descartes' Error: Emotion, Reason and the Human Brain*. New York: Avon Books.

Damasio, A.R. (1999). *The Feeling of What Happens: Body, the Emotions in the Making of Consciousness*. New York: Harcourt Brace.

Debs, N. (2017) Ongoing Mourning as a Way to Go Beyond Endless Grief-Considerations on the Lebanese Experience. In Auestad, L. (ed.) *Shared Traumas, Silent Loss, Public and Private Mourning*. London: Karnac Books.

Douglas, M. (1966). *Purity and Danger. An Analysis of Concept of Pollution and Taboo*. London and New York: Routledge.

Douglas, M. (1968). Pollution. In *Encyclopaedia of the Social Sciences*. XII, pp. 336–341.

Eliade, M. (1969). *The Quest, History and Meaning in Religion*. Chicago and London: The University of Chicago Press.

Freud, S. (1914). Remembering, Repeating and Working-Through. (Further Recommendations on the Technique of Psycho-Analysis, II). *Collected Works*, Vol. 12. London: Hogarth.

Eliade, M. (1958). *Rites and Symbols of Initiation. The Mysteries of Birth and Rebirth*. Woodstock, CT: Spring Publications, 1995.

Fortes, M. (1949). *The Web of Kinship Among the Tallensi*. London: Oxford University Press.

Fraser, J.G. (1922). *The Golden Bough, A Study in Magic and Religion*. Abridged Ed. London and New York: Penguin Books.

Gillison, D. (2002). *New Guinea Ceremonies*. New York: Abrams.

Gluckman, M. (1965). *Politics, Law and Ritual in Tribal Society*. Chicago: Aldine Publisher.

Goodwyn, E. (2016). *Healing Symbols in Psychotherapy: A Ritual Approach*. London and New York: Routledge.

Harrison, J. (1903). *Prolegomena to the Study of Greek Religion*. London: Cambridge University Press.

Haule, J.R. (2011). *Jung in the 21st century, Vol. 1: Evolution and Archetype*. London and New York: Routledge.

Hernlund, Y. and Shell-Duncan, B. (2007). *Transcultural Bodies: Female Genital Cutting in Global Context*. New Brunswick, N.J: Rutgers University Press.

Hertz, R. (2009). A Contribution to the Study of the Collective Representation of Death. In (2009) Robben, A.C.G.M. (ed.) *Death Mourning and Burial: A Cross-Cultural Reader*. Malden, MA: Blackwell, pp. 197–212.

Jung, C.G. (1911–12/1952). Symbols of the Mother and Rebirth. In *Collected Works*, Vol. 5. *Symbols of Transformation*, 2nd edn. London: Routledge and Kegan Paul, 1995.

Kuper, H. (1947). *An African Aristocracy*. New York: Oxford University Press.

Lessa, W.A. and Vogt, E.Z. (eds.) (1979). *Reader in Comparative Religion, An Anthropological Approach*, 4th edn. Harvard: Harper Collins Publisher.

Lifton, R.J. and Olson, E. (2009). Symbolic Immortality. In Robben, A.C.G.M. (ed.) *Death, Mourning, and Burial: A Cross-Cultural Reader*. Malden, MA: Blackwell, pp. 32–38.

Mannix, K.M. (2017). *With the End in Mind: Dying, Death and Wisdom in the Age of Denial*. London: William Collins.

Meade, M. (1995) Introduction to Eliade, M. (1958). *Rites and Symbols of Initiation. The Mysteries of Birth and Rebirth*. Woodstock, CT: Spring Publications, 1995.

McCulloch, J.A. (1913). Monsters. In *Hastings Encyclopeadia of Religion and Ethics*. Edinburgh: T & C Clark.

McCauley, R.N. and Lawson, E.T. (2002). *Bringing Ritual to Mind*. Cambridge: Cambridge University Press.

Neumann, E. (1955). *The Great Mother.* Trans. Manheim, R. Princeton: Princeton University Press, 1991.

Radcliffe-Brown, A.R. (1952). *Structure and Function in Primitive Society. Essays and Addresses.* Glencoe Ill: The Free Press.

Rand, N.T. (ed.) (1994). *The Shell and the Kernel.* Chicago, IL: University of Chicago Press.

Robbens, AC.G.M. (ed.) (2009). *Death Mourning and Burial: A Cross-Cultural Reader.* Malden, MA: Blackwell.

Roth, W.E. (1897). *Ethnological Studies among the North-West-Central Queensland Aborigines.* London and Brisbane: Cornell University Press.

Shakespeare, W. (c. 1603). *King Lear.* London: Arden Shakespeare, Methuen, 1997.

Taylor, T. (2002). *The Buried Soul: How Humans Invented Death.* Boston: Beacon.

Turner, V.W. (1964). Betwixt and Between: The Liminal Period in Rites De Passage. In (1979) Lessa, W.A. and Vogt, E.Z. (eds.) *Reader in Comparative Religion, An Anthropological Approach*, 4th edn. Harvard: Harper Collins Publisher, pp. 234–243.

Turner, V.W. (1969). *The Ritual Process. Structure and Anti-Structure.* New Brunswick and London: Aldine Transaction.

Van Gennep, A. (1960). *Rites of Passage.* Chicago: University of Chicago Press.

Walker, B. (1983). *The Women's Encyclopaedia of Myths and Secrets.* San Francisco: Harper Collins.

Winthuis, J. (1929). Das *Zweitgeschlechterwesen* Leipzig: Hirschfeld Verlag.

Zeavin, H. (2017). War games-Mourning Loss Through Play. In Auestad, L. (ed.) *Shared Traumas, Silent Loss, Public and Private Mourning.* London: Karnac, pp. 1–13.

Chapter 8

Taboo, shamanism, and Jungian psychoanalysis

Introduction

Rites of passage leading to a new developmental status discussed in chapter 7 take place away in secluded darkness, similar to working with unconscious processes at night-time through dream work. Within this dark and invisible frame, one enters the liminal night-time journey of transformation, analogous to the sun as it sets in the west and disappears into the darkness of the 'other' side to arise anew the next day (Jung, 1911–12/1952a, paras. 251–253). This chapter explores the colour black as a night-time colour, which is not considered negative, but as an undifferentiated potential to be explored in the unconscious, not yet realised in consciousness. Blackness, itself, has many shades: there is black that recedes and absorbs; black that dampens and softens; black that sharpens and etches; and black that shines with an effervescence (Hillman, 1997, p. 11). From the analysis of black, I examine the role of shamans who undertake the difficult journey into the unconscious (as the land of the dead) to restore lost or stolen soul aspects of the self. I give two examples of this imaginal fete and compare their journey to the work of psychoanalysis, in particular, Jungian analysis.

Black as invisibility

When Hillman (1979, 1997, 1999) discusses the colour black, he suggests that this particular colour deepens our perception of unconscious material, hidden and tabooed, attached to sorrow and the loss of missing parts of the self, which when found in this blackness, paradoxically restores soul elements to the psyche as a whole. We discuss in chapter 4 the relationship of the miscegenation taboo attached to racism and the colour black. In this chapter, I want to examine black as the alchemical *nigredo*. Of the four alchemical substances, black, white, red, and gold, black plays an especially important role as the basis of the work because it enters into the genesis of the word alchemy. The word *khem* refers to Egypt as the black land, land of black soil; the art of alchemy was called the black art or science (Hillman, 1997, p. 5).

Any substance to enter the nigredo phase and blacken the operation includes in alchemical language: *mortification, putrefaction, calcination, iteration,* and *separation*. Separation means a decapitation (cf. Jung, 1954a, para. 730) by making distinctions that free the mind from a too literal, naturalistic, and reductive identification with nigredo. Separation and distance allow the mind to cognate the darkness and form imaginal appreciations of the material. The process is slow and pulverising, indicating a depressed melancholia already at work and broken down through the loss of comforting and safe paradigms, just as charcoal is the result of fire acting on wood, black faeces the result of digested food mixed with blood, and blackened fungus the result of putrefaction and decay.

Raff (2000, pp. 100–101) warns the initiate not to underestimate the dangers involved in working with unconscious processes, either by taking a naïve view that the imaginative world is full of good will, or that imaginative images should be unconditionally trusted. The ego that approaches the unconscious needs to be willing to hold its independent position, otherwise it will be overwhelmed by the undifferentiated unconscious emotions. The tension of holding the opposites between the ego and the unconscious is frightening, filled with terror and dread. These feeling of dread correspond to the definition of taboo as stepping over the border from one known state into the chaos of the unstructured unknown. The ego may be taken over by undifferentiated affect, particularly loss, abandonment, and guilt, which takes time to process.

Hillman (1997, p. 7) suggests that the two processes most relevant for producing blackness, that of putrefaction and mortification, break down the inner cohesion of a fixed state: putrefaction by decomposition or falling apart, mortification by grinding down as seeds in mortar refined into ever thinner and smaller particles. Black steers all variety of colour into the shade. The shade that black inflicts pertains to the deeper and invisible realms of darkness, carrying the meaning of random and formless. Like a black hole, it sucks into form and makes it vanish along with the fundamental security of consciousness. By deconstructing presence into absence, black breaks the paradigm of comfort and security, making psychological change possible by entering into taboo, liminal, border*land* states. For Hillman (1997 p. 14) blackness means the incorporation of invisibility within all perceptions, never losing the dark eye or ignoring the soul's desire for shades and sorrow. By means of black, concrete fixities shift into metaphorical images. We cure depression by becoming blacker than black, that is, *archetypally* black, not concretely black, so that we are no longer influenced by the prejudice of colour, but step in the underworld to explore these dreaded taboo images.

Hillman (1997, pp. 5–10) stresses that one of the main tasks of psychoanalysis is not to eliminate the black mood of depression, but to carefully reconvert it into melancholy, with an increased understanding of all its underworld moods, beauty, longing, nostalgia, losses and sadness. Sadak and

Weiser (2017, pp. 434–444) movingly depict the process of grieving, lamentation, and loss by personifying the emotional content as *Penthos*, the Greek spirit of mourning, who is related to the Algea spirits of sorrow and suffering. Gender fluid, sable skinned *Penthos* (or Roman *Luctus*) keeps close company with dread, terror, and madness. His/her bed sits outside the entrance to the underworld next to disease, old age, and fear. In Statius' *Thebaid 3, Penthos* as a composite image, expresses the inconsolable grief and sorrow of mothers who have lost their sons in warfare, as well as imaging the slain sons' injuries through her torn and bloody clothes and pierced breast. In Seneca's *Oedipus, Penthos* tears out her hair in misery and desolation. These vivid archetypal images offer containment and legitimacy for such inconsolable emotions, reconnecting individual lonely melancholy to the communality of collective grieving and loss that is embedded within the collective unconscious.

Blackness is associated positively with black clouds, which bring rain and much needed moisture (Fraser, 1922, p. 87). Brewster (2017, pp. 58–59) points out that pollution (or a taboo element) is considered in Zulu's beliefs to have special powers and two situations dominate: red and black. Red is associated with fertility, child birth, and menstruation; black with faeces, nighttime, and death. Black medicine is considered necessary to restore health and provides a time for resting. Brewster alludes to Hillman's insistence on darkness to putrefy matter as a return to the undifferentiated *prima materia*. The journey to the underworld is a rite of passage to overstep the margins that separate the known (consciousness) from the unknown (the unconscious) to widen consciousness. Passage through the underworld is held within a hidden precinct (*temenos or Hort*) connected to the womb and rebirth (Jung, 1911–12/1952b, para. 570). A basic tenet of Jungian analysis is to explore the unconscious for missing, undeveloped, or disassociated aspects of the personality that are stuck at the margins between outdated authoritarian blocking mechanisms and legitimatise their presence within the psyche.

Hades

In describing working with unconscious processes such as dreams, Hillman (1979, pp. 27–32) depicts Hades rather than *Penthos* as the spirit of the depths, the god of invisibles. Hades, himself invisible, is said to have no temples or altars and, thus, no representative attributes except an eagle. Hades hides invisibility in things. Hidden itself is an attribute of being buried, shrouded, and concealed from eyesight. Whether as a corpse of a *mysterium or* concealed in the sense of a secret, that which is hidden cannot be seen on inspection; it is blocked, censored or forbidden. In short, Hades is nature's 'tabooed hidden hider.' Hillman's description of Hades is that of nonbeing, that liminal state after separation in the darkness, the putrefying, indeterminate state in which the neophyte navigates the individuation process as a voluntary death process to reassimilate tabooed soul elements that have been disassociated as either lost or stolen and restore order.

The rites of passage at puberty discussed in the previous chapter use the properties assigned to Hades: first, the neophytes are buried or shrouded as a corpse; second, they are concealed in the sense of having a secret; third, they are nonvisible and hidden from view; fourth, they are without sunlight in dark places, sometimes painted black; fifth, they are hidden in a subterranean storeroom, cellar, or cell. Sixth, they are taboo, untouchable and experienced with dread and terror. Seventh, the rites are imbued with stealthy, hidden motives and linked by unseen connections. Hillman suggests that all psychic events and rites of passage have these aspects of Hades when we ask what these events mean for one's life and death process.

Hillman (1979, pp. 24–32) is correct when he maintains that dream analysis has moved from the Freudian attention of taking things apart and reducing them to wayward bits and pieces that have fallen through the cracks of the ego. Visibilities are never enough for the soul in search of meaning. Invisible connections are stronger: to arrive at the basic structure of things, one must go into their darkness because the real constitution of each thing is accustomed to hiding itself. Nature loves to hide. It is in the operation of penetrating, an in-sighting into depth that is soul making as it proceeds. If soul is the prime mover, then its primary movement is deepening and penetrating; it increases its dimension and all things become soul. The movement from the material to the psychic perspective often presents dream imagery of sickening and dying (mortification) because the conscious perspective of the ego is one-sided.

Jungian analysis has been likened to shamanism (cf. Smith, 1997; Noel, 1999; Duran, 2012). Apart from the long intensive training and exposure to unconscious processes required by both disciplines, their salient similarity lies in the use of nature, particularly animal energy, as a transitional tool to reconnect unconscious tabooed disassociated elements of the psyche to enrich and benefit both the personal and collective consciousness. Theriomorphic symbols allow for a wider range of differentiated emotional expression than human form and restore animal totem ancestral imaginary, bringing that disassociated root instinct in-line with ego consciousness (Jung, 1951, para. 291; Hannah, 2006, pp. 3–19; Bernstein, 2005, pp. 15–32).

Depictions of shamanism

Eliade (1964, p. 4) states that shamanism is pre-eminently a religious phenomenon of Siberia and Central Asia as the practice was described and documented by the earliest travellers to these regions. Later, similar magico-religious shamanic practices were observed in North America, Indonesia, Oceania, Africa, and elsewhere. To differentiate shamanism from magic and magicians found worldwide, shamans exhibit a particular speciality, such as mastery over fire and magical flight. The shaman, as distinct from a magician, specialises in an imaginal trance whereby his soul is believed to leave his body and ascend to the sky or descend to the underworld in search of lost or stolen souls. The Central and Northeast Asian methods of recruiting shamans are first, through heredity transmission, second, by spontaneous vocation through a call or election, and third, through his/her own free will; the self-made shaman is not considered as powerful as the other two accesses to the shamanic profession.

Future shamans are expected to pass through certain initiatory ordeals and receive a highly complex twofold education: ecstatic through dreams and didactic through instruction. Eliade (1964) stresses that it is not the point of departure for obtaining shamanic powers (heredity, bestowal of spirits, voluntary quest), but the technique and its underlying theory, transmitted through initiation, that is important. All the ecstatic experiences that determine the future shaman's vocation involve the traditional schema of the initiation ceremony: suffering, death, and resurrection. Suffering includes the symbolic dismemberment of the body, followed by a renewal of the internal organs and viscera: ascent to the sky and dialogue with the gods and spirits, descent to the underworld to dialogue with souls of the dead and the ancestors.

These ordeals appear in the dreams of the shaman initiate who experiences his/her initiatory sickness, cured through the initiation process of becoming a shaman. The initiation process includes the fundamental pattern of all initiations: first, torture at the hands of demons or spirits who play the role of masters of initiation; second, ritual death experienced by the candidate as a descent into hell or an ascent into heaven, and third, the resurrection of a new mode of being as someone who can personally communicate with the spirit. The shaman's integration of a new personality is largely dependent on his/her being cured. The initiatory imaginal death forms an integral part of the mystical process by which the neophyte becomes *another* fashioned in accordance to the spiritual ancestors and made by the old masters to reveal the deep meaning of existence to new generations in participating fully in their culture.

The key to the esoteric training of the novice shaman is to develop enhanced skills in mental imagery with an auditory component. The novice is trained to increase the vividness of his internal imagery through various psychological and physiological techniques, some of which are extreme, such as pain stimulation, hypoglycaemia, dehydration, acoustic stimulation, restricted mobility, and hyperventilation, all of which induce an alteration in consciousness. It is as if the vibrant world within blocks out the light from the outside world (Noll, 1987, pp. 47–61).

Once novices have access to such internal imagery, they learn how to master their transpersonal energies that convey crucial information and wisdom beyond the normal constraints of space and time. Guardian spirits in the form of animal helpers, spirit ancestors, and teachers are invoked by the shaman who believes he/she is tapping into collective repository of the wisdom of the human species, which Jung called the collective unconscious.[1] Thus, instructions from such spirits existing in the imaginal realm of reality that coincides and interacts with ordinary states of consciousness can facilitate spiritual transformation.

Above all, shamans are able to contribute imaginatively to the *knowledge of death*. Through the features of funerary geography, the unknown, terrifying, and taboo assume imaginative form as animals or supernatural humans organised in accordance with particular patterns that become familiar and acceptable. The invisible as tabooed become visible, even knowable, and death itself is elevated primarily as a rite of passage on a spiritual mode of being. Shamans' ecstatic journeys, above all, enrich death with their imaginative forms and figures, making the final liminal crossing into the unknown knowable, bearable, and meaningful.

The usual shamanistic performance is carried out in an inner room with the light extinguished (Bogoras, 1904–1909, pp. 443–441). In some cases, after the shaman has sung, beaten the drum, and conversed with his accompanying animal spirits, s/he sinks into a trance during which his body lies unconscious on the ground while his/her soul visits spirits in their own world and asks for advice, chiefly to find the missing soul of his/her patient. Among the northwestern branch of the Koryak and the Asiatic Yupik, the spirits use a special kind of language or pronunciation. During the shamanic ritual, it is strictly taboo to attempt to touch any of the 'spirits.' If the taboo is broken, the spirits might kill the shaman on the spot, or kill the transgressor with a knife thrust through his/her ribs in the dark. Needham (1967, pp. 606–614) argues that there is a connection in human life between percussion and transition. The percussion instruments used by the shaman, such as drum, gong, bell, tambourine, rattle, rasp, and resounding rocks, and the sounds they produce, communicate with the spirits of the other world. Dworakowski (1938) through a comparative study of the drum, the bell, and the gong, suggests that there is a close relationship between these instruments and cults of the dead. She does not, however, explain sufficiently the symbolic nature of that connection.

Crawley (1912, p. 91) earlier bridged that gap by suggesting that the sound of the drum is complete enough to cover a whole range of human emotion. Following on from this observation, Needham argues that there is an immediate connection between the type of sound and the type of rite being performed, leading to the conclusion of a significant connection between percussion and transition. Percussion is a transition marker and displays fundamental features: first, its affective impact; second, as the go-between two structures of category change. Huxley (1967, p. 286) points out that the drummer provokes disassociation by quickening, altering, or breaking rhythm, which meets and balances the emotional disorientation of the oncoming separation and status change. Firecrackers used during Chinese wedding ceremonies similarly act as neutral sound markers to punctuate separation.

In Yakut shamanism in Siberia, the future shaman 'dies' and lies in the yurt for three days without eating or drinking. The candidate dreams that his/her limbs are symbolically removed and disjointed with an iron hook. The bones are cleaned, the flesh scraped, body fluids thrown away and the eyes torn from their sockets. After the operation, all the bones are gathered and fastened together with iron. The operation lasts seven days, and during that time, the initiate remains like a dead person, solitary and scarcely breathing. Each candidate has a great Bird-of-Prey Mother with hooked claws and a long tail who shows itself twice: at the shaman's spiritual birth and at his/her death. It carries her/his soul to the underworld and leaves it to ripen to gain maturity. The bird carries it back to earth, cuts the candidate's body into pieces and distributes to the evil spirits that bring disease and death. Each spirit devours his/her share and departs, which gives the future shaman his/her power to cure the corresponding diseases. The Bird-of-Prey Mother restores the bones to their places and the candidate wakes up as if from a long sleep. An alternative account depicts the Bird-of-Prey Mother alighting on a giant fir tree, laying eggs, then brooding and hatching shamans respectively in three-, two-, and one-year intervals depending on their respective status.

The descent to the underworld is initiated by shamans searching for the soul of a sick person that has strayed or been abducted (Eliade, 1964, pp. 308–309). The theory of the loss of soul as a cause of illness is comparatively ancient and found in shamanic practices worldwide. It is principally in searching for a patient's lost soul that the shaman uses his/her knowledge of infernal topography and his/her capabilities of ecstatic clairvoyance. The shaman's journey to the underworld takes on dramatic aspects. For example, among the tribes of British Columbia, the shaman takes the old path to the land of the dead and has to fight ghosts before s/he can wrest the patient's soul from them. Since the Nootka attribute the theft of the soul to marine spirits, the shaman in ecstasy dives to the bottom of the ocean and returns wet, sometimes streaming with blood from his nose and temple, carrying the stolen soul in a bunch of eagle feathers. Shamans are believed capable of not only bringing strayed souls of the sick but also of restoring the dead to life. Those who are thus restored on their return from the underworld tell the living what they have seen in the land of the dead in 'spirit.' Shamanism implies the possibility of returning to the origins of time to recover that prelapsarian innocence that existed before the 'fall,' that is, the breakdown of communication between heaven and earth, humans and animals. This primordial state is reaccessible only through ascent and descent.

To rectify any notion that shamans suffer from defective or a too diffuse, magical, associative thinking, Shweder (1969, pp. 327–331) researched into 33 Zinacanteco South American shamans and contends that, in comparison to nonshamans, shamans, in fact, possess special cognitive skills, such as inner directedness and clear-headedness. They avoid bafflement and confusion more efficiently than nonshamans. Shamans easily impose form and structure on diffuse sense data, are productive in their responses, and generative to different responses. To sum up, shamans are better capable of imposing a differentiated order on chaos than nonshamans and emerge as effective agents of control on unstructured stimuli, which, in turn, produces highly productive, creative, and generative response patterns.

Robbins (2011, pp. 89–93) underscores the view that shamans are unusually mature persons who have undergone rigorous and stressful training that enables them to negotiate in a controlled way between the mental world of thought and trance or ecstasy and translate the experiences from one context to another. The spirit is believed to be an essence, not isomorphic, within the body and able to travel independently of time and space. Halifax (1979, 1982) concludes that shamans develop an unusual sensitivity and compassion because they continually confront and struggle with their own deepest suffering and despair and, thus, are able to contact and help heal others on that deep level without disassociating from that suffering. Eliade (1958, p. 102) also emphasises that the shaman is powerful because he/she *knows* and *remembers*. The initiatory death evokes courage and strengthens memory and mental faculties. S/he is not only an ecstatic who shares in the spirit life, but is also a contemplative thinker, passionately interested in the intertwining mysteries of outer and inner life.

Two examples of shamanism in practice

A shaman journey to the underwater Sea Spirit

In this moving account, Knud Rasmussen (1929/1979, pp. 308–311) one of the foremost authorities on Inuit people, describes a chief shamanic ritual to propitiate the spirit of the sea called Sedna or the sea goddess. The Inuit believe that the sea goddess controls the sea mammals, which, in turn, provide the Inuit with their food, fuel, and clothing, and sends the worst misfortunes when a misdeed or an offense is committed. These offenses gather dirt and impurities over the body of the goddess. It is necessary for the shaman to travel to the body of the sea to meet the sea goddess, comb her hair from dirt and lice, and report the difficulties of his people. The goddess replies by relating which breaches of taboo have caused the misfortunes. The shaman returns to his people to hear their confessions and, presumably, when all the taboo violations are confessed, the goddess releases the game, returns lost souls, cures illnesses, and restores equilibrium and prosperity to the Inuit.

The sea goddess was once a girl who was thrown into the sea by her own father, who cruelly cut off her fingers as she clung in terror to the side of the boat. Feminist anthropologist, Sonne (1992, pp. 172–174) suggests the father was so angry with his daughter because she tenaciously refused to marry.

Her cut-off fingers become various species of sea mammals while the fingerless girl sinks to the bottom of the sea and is transformed into the giant mistress of the species that sprang from her hands. When a shaman wishes to visit Sedna on behalf of the community or a particular family experiencing sickness, s/he sits on the inner part of the sleeping place behind a curtain and 'drops down,' wearing almost nothing, to the bottom of the sea. No one knows how this imaginal feat is accomplished; some evidence suggests that the earth 'opens up' like a wormhole under the shaman with the help of his/her deceased ancestor spirits. In the darkened room, one can hear sighing and puffing noises as if the spirits were deep in the water and coming up to breath as if they were sea mammals.

The shaman experiences many difficulties on the way to the bottom of the sea to visit the sea goddess, the most dreaded being the three large rolling stones, which can easily crush the shaman, that leave very little space to pass between them. Once past them, the shaman follows a coastal path and enters a great plain where Sedna lives, guarded by a snarling dog seated at the doorway of her house. If a large shelter wall is built outside the house, this means that Sedna is very angry and implacable and the shaman has to kick the wall down. Some say that the house has no roof so that Sedna can better observe the behaviour of humans. To the right of her lamp, all different kinds of game, such as seals, walrus, and whales collect in a great pool. When the shaman enters, s/he sees at once Sedna sitting with her back to the lamp and with her back to all the animals in the pool. Her hair hangs down loosely in a tangled untidy mass hiding her eyes so that she cannot see. It appears as if all the human misdeeds and offenses have gathered as dirt and impurity over her body with her hair filled with dirt and lice.

The shaman's task is to grasp Sedna by the shoulder to turn her face toward the lamp and the animals. S/he then strokes and combs Sedna's hair because she is unable to comb it herself as she has no fingers. Once Sedna is calmer and soothed, the shaman relates to her that 'those above can no longer help the seals up by grasping their fore flippers.' Sedna tells the shaman that certain breaches of taboo have barred the way for the animals. The shaman appeases her anger and when, at last, she is in a friendlier mood, she frees the animals into a whirlpool to return into the sea. The shaman returns to those awaiting him through the tube kept open for him by the spirits. Those above can hear him/her returning from the sea as if to take a deep pressured breath. All in the house must confess to any breaches of taboo. One particular breach of taboo concerns a young woman who has not admitted to a miscarriage, but kept it secret because of all the consequences involved, such as throwing away all the soft skin contents in her house including the sealskin used to line the whole interior of the snow hut. The main cause of Sedna's anger is the hidden 'thick blood' on a menstruation cloth pointing to a miscarriage that has escaped the necessary purification rites. Once the rites have been exercised, they can be assured of an abundance of game the following day.

The sea goddess, herself, is a personification of taboo who absorbs all the dirt accumulated at the margins between consciousness and the collective unconscious. Most of the taboos in Inuit culture affect women during menstruation. They are not allowed to work, to wash, comb their hair, move out of doors, eat meat from freshly killed animals, or even use their own drinking cup. In Greenland, a woman spends this period sitting on a platform facing the wall. In Canada and Alaska, a separate hut is made to isolate her completely. A breach of these rules would contaminate the souls of killed sea mammals and hinder their rebirth from the house of the Sea Woman. As Sonne (ibid, p. 173) correctly surmises, the depiction of the Sea Woman's helpless state is modelled on the actual woman under taboo. Like her, the Sea Woman is unable to look after her own hair because of the taboos. The shaman performs the purification for her so that she emerges calmer, cleaner, and able to free the animals.

The burden of taboo is much harder on women than men because women, by their biological nature, are the vehicles of human life who pass through two main perilous transitional stages: birth and death. Within these transitional stages, there lies the danger that the life cycle of sea mammals would become entangled with that of humans with the result that the reciprocity between animals and human could become damaged. The shaman's task is to ensure that the exchanged relationship continues. In indigenous beliefs, the true nature of every animal was considered to be human-like and sea mammals even more so because they spring from the hands of a human girl. Sonne (p. 174) asks why from the girl's hands and not from another part of the human body? She suggests that 'hands' signify a meat-sharing relationship. Meat shared and exchanged is offered by sea mammals, whose reincarnation depended upon the behaviour of humans. Humans alone are responsible for keeping in motion the rebirth cycle of sea mammals. One can interpret the myth of Sedna as follows: in her refusal to marry, she denies her parents the proper use of her hands, draining the meat supply procured within the family. Sedna removes herself to the margins of society (the liminal state) but still remains tied to it through her severed fingers, as a token of the meat-sharing alliance. Human members now hunt the animals into which the productive capacity of her fingers is transformed. In Canada and Greenland, Inuit adult women are primarily responsible for maintaining and mediating between both life cycles: human and animal. The two are interchangeable. By refusing to conform to societal gender forms of marriage and childbearing, Sedna remains in that intermediate, liminal zone as the caretaker of taboo.

This interpretation stresses that Sedna both absorbs and personifies the taboo and its violation for the collective in the collective unconscious, that is, in the land of the dead. Van Gennep (1960, p. 146) gives graphic descriptions of the journey into this domain, similar in topography undertaken by the shaman when s/he crosses the shoreline into Sedna's house. Sedna is the composite archetypal image of taboo combining a wide spectrum of affect in her disorderly appearance. The shaman needs enough courage to handle Sedna's strongly ambivalent disassociated emotions (dissent, anger, injustice, jealousy, shame) empathically, by touching and caring for them in the form of her tangled, matted hair, thereby soothing, understanding, and healing her psyche in the process. The role of a psychoanalyst is similar to that of a shaman: s/he must enter the unconscious terrain of the dead or the disassociated others by dialoguing and touching the tabooed emotions that hinder ego enrichment.

Shaman's symbolic journey into the womb

The second example of shamanism shows the therapeutic use of vivid symbols. Illness and disease are not merely physiological phenomena; anthropologists and depth psychologists have long noted the widespread use of curative symbols and their effect on patients. Such symbols organise the ways in which physiological illness is perceived, experienced, and dealt with. Beginning with this premise, Levi-Strauss (1963, pp. 186–205) analyses a song used by Cuna Indian Shamans to facilitate difficult childbirth.[2] He suggests that the effectiveness of the song lies in its power to psychologically manipulate the patient's generative organs. The shaman's song provides a mythic language by which the patient can express the inexpressible incoherence of pain and disorder. By attaining this psychological release, the shaman also affects the physiological cure. Levi-Strauss draws a parallel between shamanism and psychoanalytic efficacy, asserting that both attempt a cure by creating a myth, which the patient must then relive. In the case of shamanism, it is a collective myth; in the case of psychoanalysis, it is the personal myth. However, Levi-Strauss stresses than both are one and the same because shamanism and psychoanalysis parallel a universal, unconscious, symbolic function regardless of cultural conditioning. Although this view has been criticised (cf. Neu, 1975) few, including Douglas (1966, pp. 88–89), would question Levi-Strauss' insight into the power of therapeutic symbols in ritual that give meaning and engender courage.

The song begins by describing the shaman's arrival and the preparation consisting of fumigations of burnt cocoa-nibs, invocations, and the making of sacred figures called *nuchu.* These images carved out of prescribed wood represent tutelary spirits whom the shaman makes his assistants and whom he leads into the abode of *Muu* (the uterus) responsible for making the foetus. A difficult childbirth has resulted because *Muu* exceeds her functions and captured the *purba,* or soul, of the pregnant woman. Thus, the song embodies a quest for the lost soul of the woman, which will be recovered after many vicissitudes, such as overcoming obstacles, a victory of wild beasts, and, finally, the great contest waged by the shaman and his tutelary spirits against *Muu* and her daughters; once defeated, *Muu* allows the purba to be discovered and freed. The delivery of the child takes place. The battle is not against *Muu* herself, who is indispensable to procreation, but against her abuse of power.

Muu is literally the vagina and uterus itself, within which the shaman penetrates and frees the child. The pregnant woman has not just lost her purba, her double, but also her *niga,*[3] meaning her strength and vitality, which needs to be restored. It appears that *Muu*, as the instigator of the disorder, has captured the souls of the other organs in the pregnant woman's body, thus destroying the cooperation that would normally exist between them in childbirth. Once these souls are liberated by finding the corresponding teeth and hair captured by *Muu*, the soul of the uterus in the form of *Muu* cooperates. At the same time, *Muu* must not escape before childbirth is accomplished, so the shaman mobilises the lords of the wild animals to guard *Muu's* opening. Golden and silver nets are fastened, and for four days, the shaman's assistants (*nelegan*) stand watch and beat their sticks to keep *Muu's* way open.

In *Muu's* way, darkened and covered in blood is situated *Muu's* abode in a dark, uterine whirlpool where she dwells. To enter the abode, the shaman's *nelegan* wearing white hats take on the appearance and the motions of an erect penis to symbolically enter the vagina. Not only does the patient feel them entering, they also light up the route that they are preparing for the delivery. The image of white hats also attributes a reflective thinking function to the *nelegan* as they penetrate to assess the difficulties of labour and bring these to attention.

The searing labour pains of contractions and dilations become embodied in images of Uncle Alligator moving about with his bulging eyes, sharp teeth, and swishing scaly tail; *Nele Ki (k) kirpanalele*, the octopus with sticky, sucking tentacles alternatively opening and closing; and many others, such as the black tiger, the red animal, and the dust-coloured animal, all tied with an iron chain, their tongues hanging out as claws tear at things 'all like blood, all red.' The *nelegan* also have to overcome other obstacles, this time in the form of material such as fibres, loose threads, and brightly coloured curtains. For this task, the shaman brings in lords of the wood-boring insects that cut and reduce the threads identified as the internal tissues of the uterus. The lords of the burrowing animals, such as the armadillo, prepare the way to the orifice. It is not only against *Muu's* elusive stray impulses that the cure must be affected, but also to offer the patient a resolution so that all the imaginal protagonists have returned to an order that is no longer threatened or frightening but now productive.

Levi-Strauss suggests (ibid. p. 197) that the cure consists of making a distressing situation, originally existing on an emotional level, acceptable to the physical pains the body hitherto refuses to tolerate. That the mythology of the shaman does not correspond to the objective reality does not matter. The patient believes in the shaman's helpers, which helps her accept the incoherent and arbitrary pains that feel like alien elements in her body but which the shaman will reintegrate as a whole to make the unbearable contractions of the uterus meaningful. In this way, her soul's vitality is restored and freed up from the overwhelming influence of uterine childbirth symbolised by the wayward and difficult *Muu*. Entering into the relationship with a living symbol (*Muu*), the shaman provides both a language and an image by which unexpressed psychic states can be immediately experienced and expressed. Progress in a difficult childbirth is further facilitated by imaginal action on the part of the shaman's helpers. During the second part of the delivery process, when the unwilling uterus in the form of *Muu* has been sufficiently contained, attention turns to the *nelegans'* feet, now with shoes on, marching in rows of four rather than two, or in single file, to coincide with and support the widening process of dilatation in childbirth. The effectiveness of such images guarantees the harmonious paralleled development between myth and action, symbolic and concrete, and mutuality of trust and accompaniment between patient and healer.

Levi-Strauss emphasises (ibid. p. 198) the role of language in this process to induce physiological release, whereas I suggest equally the Jungian definition of a symbol[4] in terms of the efficacy of an *image* as preverbal communication. All the shaman's helpers (*nelegan*) have specific emotional images, such as white hats, white shoes, and specialised animals, such as crocodile, octopus, armadillo, and tigers, which help absorb and restructure physical pain so that the patient can simultaneously cope better psychologically. Levi-Strauss (ibid, pp. 201–203) compares shamanism to psychoanalysis in that both methods involve a genuine abreaction through a double transference mechanism whereby both the shaman and analyst serve as flesh and blood protagonists with whom the patient can restore and clarify an initial situation, which has remained unconscious, unexpressed, and unformulated. The precise differentiated images evoked by the shaman reverberate in the unconscious to affect the cure.

Taboo, shamanism, and Jungian analysis

Both the above examples of shamanist practice illustrate the skill and courage shamans show by entering the realm of taboo and dialoguing with the disassociated emotional contents, such as fear, grief, and loss (as lost souls), which are impoverishing ego agency. Their analytical and detailed exploration of the emotions involved and the precise images they create to express and absorb their patient's unconscious pain is remarkable. In both cases illustrated above, soul energy is either missing or stolen because a taboo has not been respected. The shaman has to find the missing soul aspect in the unconscious and restore it to consciousness so that an actual birth or an imaginal rebirth, depending on the case involved, can effectively occur.

The relationship between taboo, shamanism, and psychoanalysis is well depicted by Merchant (2012, p. 25) who compares the vocation of the shaman (cf. Eliade, 1964) to that of a psychoanalyst as wounded healers who have both entered the realm of taboo, that is, into the unspeakable, and survived the ordeal. Both the shaman and the analyst during their training have been symbolically killed, dismembered, and put together again, so they are able to retrieve lost souls in the underworld of Penthos, Hades, or Sedna. They traversed that tabooed, invisible, border*land* realm to recover lost energy caught up in that unconscious realm. Both return safely and restore what was lost, or disassociated, for the benefit of the individual and the collective consciousness. The process leads to a widening of ego consciousness through abreaction, differentiation, and the courage to bear previously tabooed, emotional material.

Guggenbuhl-Craig (1999, pp. 408–411) alludes to the shaman archetype as an important element in a good Jungian analyst and is a talent that one is born with. The shaman archetype ensures that dreams from the unconscious are imaginatively dialogued. Jung (1954b, para. 411, 448) defines the process of individuation in his definition as a series of painful initiatory ordeals. It is only in initiation ceremonies that death is given a positive value. Symbolic death prepares the new spiritual birth access to a mode of being not subject to the destroying action of time. Jung defined shamans as those who leave their bodies and make contact with the transpersonal archetypal realm of the collective unconscious, showing patients these other dimensions, especially through dream work. Consequently, Jung sees a shamanic initiation as central to the vocation of being an analyst. In indigenous tribes, the shamanic initiate is the one who experiences a breakthrough of the collective unconscious and is able to master the overwhelming experience, a feat those psychically wounded cannot achieve on their own.

Groesbeck emphasises (1989, p. 274) that those analysts who directly communicate with the emotions within a patient's illness to produce a transformational experience can be considered as effective analysts. Merchant (2012) suggests that given the more recent contemporary views on neuroscience research, not available to Jung when he wrote about archetypes as an innate, *a priori* disposition, the shaman archetype could be better understood as an emergent and developmentally produced mind/brain structure forged out of intense affective experiences in infancy and, once in existence, has the capacity to directly influence psychological life. Merchant (2012, p. 162) thus argues that shamanism is not an innate talent as Guggenbuhl-Craig suggests, but an emergent one having more to do with the individual's capacity to process and use early preverbal infant trauma associated with the development of the proto-borderline model. Merchant believes that the proto-borderline model, when applied to particular analysts, explains why they are drawn to their own psychotherapy and what kinds of wounds predispose them to the analytical vocation.

An effective analyst must have a similar prototype borderline psychological structure as shamans, that is sufficiently wounded at a core level of their personality, but without further gross psychopathology deriving from other chaos, which would impede their all-important self-cure. This also explains how analysts use this psychological construction in their countertransference because the analysts' own pocket of early infant damage becomes activated and resonates with that of their patient. The self-cure through their own analytical work enables them to engage with unconscious complexes as a wounded healer without being possessed by them. It is only those analysts who have been wounded in the earliest stages of infancy who have the essential porosity and susceptibility to the psychic infection kind of embodied countertransference experiences. Jung (1946, para. 364) suggests that the analyst 'by voluntarily and consciously taking over the psychic suffering of the patient, exposes himself to the overpowering contents of the unconscious and their reductive action.' Jung stresses that the transference bond (conscious/unconscious) demands the whole person of the analyst in his/her preparedness to enter into the suffering of the other and become affected by it.

Hillman (1977, p. 117) emphasises that the wounded healer is a personification of a consciousness that has broken through dismemberment and allows a dialogue between two people through their wounds: 'My wounds speak to yours; yours to mine.' Hillman equates such moments of localised, dismembered, disassociated consciousness as the 'healers in the wounds.' These statements resonate with the work of shamans who enter into difficult taboo, unconscious terrain between the margins where aspects of the self are lost or stuck in transit. As shown in the two illustrations of shamanic intervention, shamans touch 'tabooed filth,' not as dirty or disgusting, but as emotional aspects that need patience, kindness, and empathy.

Conclusion

Working with dreams where the animal psyche often appears as a helpful guide, as I describe in chapter 6 (two clinical cases), links unconscious processes to shamanism and Jungian analysis. The animal psyche bears witness to the efficacy of indigenous animal totems as vital energy sources that link us to our instincts and our evolutionary past, as I have described in chapter 4.

The analytical work involved is difficult because certain emotions have been tabooed for good reason; to uncover them feels like a betrayal to the collective rules that are meant to keep us safe but at the expense of independent thinking and freedom of expression. Questioning religious or secular authority is a courageous act filled with anxiety and dread. Animal totemic energy provides a method of differentiation, which can lead to change and how we view working with taboo as a creative, rather than a punitive phenomenology.

Working with taboo is important in clinical practice because the analyst and the patient gain insight into the taboo unconscious areas that have not yet entered the symbolic death process of independent thinking and separation, but become stuck in a never ending liminal ritual of cleansing and purification of dirt and contamination. Such patients have not been able to traverse their margins into a new consciousness because of societal or religious pressure to conform; taking risks into unchartered territory would be seen as 'sinful.'

Each culture performs its rites of passage in different ways using different taboos, depending on climate and topology (cf. Brodersen, 2016, pp. 20–27). An analyst from a different culture, as I show in the two client cases in chapter 6, can help overcome an outdated set of taboos in a more conservative, authoritarian culture that is causing considerable psychological distress. The severity of the taboo in the form of a symptom gives an indication of the ambivalence between not overstepping a particular margin and the overriding wish and need to do so.

Notes

1. The concept of collective unconscious as defined by Jung (1936, paras. 87–110) differentiates the personal unconscious consisting of mainly of complexes, and the collective unconscious made up essentially of archetypes. Archetypes are primordial categories of imaginative thought made visible and dynamic through motifs that become clothed as images that enact their energetic charge.
2. Levi-Strauss places stress on the words in the song of the shaman, whereas I suggest that the specific physicality of the images evoked by the shaman in animal form as helpers meet and assuage the difficult painful labour.
3. The word *Niga* is used nonpejoratively by Levi-Strauss, where its original indigenous meaning of positive vitality and resistance is stressed.
4. Each of the shaman's helpers embodies a specific image that constellates a preverbal somatic communication. These are immediate and empathic, similar in nature to affect attunement in the mother-infant dyad before the child is able to speak (cf. Stern, 1998, pp. 138–61).

References

Bernstein, J.S. (2005). *Living in the Borderland, The Evolution of Consciousness and the Challenge of Healing Trauma.* London and New York: Routledge.

Bogoras, W. (1904–1909). Shamanistic Performance in the Inner Room. In Boas, F. (ed.) *The Chuckhee*, Vol. VII. *The Jesup North Pacific Expedition.* Leiden: Brill.

Brewster, F. (2017). *African Americans and Jungian Psychology, Leaving the Shadows* London and New York: Routledge.

Brodersen, E. (2016). *Laws of Inheritance, A Post-Jungian Study of Twins and the Relationship Between the First and Other(s).* Abingdon and New York: Routledge.

Cater, N. (ed.) (2012). *Native American Culture and the Western Psyche: A Bridge Between.* New Orleans; Louisiana: Spring Journal.

Crawley, A.E. (1912). Drums and Cymbals. *Encyclopedia of Religion and Ethics*, V. London: T&T Clark, pp. 89–94.

Douglas, M. (1966). *Purity and Danger. An Analysis of Concept of Pollution and Taboo.* London and New York: Routledge, 2002.

Duran, E. (2012). Medicine Wheel, Mandala, and Jung. In Cater, N. (ed.) *Native American Culture and the Western Psyche: A Bridge Between*. New Orleans; Louisiana: Spring Journal.

Dworakowska, M. (1938) The Origin of Bell and Drum. *Pr Etnol. Warsaw* Vol. 5, Warsaw: Nakladem Towarzystwa Nankowego Warszawskiego.

Eliade, M. (1958). *Rites and Symbols of Initiation. The Mysteries of Birth and Rebirth*. Woodstock, CT: Spring Publications, 1995.

Eliade, M. (1964). *Shamanism, Archaic Technique of Ecstasy*. Princeton: Princeton University Press.

Fraser, J. (1922). *The Golden Bough. A Study of Magic and Religion*. Abridged Version. London and New York: Penguin Books.

Groesbeck, C.J. (1989). C.G. Jung and the Shaman's Vision. *Journal of Analytical Psychology* 34, 225–275.

Guggenbuhl-Craig (1999). The Necessity of Talent. In (1999) Mattoon, M.A. (ed.) *Florence 98, Destruction and Creation; Personal and Cultural Transformations. Proceedings of the Fourteenth International Congress for Analytical Psychology*. CH-Einsiedeln: Daimon Verlag, pp. 408–411.

Halifax, J. (1979). *Shamanic Voices: A Survey of Visionary Narratives*. New York: Arkana.

Halifax, J. (1982). *Shaman: The Wounded Healer*. London: Thames and Hudson.

Hannah, B. (2006). *The Archetypal Symbolism of Animals. Lectures given at the CGJI Zürich 1954–1958*. Wilmette, Illinois: Chiron Publisher.

Hillman, J. (1977). Puer Wounds and Ulysses' Scar. In Hillman, J. (ed.) *Puer Papers*. Dallas: Spring Pubs, 1979.

Hillman, J. (1979). *The Dream and the Underworld*. Toronto: Harper Collins.

Hillman, J. (1997). The Seduction of Black. In (1997) Hillman, Hogarth, et.al. (eds.) *Haiti or the Psychology of Black*. Woodstock, Conn: Spring Publication.

Hillman, J. (1999). A Note on Hermes Inflation. In (1999) Hillman, Burns, Grimaldi-Craig, Smith, et al (eds.) *Lost Souls*. Woodstock Conn: Spring Journal.

Hillman, J. (ed.) (1979). *Puer Papers*. Dallas: Spring Pubs.

Hillman, J., Hogarth, H. et al. (eds.) (1997). *Haiti or the Psychology of Black*. Woodstock, Conn: Spring Publication.

Hillman, J., Burns, J., Grimaldi-Craig, S., Smith, A., et al. (eds.) (1999). *Lost Souls*. Woodstock Conn: Spring Journal.

Huxley, F. (1967). Anthropology and ESP. In (1967) Symthies, J.R. (ed.) *Science and ESP*. London: Routledge and Kegan Paul.

Jung, C.G. (1911–12/1952a). The Origin of the Hero. In *Collected Works*, Vol. 5 *Symbols of Transformation*, 2nd edn. London: Routledge and Kegan Paul, 1995.

Jung, C.G. (1911–12/1952b.) The Dual Mother. In *Collected Works*, Vol. 5 *Symbols of Transformation*, 2nd edn. London: Routledge and Kegan Paul, 1995.

Jung, C.G. (1936). The Concept of the Collective Unconscious. In *Collected Works*, Vol. 9i, *The Archetypes and the Collective Unconscious*, 2nd edn. London: Routledge and Kegan Paul, 1990.

Jung, C.G. (1946). The Psychology of the Transference. In *Collected Works*, Vol. 16. *The Practice of Psychotherapy*, 2nd edn. London: Routledge and Kegan Paul, 1993.

Jung, C.G. (1951). Gnostic Symbols of the Self. In *Collected Works*, Vol. 9ii. *Aion*, 2nd edn. London: Routledge and Kegan Paul, 1989.

Jung. C.G. (1954a). The Conjunction. In *Collected Works*, Vol. 14, *Mysterium Coniunctionis*, 2nd edn. London: Routledge and Kegan Paul, 1992.

Jung, C.G. (1954b). Transformation Symbolism in the Mass. In *Collected Works*, Vol. II, *Psychology and Religion*, 2nd edn. London: Routledge and Kegan Paul, 1991.

Larrington, C. (ed.) (1997). *The Woman's Companion to Mythology*. London: Harper Collins.

Lessa, W.A. and Vogt, E.Z. (eds.) (1979). *Reader in Comparative Religion. An Anthropological Approach*, 4th edn. New York: Harper Collins.

Levi-Strauss, C. (1963). *Structural Anthropology*. Trans. Jocobson, C. & Schoepf, B.G. New York: Basic Books.

Merchant, J. (2012). *Shamans and Analysts: New Insights on the Wounded Healer*. Hove and New York: Routledge.

Mattoon, M.A. (ed.) (1999). *Florence 98, Destruction and Creation; Personal and culTural Transformations. Proceedings of the Fourteenth International Congress for Analytical Psychology*. CH-Einsiedeln: Daimon Verlag.

Needham, R. (1967). Percussion and Transition. *Journal of the Royal Anthropological Institute* (Man) II(4), 606–614.

Neu, J. (1975). Levi-Strauss on Shamanism. In *Man*, n.s., 10(2), 285–292.

Noel, D.C. (1999). *The Soul of Shamanism, Western Fantasies, Imaginal Realities*. New York: Continuum Press.

Noll, R. (1987). The Presence of Spirits in Magic and Madness. In (1987) Nicholson, S. (ed.) *Shamanism: an Expanded View of Reality*. Wheaton, IL: The Theosophical Publishing House.

Raff, J. (2002). *Jung and the Alchemical Imagination*. York Beach, US: Hays Ltd.

Rasmussen, K. (1929). A Shaman's Journey to the Sea Spirit. *Report of the Fifth Thule Expedition 1921-1924*, Vol. VII, *No.1 Intellectual Culture of the Iglulik Eskimos*. Copenhagen: Gyldendalake Boghandel, Nordisk Forlag, pp. 123–129.

Robbins, M. (2011). *The Primordial Mind in Health and Illness*. London and New York: Routledge.

Sadak, B.B. and Weiser, L. (2017). Acknowledging the Archetypal Elements of Grief. *Psychological Perspectives, a Quarterly Journal of Jungian Thought* 60(4), 434–444.

Seneca (1st C). (2010) Boyle, A.J. (ed.) Oxford: Oxford University Press.

Shweder, R.A. (1967) Aspects of Cognition in Zinacanteco Shamans: Experimental Results. In (1979) Lessa, W.A. and Vogt, E.Z. (eds.) *Reader in Comparative Religion. An Anthropological Approach*, 4th edn. New York: Harper Collins. pp. 327–331.

Smith, C.M. (1997). *Jung and Shamanism in Dialogue*. New York and Mahwah, N.J: Paulist Press.

Sonne, B. (1997). Mythology of the Eskimos. In (1997) Larrington, C. (ed.) *The Woman's Companion to Mythology*. London: Harper Collins, pp. 162–185.

Statius (1st C). *Thebaid 3*. (2004). Shackleton Bailey, D.R. (ed.) Harvard: Loeb Classical Library, Harvard University Press.

Stern, D. (1998). *The Interpersonal World of the Infant. A View from Psychanalysis and Developmental Psychology*. London: Karnac Books.

Symthies, J.R. (ed.) (1967). *Science and ESP*. London: Routledge and Kegan Paul.

Van Gennep, A. (1960), *The Rites of Passage*. Chicago: University of Chicago Press.

Chapter 9

Conclusion

I want to conclude by not tying the chapters on taboo too tightly together, but rather open them to allow new thoughts and ideas to develop as a concept that has great relevance today. As a springboard for further investigation, it is interesting to note how the meaning of taboo has changed over time, from the practically forgotten rich and emotional indigenous meanings later applied negatively as the miscegenation taboo to the popularised misleading application of the Oedipus complex as the Freudian sexualised use of the term incest taboo.

While I was writing this book on taboo, the BBC television series *Taboo* became available on DVD, its narrative underlining much of the material I emphasise in chapter 4 on miscegenation taboo: the colour black in African slavery or the shades of black in Native American indigenous people depicted as dirt and impure, particularly among mixed-blood offspring who as in-between analogous beings belong to neither race. Taboos exist in the present when we dehumanise others and *mark them* as *dirt* because they do not fit cultural, racial, or gender expectations. Taboos serve to protect the self against contamination from a perceived internal *and* external, dangerous, invasive force, but they have lost their original benign function. I would like to highlight the following aspects of taboo for further thought.

First, as we have seen throughout the chapters, the term taboo, itself, is open to many interpretations and ambiguities that change over time. The concept, itself, falls in between the margins of academic and therapeutic disciplines, not belonging to one specific discipline. Apart from Fraser's (1922) mainly descriptive definition of taboo, defined as sympathetic and homoeopathic magic, Steiner (1956) points to a more complex understanding and definition, but both agree that the premodern mind does not distinguish between the concept of holiness and pollution. Their common feature is more important: they are dangerous and in danger, and the danger in which they stand and to which they can expose others is what we could describe as spiritual and imaginary. The term taboo, thus, covers both sacred/pure and profane/impure elements. Steiner suggests that taboo means 'marked thoroughly' and embraces ritual impurity that implies awe, obedience, abstention, and keeping at a distance. The opposite of taboo is *noa,* which means unspecific and common. Two salient features of taboo are its *untouchability* and *contagiousness*, which attest to the danger inherent within its meaning: if a taboo is touched, be it involving a person or object, both become taboo and untouchable until the appropriate rite is performed. Another aspect of taboo involves its relationship to the unexpected, that dangerous emotional *shock* factor involved with any unpredictable happening that upsets the normal classification of natural events. Steiner (1956, p. 21) classifies taboo under the *sociology of danger.*

Second, taboos protect a strong and vital life force that indigenous people called *mana. Mana,* as energy, is dangerous, powerful, effective, productive, awesome, and terrible; it is a psychic phenomenon perceived as inseparable from the object. On contact with such power, taboos are necessary as a *regulatory structure.* Taboos not only embody the prohibitive energy, they contain and structure it at its margins so that it does not escape without proper observation and control. Energy in the form of any essence that flows through bodily margins is particularly dangerous in times of transition and needs specific rites to contain and move that energy safely across old margins into new terrain. Spilt blood, as *mana*, is particularly dangerous as it contains all life-preserving ingredients, as I discuss specifically in chapters 2, 3, 4, and 7. The protection of *mana* through taboo prohibitions involves carefully controlling that essence from escaping through the bodily orifices, which include the mouth, ears, eyes, vagina, anus, and penis. Such exits are carefully controlled and guarded through painful taboo rituals. Totems discussed in chapter 4 developed to protect sacred ancestor blood from being spilt and mixed with nonpurified blood, which forms the basis of all blood taboos, including the miscegenation taboo and religion taboos to blood transfusion.

Menstrual blood emanating from fertile women has the most *mana* and, thus, incurs most taboo protection because their blood intimately involves the generation of life. Fertile women are automatically tabooed and untouchable. As I show in chapter 5, the colour red considered in earlier Palaeolithic-Neolithic times as sacred, connected to female blood and reproduction, became negatively cursed after 3000 BCE with the onset of patrilineal primogeniture. Women became male property, their reproduction powers subjugated to produce first born male heirs.

The protection of *mana* also involves deep concern about *soul elements* of the self, thought to be migratory and open to loss or theft. Indigenous people believe that the soul of a person takes the form of an inner animal, a manikin, a shadow or a reflection that has a life of its own and embodies life energy (Fraser, 1922, p. 215). When a person is inactive, as in sleep, the soul as her/his double leaves the body and can be stolen or expropriated by others, leading to sickness or death. To safeguard his/her soul, a person might put it in a safe, hidden, tabooed place far away so that it comes to no harm. Moving to a new country might mean that the soul is left behind with a person suffering from acute attacks of homesickness because his/her soul cannot find its way into its body. This aspect of soul-making is particularly relevant in clinical practice today with people moving across their physical borders and losing aspects of their core identity. Analysis, itself, as a soul-making activity with access to unconscious processes can act as a temporary, symbolic container for the tabooed soul aspects until they can be found, re-examined, and reincorporated into the ego.

Third, indigenous taboo practices are as equally preoccupied with life after death and its imagined landscape as modern organised religions. As Malinowski (1931), Durkheim (1915), and others have stressed, the difference between religion and indigenous magic is minimal. Animism, expounded by Tylor (1903, pp. 6–9), is concerned with the difference between a living person and a dead one and the causes of waking, dreams, trances, disease, and death. Animism believes that the soul as phantom is able to exist after death in the form of a shadow or ghost-soul. Taboos involved in the rites of passage concerning the souls of the dead, the mourning process, and the successful passage to the land of the dead are of great relevance today as in indigenous cultures as I stress in chapter 7. Tylor importantly sees a continuum between early indigenous animistic beliefs about the existence of spiritual beings after death and later monotheisms, such as Buddhism and Christianity (Jong, 2017, pp. 47–61). The idea of bodily resurrection in Heaven or Hades is technically an indigenous transmigration of the soul: both exist on a detailed cognitive level. Indigenous beliefs about afterlife and their detailed description of the land of the dead illustrated through shamanic journeys to retrieve lost souls from the underworld, which I describe in chapter 8, are of equal healing efficacy, if not superior, as those of organised religions. The idea of religion first, propounded by the *OT* Genesis myth of a father in heaven who gives birth to a son, Adam, and then Eve, second-born of Adam's rib, and, second, in the *NT* depicting the miracle of the virgin birth followed by Christ's ascension are based on *nonlogical* phenomena qualitatively comparable to magical beliefs.

Fourth, Jung's analytical framework has much to offer the study of taboo. His inclusion of indirect *associative* thinking (Jung, 1911–12/1952, paras. 21–46) gives a legitimate frame to expand upon the mythological, associative thinking found in taboo practices, and supports structural anthropologists Eliade (1958), Tambiah (1973), and Levi-Strauss (1962, 1963) in their work on symbol formation and associative thinking that challenges Fraser's original definition of sympathetic and contagious magic as misapplied logic. Associative thinking has its own logic. Jung and Jungian analysts, such as Adams (2001, p. 121, 2004, pp. 2–19) and Hillman (1997, 1999), use associative, indirect, imaginative thinking through amplification as a *directed* analytical tool to sharpen fantasy and dream *images* to transform subjective, disassociated taboo emotions into legitimate ego and cultural/collective analytical discourse. Through contact with indigenous, primordial, shamanic practices described fully in chapter 8, a reconnection with nature and ancestral memories revitalises an anxious, dried-out, hierarchical thinking into an emotional associative immediacy and intensity for life (Jung, 1961, p. 270). Analysis can provide that necessary temporary container for patients initially unable to enter the rites of passage or complete the final stage of parental separation.

Jung's theory of *archetypes* is applicable to the nature of taboo, as taboos deal with the universal fabric of human emotions and are found not only in indigenous cultures but worldwide. Taboos give form, pattern, and containment to the *unfinished business* of intense personal and collective complexes attached to the grief and anxiety of unexpected changes within developmental processes worldwide since time immemorial. Jung's willingness to personify archetypes as animate beings with purposeful properties brings to life these primordial experiences. In chapter 6, I show how the archetypal images of *puer/puella* are constellated in two client cases belonging to incomplete rites of passage where individuation has been tabooed. In chapters 7 and 8, I elucidate how taboo is personified through the images of Hades, Sedna, and Penthos to describe their intense emotional mutuality and communality.

Jung (1947, paras. 408) suggests that 'psychic processes behave like a scale along which consciousness slides.' At one end, instincts dominate and at the other, the spirit. Taboos move along this spectrum easily by incorporating the physical, affective, as well as the spiritual dimension, particularly attached to painful *rites of passage*. The harsh emotional physicality of taboo rituals are met with their profound developmental and spiritual significance.

Hillman (1983, p. 1) argues that archetypes personify not just the human psyche but simultaneously constellate in physical, sociocultural, linguistic, aesthetic, affective, and spiritual form (cf. Brodersen, 2016, pp. 3–5). Jung's concept of *synchronicity* (Jung, 1952, paras. 818–871) can be applied to Fraser's concept of sympathetic and contagious magic and better explains both types of occurrence. Through the *affective* creative tension of opposites found in the polarising activity between conscious and unconscious processes, a bridge or transcendent function is formed between psyche and matter: a synchronistic, interactive field is constellated, which breaks through the barriers of space and time, between the ego and the collective unconscious. Synchronicity seems magical: each person has an electrical and magnetic field, an attractive and/or repellent force, which activates when touching something or someone with a similar affective charge (Jung, ibid. para. 860). Von Franz (1994, p. 386) stresses the importance of Jung's discovery of the synchrony principle, that is, that 'symbols produced sporadically and spontaneously by the unconscious through the action of the archetypes tend to coincide in a meaningful way with the material occurrences in the external world.' Synchronicity incorporates an objective psyche that organises psyche and matter simultaneously in a form called *magical consciousness* (cf. Greenwood and Goodwyn, 2016).

Fifth, in order to explore the painful *miscegenation taboo* associated with people of dark hair or complexion as dirt or garbage, Hillman's (1979, 1997, 1999) work on blackness and invisibility in *rites of passage* described in chapter 8 is a helpful guide to understand and ameliorate the taboos surrounding blackness. New developmental statuses gained through rites of passage discussed in chapter 7 take place in secluded darkness. Within this dark and invisible frame, one enters the liminal night-time journey of transformation, analogous to the sun as it sets in the west and disappears into the darkness. The colour black as a night-time colour of invisibility, personified by Hades, is considered a potential to be explored in the unconscious, not yet realised in consciousness. The imaginative role of a shaman is recognised as one who undertakes the difficult journey into the unconscious (the land of the dead) to restore lost or stolen soul aspects of the self. These imaginal fetes can be likened to the work of psychoanalysis, particularly Jungian psychoanalysis (Merchant, 2012).

Sixth, Meade (1995) and Bell (1992) suggest that the radical dismantling of institutions, boundaries, and older indigenous belief systems, have left modern cultures unable to handle loss, grief, and death, and still fully embrace life. I examine the rites of passage of indigenous people because in such initiation rites, a person is structurally defined as a tabooed *transitional being* or neophyte; she/he has a physical, not a social reality, hence they are invisible, hidden and symbolically dead. They have no status, rank, personal clothing, or kinship position to demarcate them structurally. As they are no longer classifiable, the *symbols* that represent them are drawn from the biology of death, decomposition, and other physical bodily taboos. Such rites accompanied through painful taboo rituals, particularly at birth, puberty, and death, give meaning and courage to endure such separations that facilitate regeneration. In indigenous beliefs, the *mother* is an active, vital, and creative force in rites of passage as the *archetypal* ambivalent Great Mother, symbol of death, rebirth, and renewal. Taboo subjects undergo change and come under new influences. In taboo rituals, margins between ritual time and space are stretched to open and introduce frightening matrilineal elements of the Great Mother, which reveal her *Ungud* primordial function. Old fixed forms dissolve as experiential androgynous features emerge through such taboo rites of transition as in-between, transborder, indeterminate states where new patterns develop.

Seventh, Douglas' (1966) experiential work on *dirt* as left over bits and pieces (hair, nail clippings, nasal discharge, saliva, menstrual blood, semen, and ear wax) that have fallen out of classification in the margin between 'me' and 'not-me,' together with Kristeva's (1982) work on *abjection,* deepens any psychosocial study of taboo concerning obsessive compulsions, which I describe in chapter 6. Both academics widen parameters of discussion about the origins and positioning of taboo as rites of *purification.* I also present material from anthropologists Leach (1964) and Radcliffe-Brown (1952) to show that, whereas language gives names to distinguish and separate things, taboo inhibits the recognition of those parts of the continuum that separates things. Under taboo, they become non-things, 'not-me' as anomalies that fall out of classification, and fill the interstices as dirt or waste products. Taking her research from Leviticus in the *OT,* Douglas shows that *holiness* is defined by strict categories of classification, cleanliness, and order. Diet is classified into clean and unclean foods with animals separated into edible/holy/clean and inedible/taboo/unclean categories. These categories are extended to kinship structures. However, dirt is necessary at the margins because purity is the enemy of change and deadens creativity. Dirt as *waste* stretches the margins of the imagination about leftover bits and pieces and whether we can find a legitimate space to recycle them. Further research into Douglas' premises suggests that rubbish can be analysed in a symbolic psychosocial sense as people's potential left at the border as rubbish.

I examine Douglas' ideas in relation to Kristeva's work on *abjection*. Kristeva maintains that contrary to what enters the mouth as forms of nourishment, what is expelled from the body—out of its pores and orifices—gives rise to abjection. Kristeva suggests that how faeces and sexuality are ritualised allows the 'two universes of filth and prohibition to brush lightly against each-other without necessarily being identified as *object* and *law.*' Kristeva argues that the rites of defilement as the anomalous 'speaking being,' stands at both edges of the unnameable as the non-object *and* the off-limits. I compare the cultural aetiologies of Douglas and Kristeva to speculate how their respective cultures have influenced their research on dirt and waste in relation to bodily fluids that have crossed the margins. How they are collectively conceived and disposed as valued or as rubbish reflects upon whether margins have been crossed over into risk and independence or whether bodily essences remain trapped as dirt.

Eighth, there is an important correlation between taboo, the development of conscience, and emotional ambivalence. Freud (1912–13) suggests a link between emotional ambivalence and a tabooed incest wish (Oedipus complex). I question Freud's overemphasis on incest wish as the basis for symptomatology, such as obsessive compulsions. Research suggests that the aetiology of such symptoms develop from the need to cross over margins into the freedom of the 'other,' a movement that is prohibited in past and present totalitarian, monistic, hierarchal cultures that interpret the 'other' as risky, dirty and sinful. I use Reddish's (2014) new theory of conscience to further question Freud's positioning of a *patrilineal* totem in relation to taboo. Authoritarian dynamics through the work of Stenner (2005), Stein (2017), and Luci's (2017) in-depth psychosocial perspectives all examine the relationship between terror, love, and brainwashing, as shown in authoritarian-totalist disorganised attachment mindsets. I compare Freudian psychoanalytic development perspectives with the Jungian archetypal positioning of taboo as *disallowed space* for independent thinking. I outline two client cases where the conflict between safety/obedience/good and freedom/disobedience/sinful is played out at the orifices/margins of the body as *illegitimate tabooed subjectivity* perceived as dirty and punishing.

One important observation concerning taboos is that they reflect cultural fears about the suddenness and unpredictability of birth, loss, and death. Taboo rituals carefully inculcate collective rules into these events to protect them, but the rules themselves contain an unpredictability that allows access to these altered states as a timeless mode of experience, which gives them meaning. For example, during ritual, unexpected percussion and monstrous appearances force the initiate to think differently about his/her cosmos, which I describe in chapter 7. Taboo rules are collective *hot spots* that show where new energy is accumulated, for example, at birth, puberty, marriage, and death. These situations are dangerous and unpredictable but, as Turner (1964) suggests, taboos give these dangers anomalous *betwixt and between* forms that contain the anxiety arising from the acquisition of new status values. The unpredictability contained by taboo rules in rites of passage conversely gives taboo its creative function. During taboo ritual, normal rules of behaviour are suspended and stretched to breaking point: the *shock factor* is emphasised to allow the *unknown* to enter.

In authoritarian monotheistic cultures, fear of death is associated with status change that is negatively translated into fear of disobedience and dissent with the resultant punishment of expulsion from paradise in afterlife. For those who want reassurance of everlasting life, blessing consists of fitting into preconceived classifications of known and safe elements which keep them in a state of obedient, abject, prelapsarian innocence even when it suffocates independent thought and action. How a society perceives its margins, and whether it allows passage across its internal and external borders, depends on how far the freedom to think independently and take risks are encouraged. When the freedom to traverse physical and psychic borders is not allowed, tabooed imaginary dirt, and garbage builds in the body and is perceived as unwanted and smelly discharge belonging to others caught between the stages of *me* but *not me*. To protect *me* from annihilation anxiety, the *not me* in the form of essences that leaves the body in hair, nail clippings, semen, menstrual blood, nasal and ear discharge, and saliva, is projected out onto others as *their* discarded, untouchable dirt and rubbish because the orifices are blocked and do not allow the rites of passage into freedom. This observation is important in accessing the anxiety triggered in obsessive compulsions.

As I discuss in chapters 2 and 4, 7 and 8, the original indigenous definition and practice of taboo does not exempt certain status groups: kings, queens, pubescent youths, warriors, mothers, and the dying are all subject to the same purification rites and painful experience. Since the late eighteenth century to the twenty-first century, however, the dehumanising of specific groups as dirt, garbage, and leftovers, undeserving of equal developmental rites of passage is a political phenomenon associated with mass migration across cultural and political borders, which is not facilitated by secure taboo outer structures (cf. chapter 4; Jahoda, 2014, pp. 13–33). Families fleeing from political and religious persecution, torture, or death, or those in search of better life prospects, are forced to traverse across borders between *me* and *not me* in containers psychically and physically inadequate to navigate that unpredictable risky, tabooed, indeterminate terrain between containment/belonging and separation/independence.

One final image of taboo and its structure could be drawn as that of a cocoon composed of dense, protective tabooed material. Inside the cocoon, a series of transformations are taking place whereby old margins are being dissolved and the material reformed into a new being. Once this process is complete, the chrysalis must find its way through the exit, which painfully squeezes its form in order to redistribute the bodily essences so it can emerge into daylight. Animal births, including human, undergo the same transformation in the uterus. Before birth, the same type of painful contractions are experienced, which paradoxically open up the vagina as an orifice and open the baby's lungs simultaneously for breath, for birth to proceed. Taboo rites of passage accomplish the same task and the necessary push of a psychic rebirth. If the outer passage is blocked, decay ensues and the material is recycled as an inner waste. When the process succeeds, however, as in the case of a silk worm cocoon, a precious waste product remains (silk of the cocoon), which is recycled as valuable material. Reflections on the concept of taboo as a cocoon for transformation interpret the waste—those silky florescent strands—as material to be utilised in the weaving of a new fabric.

References

Adams, M.V. (2001). *The Mythological Unconscious*. Putnam, Conn: Spring Publications, 2010.

Adams, M.V. (2004). *The Fantasy Principle, Psychoanalysis of the Imagination*. Hove and New York: Brunner-Routledge.

Bain, P.G., Vaes, J., and Leyens. J-P. (2014). *Humanness and Dehumanisation*. New York and London: Routledge.

Bell, C. (1992). *Ritual Theory, Ritual Practice*. Oxford: Oxford University Press.

Bible (1989 ed.) *The Revised English Bible*. Oxford and Cambridge: Oxford University Press.

Brodersen, E. (2016). *The Laws of Inheritance. A post-Jungian Study of Twins and the Relationship Between the First and the Other(s)*. London and New York: Routledge.

Douglas, M. (1966). *Purity and Danger*, (new preface, 2002) Abingdon, Oxon, and New York: Routledge, 2002.

Durkheim, E. (1915). The Elementary Forms of Religious Life. In (1979) Lessa, W.A. and Vogt, E.Z. (eds.) *Reader in Comparative Religion. An Anthropological Approach*, 4th edn. New York: Harper Collins, pp. 27–35.

Eliade, M. (1958). *Rites and Symbols of Initiation. The Mysteries of Birth and Rebirth*. Woodstock, CT: Spring Publications, 1995.

Fraser, J.G. (1922). *The Golden Bough, A Study in Magic and Religion*. Abridged edn. London and New York: Penguin Books.

Freud, S. (1912–13). Taboo and Emotional Ambivalence. In *Collected Works*, Vol. 13. *The Origins of Religion*. Trans. Strachey, J. London and New York: Penguin Books, 1990.

Greenwood, S. and Goodwyn, E.D. (2016). *Magical Consciousness. An Anthropological and Neurobiological Approach*. New York and London: Routledge.

Hillman, J. (1979). *The Dream and the Underworld*. Toronto: Harper Collins.

Hillman, J. (1983). *Archetypal Psychology: A Brief Account*. Dallas: Spring Pubs, 1993.

Hillman, J. (1997). The Seduction of Black. In (1997) Hillman, Hogarth, et. al. (eds.) *Haiti or the Psychology of Black*. Woodstock, CT: Spring Publication.

Hillman, J. (1999). A Note on Hermes Inflation. In (1999) Hillman, J., Burns, J., Grimaldi-Craig, S. et al (eds.) *Lost Souls*. Woodstock, CT: Spring Journal.

Hillman, J., Hogarth, H. et al (eds). (1997). *Haiti or the Psychology of Black*. Woodstock, CT: Spring Publication.

Hillman, J., Burns, J., Grimaldi-Craig, S. et al (eds.) (1999) *Lost Souls*. Woodstock, CT: Spring Journal.

Horton, R. and Flannigan, R. (eds.) (1973). *Modes of Thought*. London: Faber and Faber.

Jahoda, G. (2014). An Anthropological History of Dehumanisation from Late-18th to Mid-20th Centuries. In Bain, P.G., Vaes, J., and Leyens, J-P. (eds.) *Humanness and Dehumanisation*. New York and London: Routledge, pp. 13–33.

Jong, J. (2017). 'Belief in Spiritual Beings:' E.B. Tylor's (Primitive) Cognition Theory of Religion. In Tremlett, P-F., Sutherland, L.T., and Harvey, G. (eds.) *Edward Burnett Tylor, Religion and Culture*. London and New York: Bloomsbury, pp. 47–61.

Jung, C.G. (1911–12/1952). Two Kinds of Thinking. In *Collected Works*, Vol. 5, *Symbols of Transformation*, 2nd edn. London: Routledge and Kegan Paul, 1995.

Jung, C.G. (1947). On The Nature of the Psyche. In *Collected Works*, Vol. 8. *The Structure, and Dynamics of the Psyche*, 2nd edn. London: Routledge and Kegan Paul, 1991.

Jung, C.G. (1952). Synchronicity: An Acausal Connecting Principle. In *Collected Works*, Vol. 8, *The Structure and Dynamics of the Psyche*, 2nd edn. London: Routledge and Kegan Paul, 1991.

Jung, C.G. (1961). Compiled and edited by A. Jaffe. *Memories, Dreams and Reflections*. London: Fontana Press, 1993.

Kristeva, J. (1982). Trans. Rondiez, L.S. *Powers of Horror: An Essay in Abjection*. New York: Columbia University Press.

Leach, E.R. (1964). Anthropological Aspects of Language: Animal Categories and Verbal Abuse. In (1979) Lessa, W.A. and Vogt, E.Z. (eds.) *Reader in Comparative Religion. An Anthropological Approach*, 4th edn. New York: Harper Collins, pp. 153–166.

Lessa, W.A. and Vogt, E.Z. (eds.) (1979). *Reader in Comparative Religion. An Anthropological Approach*, 4th edn. New York: Harper Collins.

Levi-Strauss, C. (1962). *Totemism*. London: Merlin Press.

Levi-Strauss, C. (1963). *Structural Anthropology*. Trans. Jocobson, C. & Schoepf, B.G. New York: Basic Books.

Luci, M. (2017). *Torture, Psychanalysis & Human Rights*. London and New York: Routledge.

Malinowski, B. (1931). The Role of Magic and Religion. In (1979) Lessa, W.A. and Vogt, E.Z. (eds.) *Reader in Comparative Religion. An Anthropological Approach*, 4th edn. New York: Harper Collins, pp. 36–46.

Meade, M. (1995) Introduction to Eliade, M. (1958). *Rites and Symbols of Initiation. The Mysteries of Birth and Rebirth*. Woodstock, CT: Spring Publications, 1995.

Merchant, J. (2012). *Shamans and Analysts: New Insights on the Wounded Healer*. Hove and New York: Routledge.

Radcliffe-Brown, A.R. (1952). Taboo. In *Structure and Function in Primitive Society. Essays and Addresses.* Glencoe, IL: The Free Press, pp. 133–152.

Reddish, E. (2014). *The Petrified Ego. A New Theory of Conscience.* London: Karnac.

Stenner, K. (2005). *The Authoritarian Dynamic. Cambridge Studies in Public Opinion and Political Psychology.* Cambridge and New York: Cambridge University Press.

Stein, A. (2017). *Terror, Love & Brainwashing. Attachment in Cults and Totalitarian Systems.* London and New York: Routledge.

Steiner, F. (1956). *Taboo.* London and New York: Routledge.

Tambiah, S.J. (1973). The Form and Meaning of Magical Acts. In Horton, R. and Flannigan, R. (eds.) *Modes of Thought.* London: Faber and Faber.

Tremlett, P-F., Sutherland, L.T., and Harvey, G. (eds.) (2017). *Edward Burnett Tylor, Religion and Culture.* London and New York: Bloomsbury.

Turner, V.W. (1964). Betwixt and Between: The Liminal Period in Rites De Passage. In (1979) Lessa, W.A. and Vogt, E.Z. (eds.) *Reader in Comparative Religion, An Anthropological Approach*, 4th edn. Harvard: Harper Collins Publisher, pp. 234–243.

Tylor, E.B. (1903). *Primitive Culture. Researches Into the Development of Mythology, Philosophy, Religion, Language, Art, and Custom.* Vol. 2. London: John Murray.

Film

Taboo. (2017). BBC One Television, January, 2017

Index

Abitur 110, 122n2
abject 53, 116
abjection 50–2; categories 52; corporeal waste 53; female body and 116; food 53; maternity and 55; objects generating 52–5; obsessive compulsions and 169–70; pregnancy and 53–4; sexual difference 53
aborigines: childbirth rituals 128–9; initiation for boys 130; totems 59–60; tribal taboos 36; warriors 26
Abramowitz, J. 106
Adam 167
Adler, A. 101
Adorno, T. 101
adultery 21, 48
Aeschylus 86
African Americans 69
Africans 69–70
Alaska 156
Algonquins 19
amnesia 98
anal rejection 51
analogical thinking 30
animal categories 9, 66–7
animal mythic ancestor 60–1
animism 28, 59, 167
annihilation anxiety 99
Annwn 136
anorexia nervosa 11, 119
Antigone 87
antisemitism 70, 73
anxiety: annihilation 99; incest and disorders of 92; primary 33; secondary 33
apes 69–70
Arabs 74
araka 34
archaic superego 99–100
archetypal 5–6, 11, 12n1, 144n1
archetypal images 12, 12n1, 168
archetypes 31, 60, 107, 168
Arendt, H. 101, 102, 104
Arunta 132
Aryan race 70, 71
asceticism 119–21
Assam 27
associationism 65, 75n3
associative thinking 8, 167–8
astrology 61
Atkinson, J.J. 79, 80, 90
Atooi 2
attachment theory 102–5
Australian aborigines: childbirth rituals 128–9; initiation for boys 130; totems 59–60; tribal taboos 36; warriors 26
authoritarianism 100–2, 171
avoidance of situations 106–7
Azande tribe 35

Bachofen, J.J. 82
Baktamen 140
baldness 29
Barasana 62
Baring, A. 134
Bataks of Sumatra 27
Bauman, Z. 4–5, 67
Bechuanas 21
Bell, C. 127, 169
bereavement 138; *see also* death
Bergner, G. 69
Bettlelheim, B. 129
betwixt and between 127, 130, 171; *see also* rites of passage
biracial people 71
Bisagni, F. 106, 113

black and blackness 12; initiation/ regeneration rites and 141; as invisibility 147–9; positive association with black clouds 149
black art 147
black medicine 149
blacks 68, 70–1
blood: of enemies 26; of killed animas 26; menstrual 24–5, 27, 46, 53, 81–2, 120, 166; spilt 25, 27, 81–2; as symbol for violence 25
bloodletting 24–5
bodily fluids 51
body orifices 41–2
borderland 6
Borneo 134
Bowlby, J. 103
Briffault, R. 82
Brickman, C. 55
brother-sister incest 79, 92–3; *see also* incest; incest taboo
Büchner, L. 70
Buckley, T. 24, 25
Buddhism 28, 167
burial 135–6
Burma 27
Butler, J. 88

calcination 148
Caldwell, L. 88
Calvary 33
Cambodia 23
Canada 156
Cannon, W.B. 37
carnivores 44
Cashford, J. 134
caste system 47, 48
Catholic Church 89
Catholic Mass 33
Catholics 70
cat's cradle 20
ceremonial healing 37
ceremonies 127; *see also* rituals
charms 20
childbirth 82, 128–9, 157
China 7; funerals in 29
Christ, death and resurrection of 136
Christianity 28, 54, 167
Christians 68
Chrysippos 86
churinga 59, 139
circumcision 130–2
clansman 80
cleansing rituals 47
cloven hoofed animals 45
cognitive fluidity 61
cognitive lock 103
collective unconscious 152
communitas 141–3
compulsions 106
conscience 10, 98
contagion 4–5
contagious magic 22–3
contra-sexual others 8
Cook, J. 2–3
Coontz, S. 83
Coorgs 48
corporeal waste 53
corpses: touching 29; as waste 53; *see also* death
Costello, M.S. 107
countertransference 114–15, 121
Crawley, A.E. 152
Crawley, E. 81
Creon 87–8
Crews, F. 101
cultural complexes 47–8
Cuna Indian 157
curse 24, 120
Cuvier, C. 68
Cynics 119

Dacotan 63
Dahomey Africa 7
Dakota Native Americans 19
Daliks 47
Damasio, A.R. 140
dangerous dead 136
Darfur 22–3
Darwin, C. 70
Davenport, C.B. 70
de Gobineau, A. 70
death: bereavement 139; double burial 135; emotional stress and 37; fear of 171; funerary rites 136; funerary taboos 29–30; grieving 149; knowledge of 152; land of the dead 136–7; life after 167; mourning rituals 37, 88, 137–9; pollution and 49; psychogenic 36; rituals 135–6
Debs, N. 138
dehumanisation 74
Deleuze, G. 51
deportation 48

Derrida, J. 51
diet 170
dirt: creation of 47; definition of 5; necessity of 48–9; pollutants 24; potency of 45–7; as waste 169–70
dirty other 50
disallowed space 11
dismissing attachment 103
disorder: anxiety 92; eating 11, 53, 98, 100, 119; garbage and 50; as pollution 5; potency of 45–7; rituals and 43
disorganised attachment 103
dispute settlement 103
dissent, taboo on 100–2
divorce 91
double burial 135
doublethinking 105
doubling act 105
Douglas, M. 4–5, 8–9, 24, 33, 41, 42, 43, 44, 45, 46, 47, 48–9, 50, 114, 129, 157, 169–70
dream work 108, 113
drive theory 102
drums 152
Du Bois, W.E.B. 69
Durkheim, E. 59
Dürr, E. 50
Dworakowski, M. 152
Dyaks 21, 134

eating disorders 11, 53, 98, 100, 119
Echion 86
edible animals 44, 66–7
edible birds 45
ego: abjection and 53; collective unconscious and 31; consciousness 150, 160; embryonic 99; ideal 99; incest and 84–5; petrified 98; super 99–100, 103; unconscious 148
Egypt 22, 147
Eichmann, A. 104
elephant hunters 21
Eliade, M. 34, 47, 93n1, 130, 131, 150
Ellenberger, H.F. 37–8
emotional ambivalence 10, 97–122, 170–1; asceticism 119–21; attachment theory 102–5; authoritarianism and 100–2; case studies 107–18; compulsions 106; Freud's interpretation of 98–100; Jungian perspectives on 105–7; obsessional neurosis and 98; washing compulsions (case study) 107–15
emotional lock 103
Engels, F. 83
Eree-taboo 3
eugenics 72
euthanasia 72
Evans-Pritchard, E.E. 35
Eve 167
exogamy 61–2, 80

faeces 49, 51
Fanon, F. 69
Farrell, J. 101
father-daughter incest 79, 91–3, 92–3; *see also* incest; incest taboo
fear 36–7
female genital mutilation 133
Ferenczi, S. 101
ferrets 21
fertilisation 80
fertility 44
First Fruit ritual 141
Firth, R. 65
Fol, H. 80
food segregation 81
food taboos 21, 119–21
Fortes, M. 143
Fox, R. 80
Fraser, J.G. 2, 6, 8, 19, 20, 25, 29–30, 32, 35, 61–2, 63–4, 128–9, 165
Freud, S. 5, 9, 10; abjection 52; drive theory 102; emotional ambivalence 98–100; incest and totem formation 61; mourning 88; Oedipus complex 83–5, 100–1, 170; taboo versus obsessional neurosis 105
funerary rites 136
funerary taboos 29–30

Ganesha 123n3
gang pressing 48
garbage 50
Genesis 44, 167
Genesis myth 84
German refugees 108
gestation 129
Gexsem clan 63
ghosts 29–30
Gidla, S. 47
Gigilqam clan 63
Gimi tribe 28
Girard, R. 6, 25, 41, 85
Gnabaia 131

Goddesses of Destiny 134
Goldenweiser, A. 83
Goodwyn, E. 35, 136, 139, 168
Gottlieb, A. 24, 25
Great Goddess 134
Great Moon Goddess 142
Great Mother archetype 133–6, 169
great name 22
Greenland 156
Greenwood, S. 35, 168
grieving 149
Groesback, C.J. 160
Gross, E. 51, 116
guardian spirits 63
Guggenbuhl-Craig, A. 160
Günter, G. 69

Hades 149–50, 167
Haeckel, E. 70
Haemon 87
Haida 60
Hailolaux 63
hair: colour 68; cutting 21, 23; shorn 22
half-person-half-animal hybrids 42
Halifax, J. 154
hausman 26
He people 62
Heaven 167
Hedman, B. 60
Henderson, P. 83
Herowana boys 26
Hertz, R. 135
hierophanies 33–4
Hillman, J. 86, 107, 115, 147, 148, 149–50, 160, 168, 169
Hindu caste system 47, 48
Hindu India 136
Hobhouse, L.T. 80
holiness 20, 44, 170
Holt, R.H. 101
Homans, G.C. 33
homeopathy 21
hominids 89
Homo erectus 89
Homo sapiens 61
Hort 149
human propagation 9, 66–7
hunter-gatherers 61
Huxley, F. 152
Huzuls 20

illegitimate tabooed subjectivity 11
imanduruakondo 34
imitative (sympathetic) magic 20–2
inbreeding 80, 89
incest: avoidance mechanisms 80, 92; brother-sister 92–3; causes of 91–2; father-daughter 92–3; frequency of 92; mother-daughter 92; mother-son 91–3, 92; revulsion of sexual difference and 53; stepfather-stepdaugher 92; symbolic 85
incest taboo 79–93; as bridge between nature and culture 90; creationist principle of 83; Freud's interpretation of 83–5; hominids and 89; inbreeding and 89; Jung's interpretation of 85; Oedipus complex and 83–8; origins of 75n3, 79–81; overview 10; psychoanalytical/psychosocial interpretations of 83–7; psychosocial-anthropological interpretation of 89–91; repression of women and 82–3; versus sex avoidance 79–81; spilt blood taboo and 81–2; totemic clan structure and 61; violations of 91–3
Incwala 141
independent thinking, taboo on 100–2
India 46, 123n3
indigenous practices 18–38; analogical/symbolic versus scientific thinking 30–5; animism 167; contagious magic 22–3; imitative (sympathetic) magic 20–2; kingship 23; *mana* 19–20; menstruating women 24–5; pubescent boys 26; soul, loss of 27–30; tabooed personages 23–7; warriors 26–7
indirect associative thinking 30
individuation 6, 85, 149, 160
inedible animals 44, 66
initiation: for boys 130–2; circumcision 130–2; female genital mutilation 132–3; for girls 132–3; great mother archetype 133–6; regeneration and 141; subincision 130–2
interbreeding 79–80, 87
interpretive paradigms 30
interracial sex 71
Inuit people 20, 156
Iroquois 62, 83
iteration 148

James, W. 30
Jewish taboos 44–5
Jews 67, 70, 72–4, 104

Jocasta (Queen of Thebes) 83–4, 86, 87
Judaism 54
Jung, , C. G. 5–6; archetypes 30–1, 168; associative thinking 30, 167–8; on emotional ambivalence 105–7; Great Mother archetype 135; on individuation 160; interpretation of incest 85; synchronicity 31–2, 168; transcendent function 13n2
Jungian analysis, shamanism and 150, 159–61

kangaroos 60, 65
Kant, I. 83
kapu 3
Karadjeri 132
Karens of Burma 27
Kerenyi, K. 86
Key Islands 21
khem 147
khuan 23
kiaimoku 32
kibbutz 89
King, J. 3
kings 171
Kings of Sheba 23
kingship 23; *see also* tabooed personages
kinship libido 88
Koryak 152
kratophanies 33–4
Kristeva, J. 8–9, 41, 50–2, 52, 53, 54, 169–70
Kroeber, A.L. 62

Lacan, J. 52
Laius 86
Laius (King of Thebes) 83, 86
land of the dead 12, 136–7
Lang, A. 80, 90
Laos 21
Lapouge, G.V.de 70, 71
Lawson, E.T. 140
LeBon, G. 69
Leach, E.R. 8, 41, 42, 66, 169–70
Lehmann, Fr. R. 4
Lele 49
Lent 32, 43
Levi-Strauss, C. 64–6, 75n2, 89, 90, 157–9
Leviticus 42–4, 170
Levy-Bruhl, L. 61
Lewis-Williams, D. 66, 136
libido 88
life after death 167
Lifton, R.J. 138
Lillooet 63
liminality 141–3
Lisiansky, U. 3
Luci, M. 11, 104, 114, 170
Luctus 149
lunar symbolism 141
Lyotard, J-F. 51

Madagascar 21
madness 49
magic: contagious 22–3; imitative (sympathetic) 20–1; overview 8; science and 35–6; versus shamanism 150–1
magical consciousness 32, 35–6
malformed births 45
Malinowski, B. 32
malocas 62
mana 4, 19–20, 23, 27, 166
manioc 36
manitu 19
Mann, D. 88
Mannix, K.M. 138
Maoris 23, 26, 81
margin 128
Maryanski, A. 79, 89, 91, 92
mass killings 72
maternity 55
matrilineal clan 80, 82
matrilineal inheritance 87
McCauley, R, N. 140
Meade, M. 126, 169
meat eating 32, 43
Mediterrese 70
Mekeo 29
Melanesians 19
menopause 118
menstrual blood 24–5; fear of 46, 82; food taboos and 120; *mana* and 166; revulsion of sexual difference and 53; warrior taboos and 27
menstruating women 24–5, 27; *see also* tabooed personages
mental health practices 36–8
Merchant, J. 159, 160
metempsychosis 60
mice 45
Middle Ages 68
Mikado 23
Miller, A. 102

mirror stage 52
miscegenation taboo 9, 67–71, 169
Mithen, S. 61
mixago 135
mixing of blood 9
Mixtex 37
Mohawk 62
Monster Barlun 131
Montezuma 23
Moors 68, 70
Morgan, L.H. 61, 62, 66, 80, 82
mortification 148
mother-daughter incest 92
mothers 171
mother-son incest 79, 91–3, 92; *see also* incest; incest taboo
mourners 29
mourning 37, 88, 137–9
multiracial people 71
Muslims 68, 74
Muu 157–9
mwadi 129
mysterium 149

Na 79
nail clippings 22, 46
Naimark, N.M. 108
names 22
Navaho 37
Nazi Germany 71–4, 119
Ndembu tribe 129, 140
Needham, R. 152
Neentsa clan 63
negative precepts 20
Nele Ki (k) kirpanalele 158
nelegan 158
neophytes 93n1, 128, 135, 169
Neumann, E. 142
New Guinea 131
New Testament 54
Newman, H.H. 6
nigredo 147
noa 4, 166
non-things 67
Nootka South Indians 81
North Cheyenne Native Americans 137
nuchu 157
Nuer 45
nuru 81
Nyakyusa tribe 49

obsessional neurosis 98, 105
obsessive compulsions 106–7, 169–70
Oedipal superego 99
Oedipus 83–8
Oedipus (Seneca) 149
Oedipus complex 10, 54, 83–8, 170
Oedipus Rex 83
Ojibwa 64
Oliver, K. 115
Omaho 135
one drop rule 71
Oneidas 62
oral disgust 53
orifices 41–2, 46
Origin of the Species 70
Osages 63
Osiris 85
Ostyaks 136
Otherworld 136

paedophilia 102
Pagans 68
Palaeolithic-Neolithic creation myths 84, 88
pangolin 49
Papua New Guinea 26, 28
parental complexes 106
Parson, T. 89
parturition 129
patrilineal inheritance 10
patrilineal totem 10, 170
Pearce, D. 66, 136
pederasty 86
Pelops 86
Penthos 149
petrified ego 98
pigs 45
poisonous pedagogy 102
pollutants 24
pollution: death and 49; re-entry 48; rules 42–3; social 46; threat from 54
Polynesians: psychogenic death 36; taboos 43; *tabu* 19; totemism 65
portrait 29
post-traumatic stress disorders (PTSD) 92, 140
pregnancy: abjection and 53–4; taboos in 20–1, 82
preoccupied attachment 103
prima materia 121, 129, 135, 141, 149
primary anxiety 33
primary ritual 33

primogeniture 82
psychoanalysis: of abjection 51; Jungian 159–61; main tasks of 148; shamanism and 157
puberty 129, 150
pubescent boys 25, 171; *see also* tabooed personages
Pueblo 62
puella 11, 107, 121, 168
puer 11, 168
puer aeternus 107, 111, 121
puer senilis 115
Punjab 129
purba 157
purification 169–70
purity 48–9
putrefaction 148
Pythagoreans 119

queens 171

Radcliffe-Brown, A.R. 2, 8, 19, 32, 43, 65, 128, 169–70
Raff, J. 148
rage 37
Ra-Osiris 137
Rasmussen, K. 154
rationalisation 33
rats 123n3
reaggregation 128
red 149
Reddish, E. 10, 98–100, 170
Reed, E. 64, 81, 87, 90
reflective triangle 104
refugees 108
regeneration 141
Renaissance 68
reptiles 45
Rhineland bastards 73
rites of passage 11, 12, 168; archetypes and 31; betwixt and between 127, 130, 171; blackness and invisibility in 169; circumcision 130–2; communication of *sacra* 139–41; *communitas* 141–3; death rituals 135–6; definition of 127–8; efficacy of 127; female genital mutilation 132–3; great mother archetype 133–6; initiation 141; initiation for boys 130–2; initiation for girls 132–3; journey to underworld 149; liminality 141–3; margin 128; mass denials and 126; neophytes 93n1, 128, 135; puberty 150; reaggregation 128; regeneration 141; ritual mourning 137–9; separation 128–33; souls of the dead 167; subincision 130–2; as symbolic intergenerational expressions of sentiments or values 128; transitional beings in 128; between two states of being 128
ritual mourning 137–9
ritual murder 49
rituals 127, 171; avoidance versus prohibition 43; secondary 33; shamanic 152
Robbins, M. 154
Roma people 72
Roman Catholicism 43
Rose, J. 102
Royal Geographical Society 2

sacra, communication of 139–41
sacred 12
sacredness 23
Sadak, B.B. 148
Samika 36
Samoa 29
Sarawak 21
Sartre, J-P. 46
Schultze, F. 69
scientific thinking 30
Scotland 29
sea goddess 154–7
secondary anxiety 33
secondary ritual 33
secure attachment 103
Sedna (sea goddess) 154–7
Self 9
Seneca 149
separation 128–33; childbirth 128–9; from mothers 130; nigredo phase 148; puberty 129
Seth 85
sex avoidance 79–81
sexual accessibility 67
sexual intercourse: with family members 66–7; female genital mutilation and 133; with near kin 79; warriors abstaining from 27
sexuality, snakes as symbol for 130
shadow 8
shamans/shamanism: cognitive skills 153–4; depictions of 150–4; descent to the underworld 153; didactic education through instruction 151; dreams of 151;

drums and 152; ecstatic education through dreams 151; esoteric training of 151–2; examples of 154–9; initiation process 151; initiatory sickness 151; journey to underwater Sea Spirit 154–7; Jungian analysis and 150, 159–61; knowledge of death 152; versus magic and magicians 150–1; performances 152; psychoanalysis and 157; recruitment of 151; as a religious phenomenon 150; rituals 152; sensitivity and compassion of 154; symbolic journey into the womb 157–8; taboo and 159–61; Yakut 152
Sheol 136
Shuwap 29
Siamese 23
sin, as pathogenic secret 37
Sisintle clan 63
skin colour 68
skin of milk 53
slime 46
social anthropology 2
social Darwinism 71–2
social groups 67–8
social pollution 46
social puberty 129
sociology of danger 2
Soemmering, S.T. 68
Sonne, B. 154
Sophocles 83, 87
soul: loss of 27–8; making 28–9, 166–7; projection into mirror reflection 29; taboo and 27–8, 166–7
South Sea Islanders 2
Spanish conquerors 68
sperm cell, discovery of 80
spilling salt 32
spirit world 61
Spiro, M. 89
spilt blood 25, 27, 81–2
Statius 149
Stein, A. 11, 44–5, 102–3, 104, 114, 170
Steiner, F. 2, 3, 19, 33, 165
Stenner, K. 11, 101, 102, 170
stepfather-stepdaugher incest 92
sterilisation law (Germany) 72
Stern, D. 55, 103
stickiness 46
Stoics 119
structural forms, symbolic usage of 130
subincision 130–2
suicides 118
Sultan of Darfur 22–3
Sumatra 21, 27
Sundanese 21
super ego 99–100, 103
supernatural beings 42
Swammerdam, J. 80
sweat house 29
symbolic thinking 30
symbolisation 33
symbols 6, 13n2, 169
sympathetic magic 20–2
sympathetic-adrenal system 37
synchronicity 31–2, 168

T4 killings 72
tabaka 3
taboo: ambiguity of meaning 1; background to study of 1–2; as a cocoon for transformation 172; contagious magic 22–3; definitions of 2, 18–19, 165–6; emotional ambivalence and 97–122; etymology of 3–5; features of 166; functions of 165; funerary 29–30; historical accounts of 2–3; as imitative (sympathetic) magic 20–2; in indigenous practices 18–38; interdisciplinary perspectives of 5; miscegenation 9, 67–71, 169; as a regulatory structure 166; shamanism and 159–61; untouchability of 2; violations 36–8
Taboo(television series) 165
taboo conscience 98
tabooed personages 23–7; kingship 23; menstruating women 24–5; pubescent boys 25; warriors 26–7
tabu 3, 19
tafu 3
Tahiti 23; childbirth rituals 129; infant's head as taboo in 23
Tallensi 65, 143
Tambiah, S.J. 34
tapa-tabu 4
tapu 3
Taylor, S. 106
Taylor, T. 136, 138
tears 46
teeth, loss of 29
temenos 149
Tepito 50
terrorists 74
Thebaid 3 149

theft 37
theriomorphic symbols 150
Third Reich 66, 67, 104, 119–20
toilet training 108–9
Tonga-taboo 3
totem and totemism 59–66; animal mythic ancestor 60–1; Australian aborigines 59–60; clan structure 61–3; clans and 59; cosmology of 61; exogamy and 61–2; guardian spirits 63; *Haida* 60; multifaceted functions of 63–6; overview 5, 9; patrilineal 170; Polynesian 65
totemisation 100
transcendent function 13n2
transference-countertransference 114–15, 121
transitional beings 11, 128, 169; *see also* rites of passage
transitional space 55
transmigration 28
Turner, J. 79, 89, 91, 92, 127
Turner, V,W. 11, 139, 143
Tuscaroras 62
Twanyirrika 131
twins 6–8
Tylor, E.B. 28, 60, 167

unborn babies 45
unclean animals 44
Ungud 61, 169
untouchables 47, 48

vagina indenta 142
Van Gennep, A. 128, 135, 156
venery 66
vermins 67
Virey, J.J. 68
Virgin Mary 42
viscosity 46
Vogt, C. 68, 70
Von den Veldon, E. 69
Von Franz, M-L. 32, 107, 111, 168
von Kotzebue, O. 3
von Krusenstern, A.J. 3
von Langsdorff, G.H. 3
voodoo 36

Walker, B. 86
warriors 26–7, 171; *see also* tabooed personages
washing compulsions 107–15
weasels 45
Webster, H. 32, 64
Weiser, L. 149
Westermarck, E. 80, 89
white Pagans 68
Wilkes, C. 3
Winder, G.M. 50
Winnicott, W. 103
wombats 65
women: childbirth 82, 128–9, 157; female genital mutilation 133; menstruating 24–5, 27, 46, 53, 81–2, 120, 166; pregnancy 20–1, 53–4, 82; repression of 82–3
Wondjina 61
Woodman, M. 107, 119, 120–1
Wundt, W. 98

Yakut shamanism 152
Yeba 62
yellow race 70
Yuin 130
Yupik 152

Zeavin, H. 138
Ziegler, A.J. 107, 119
Zinacanteco shamans 153
Zulu 149

For Product Safety Concerns and Information please contact our EU representative GPSR@taylorandfrancis.com Taylor & Francis Verlag GmbH, Kaufingerstraße 24, 80331 München, Germany